SMITH'S REVIEW SERIES

Family Law
SECOND EDITION

MYRON G. HILL, JR.
Associate Professor of Law,
Antioch School of Law
Member of District of Columbia,
Ohio and U.S. Supreme Court
Bars

HOWARD M. ROSSEN
Director, Ohio Bar Review and
Writing Seminar
Member of Ohio,
District of Columbia,
Florida, Pennsylvania and
U.S. Supreme Court Bars

WILTON S. SOGG
Adjunct Professor of Law,
Cleveland-Marshall
College of Law,
Cleveland State University
Lecturer on Law,
Harvard Law School
Member of Ohio,
District of Columbia,
Florida, U.S. Tax Court and
U.S. Supreme Court Bars

SMITH'S REVIEW SERIES

Family Law
Second Edition

for Law School, Bar and College Examinations

WEST PUBLISHING COMPANY
St. Paul, Minnesota © 1981

Library of Congress Cataloging in Publication Data
Smith, Chester Howard, 1893–1964.
    Smith's Review of family law.

    (Smith's review series)
    Includes index.
    1. Domestic relations—United States—Outlines,
syllabi, etc.   I. Hill, Myron G., 1936–
II. Rossen, Howard M., 1936–   .   III. Sogg,
Wilton S., 1935–   .   IV. Title.   V. Title:
Review of family law.
KF505.Z9S5   1981   346.7301′5   81-401
ISBN 0-8299-0515-4   AACR1

    2nd Reprint—1985

To The Memory Of
MARIAN S. HILL

PREFACE

This revised volume in the Smith's Review Series covers the subject matter of Family Law. This Review is structured to cover the subject matter as presently taught in its modern form in law schools today. Thus, the subject matter covers not only the traditional content of Domestic Relations courses, but also includes tort actions among family members, the legal position of minors, no-fault divorce, tax aspects of divorce, and trends in family law, including those with respect to adoption, illegitimacy, marriage, the rights of women, and the proposed Equal Rights Amendment which is still awaiting final ratifications as this Review goes to press.

This Review contains an Outline of Family Law at pages xvii to xxv. In this Outline, the authors have attempted to provide a structural outline of the subject matter, together with a word-phrase presentation of the elements of key concepts and principles of law in each of the basic subject areas.

To assist the student in preparing for examinations in Family Law, the authors have included materials on a Suggested Approach to Answering Essay Examinations in Law, together with some selected essay questions in Family Law and the authors' suggested answers to them. This book would not be complete without thanks to Professor Paul McLane Conway of Georgetown Law Center, Washington, D.C., for his gracious permission to reprint these questions.

The authors have made use of the CAVEAT and NOTE throughout, to alert the student to important areas of difficulty, change and development.

The authors have combined their teaching experience and practical knowledge to make this Review the clearest, most complete and accurate study guide available to students of Family Law. Suggestions for further improvement of future editions may be directed to the authors in care of West Publishing Company.

Apart from the cases cited, the citations in this Review are as follows:

"Areen" refers to Judith Areen, Cases and Materials on Family Law, 1978, by The Foundation Press, Inc.; "Burby" refers to William E. Burby, Law of Property Third Edition, 1965, by West Publishing Co.; "Calamari and Perillo" refers to Joseph D. Calamari and Joseph M. Perillo, The Law of Contracts, 1970, by West Publishing Co.; "Clark" refers to Homer H. Clark, Jr., The Law of Domestic Relations in the United States, 1968, by West Publishing Co.; "Foote" refers to Caleb Foote, Robert J. Levy and Frank E. A. Sander, Cases and Materials on Family Law, 1976, by Little, Brown and Company; "Goodrich" refers to Eugene F. Scoles, Handbook of the Conflict of Laws, Fourth Edition, 1964, by West Publishing Co.; "Katz" refers to Joseph Goldstein and Jay Katz, The Family and The Law, 1965, by The Free Press; "Krause" refers to Harry D. Krause, Family Law Cases and Materials, 1976, by West Publishing Co.; "Mucklestone" refers to John Huston, Robert S. Mucklestone, and Bruce M. Cross, Tax Management, Estates, Gifts, and Trusts, Portfolio 212, Second Edition, 1974, by The Bureau of National Affairs, Inc.; "Paulsen" refers to Monrad G. Paulsen, Walter Wadlington and Julius Goebel, Jr., Cases and Other Materials on Domestic Relations, 1970, by The Foundation Press, Inc.; "Prosser" refers to William L. Prosser, Law of Torts, Fourth Edition, 1971, by West Publishing Co.; "Wadlington" refers to Walter Wadlington and Monrad G. Paulsen, Domestic Relations Cases and Materials, 1978, by The Foundation Press, Inc.

Myron G. Hill, Jr.
Howard M. Rossen
Wilton S. Sogg

Washington, D.C.,
Cleveland, Ohio
February, 1981

SUMMARY OF CONTENTS

TABLE OF CONTENTS

OUTLINE OF FAMILY LAW

I. INTRODUCTION AND ANALYSIS

A. The Marriage Relationship
  1. Primary concern of Family Law is the marital relationship
    a. formation of the marriage
      i. formalities
      ii. types of marriage
    b. rights and duties flowing from marriage
B. Annulment
C. Family Relationships
D. Divorce
E. Adoption And Illegitimacy
F. Trends In Family Law
  1. Rights of women
  2. Rights of children

II. THE INSTITUTION OF MARRIAGE

A. Historical Background Of Marriage—English matrimonial law influenced statutes in United States
  1. Ecclesiastical courts
    a. established formalities
      i. publish marriage banns
      ii. wedding ceremony
      iii. giving of ring to bride
    b. canonical disabilities
      i. marriage of relatives
      ii. impotence
  2. Common law (civil) courts
    a. civil disabilities
      i. prior marriage
      ii. age
      iii. fraud
      iv. duress
      v. insanity
B. Nature of The Marriage Relationship
  1. Contractual by nature, but has special status because it is institution upon which the "family" is based
  2. Importance to society—state laws foster, protect, and provide for dissolution
C. Elements of A Valid Marriage
  1. Competency of parties
  2. Present agreement to become husband and wife
  3. Compliance with regulations governing marriage
    a. blood tests
    b. banns
    c. licensing
    d. solemnization
    e. officiation
    f. registration
NOTE—Regulations may be *mandatory*, in which case they are necessary

for a valid marriage, or *directory,* in which case they are not necessary for a valid marriage but non-compliance may subject party to civil or criminal penalties.

  D. Contracts Preventing Or Promoting Marriage
    1. General restraint preventing marriage usually invalid
    2. Partial restraint usually valid
    3. Contracts promoting marriage for profit unenforceable
  E. Contracts Made Prior To Marriage
    1. Antenuptial Contract—signed writing required if marriage is part of consideration because of statute of frauds
    2. Requirements
      a. full disclosure
      b. fair and reasonable provisions
      c. valid consideration
    3. Prohibitions
      a. may not regulate marital rights, such as right to support and maintenance, during marriage
      b. void to extent it provides for compensation for performance of marital duties
  F. Formalities Of The Marriage Relationship

III. TYPES OF MARRIAGES

  A. Introduction
  B. Common Law Marriages
    1. Requirements
      a. agreement by parties to enter marriage, usually implied from conduct
      b. representation to public that couple is married
      c. cohabitation as husband and wife
    2. No civil or ecclesiastical ceremony
  C. Recognition Of Common Law Marriages—
    1. Most states do not recognize—law of parties' domicile controls
  D. Proxy Marriages—
    1. Agent contracts for party
    2. Validity depends on state law
  E. Putative Marriages—marriage contracted in good faith, and in ignorance of existing impediment by at least one party
    1. Recognized by some states to permit spouse who "married" in good faith to
      a. claim interest in community property
      b. inherit from spouse
      c. sue for wrongful death of spouse
  F. Successive Marriages—bigamy and polygamy
    1. Second marriage void if party has spouse of previous marriage still living and is undivorced
    2. Enoch Arden statutes permit court to declare absent spouse dead or to dissolve marriage after specified period of time of absence, thus permitting lawful second marriage

IV. ANNULMENT

  A. Historical Background—annulment—legal process by which a marriage is invalidated retroactively to the date of the inception of the marriage
  B. Annulment As Distinguished From Divorce
    1. Annulment results from invalid marriage, either void or voidable, and divorce is based on valid marriage
    2. Annulment terminates marriage retroactively to date of inception, and divorce terminates marriage as of date of decree

    3. Grounds for annulment, unlike divorce, must have existed at time of marriage

    4. Usually permanent alimony is not granted in annulment decree, unlike divorce

  C. Jurisdiction In Annulment Actions—normally based on domicile of one or both spouses

  D. Grounds For Annulment

    1. Similar to grounds for divorce, so time which ground arose determines whether annulment or divorce is sought

    2. Generally grounds include

      a. impotency

      b. fraud

        i. misrepresentation going to essentials of marriage is valid ground

        ii. misrepresentation as to sterility, venereal disease or mental illness is valid ground

      c. dare or jest

      d. prior existing marriage

      e. mental incapacity

      f. duress

        i. threat of force is valid ground

        ii. threat of legal action is not ground regardless of whether the legal action is justified

  E. Defenses To An Annulment Action

    1. Ratification—continued cohabitation after learning of ground for annulment

    2. Clean hands—inequitable conduct or bad faith may be asserted in some jurisdictions

    3. Antenuptial knowledge—knowledge of marital defect before the marriage

    4. Res judicata—where claim has been litigated to final judgment before

    5. Statute of limitations—time within which action for annulment must be brought

  F. Property Settlements in Annulment Actions

    1. Temporary alimony may be awarded defendant spouse if she contends the marriage is valid

    2. Permanent alimony traditionally not awarded, but many states permit it in court's discretion or to prevent injustice

V.   FAMILY RELATIONSHIPS

  A. Introduction

  B. Support Obligations In A Family

    1. Types of statutes which impose support obligations:

      a. common law type statutes which obligate the husband to support his wife

      b. family expense statutes which charge expenses against the property of both the husband and wife

      c. family responsibility statutes which obligate the husband to support his wife, but obligate the wife to support the husband only if he is unable to support himself

NOTE—Under recent Supreme Court decisions the constitutionality of any support statute which discriminates on the basis of sex must be questioned because of the Equal Protection Clause of the Fourteenth Amendment

    2. Support always includes necessities

    3. Support includes all expenses in some states

    4. Uniform Reciprocal Support Act allows reciprocity between states to obtain and enforce support obligations (See CHART II)

2. Doctrine of comparative rectitude
   a. used when both spouses commit acts which are grounds for divorce
   b. under the doctrine the spouse committing the less serious act is granted the divorce
F. No Fault Divorce—present law in almost all states
   1. Determined by state statutes, which may include
      a. evidence of irreconcilable differences
      b. voluntary separation for a certain period
      c. separation caused by incompatibility where reconciliation is improbable

VII. FINANCIAL AND OTHER ASPECTS OF DIVORCE

A. Introduction
B. Property Division In Divorce
   1. Most states divide property according to what is "just and reasonable"
   2. Community property states require equal or equitable division of all property acquired during marriage
C. Historical Background Of Alimony—money paid for maintenance and support
D. Temporary Alimony—may be awarded for the period of litigation, and
   1. Is a decree in personam
   2. Ends with termination of divorce action
   3. Is within the discretion of court
   4. Amount depends upon circumstances of parties
E. Permanent Alimony—may be awarded when divorce is final
   1. Different forms:
      a. periodic payments
      b. lump sum payment
      c. annuity purchase
      d. alimony trusts
   2. Form dependent upon
      a. circumstances of parties
      b. statutes in jurisdiction
      c. negotiations
      d. discretion of court
   3. Alimony is usually based on needs and abilities of parties, considering
      a. age of the parties
      b. health and physical condition of the parties
      c. the earning capacity of the parties
      d. present income of the parties
      e. in some jurisdictions, the duration of the marriage
F. Enforcement Of Alimony And Support Decrees—through contempt proceedings integrated divorce decree
   1. Rehabilitative alimony provides support until spouse can be self-supporting
   2. Alimony may be awarded to either spouse
G. Termination Of Duty To Pay Alimony
   1. Death or marriage
   2. Changed circumstances of party
   3. In some jurisdictions, cohabitation without marriage
H. Determination of Child Custody—by court according to best interests of child
   1. Factors considered
      a. the age of the child
      b. the health and emotional stability of the child
      c. fitness to care for the child, including
         i. the emotional stability of each parent
         ii. the misconduct of one spouse

5. Legal fees are not deductible except
   a. when rendered for tax purposes
   b. to the extent they are for the collection of alimony, which is taxable income

VIII. **ADOPTION—legal procedure by which the status of parent and child is conferred upon persons not so related naturally**

A. Introduction
B. Types Of Adoption Placement Procedures
   1. Agency placement
      a. adoption agency makes arrangements and is responsible for placing children
      b. usually extensive investigation made of adoptive parents
      c. usually adoptive parents pay fee to agency
   2. Independent placement
      a. arrangements made directly by natural parent or interested intermediary representing prospective or natural parents
      b. usually no investigation made unless required by statute
      c. usually adoptive parents pay medical expenses of mother and legal fees
C. Subsidized Adoption—adoptive parents receive reimbursement for certain expenses in connection with rearing hard to place children, children with physical or mental handicaps
D. Privacy Of Adoption Records—adoption records noramally sealed to the child, the natural and adoptive parents
E. Consent In Adoption
   1. Consent of natural parents or guardian required
   2. Form and procedure set out in each jursidiction
   3. Revocation of consent permitted in some cases
      a. fraud or duress
      b. any time prior to a final decree of adoption
      c. within the discretion of the court whose chief consideration is the welfare of the child
   4. Natural father of illegitimate child has constitutionally protected rights
F. Termination Of Natural Parent-child Rights And Duties
   1. Two step process
      a. termination of rights and responsibilities between child and natural parent
      b. creation of rights and responsibilities between child and adoptive parents
   2. Termination can be
      a. voluntary by natural parents in accordance with applicable statute
      b. involuntary where natural parents are unable or unfit
   3. Custody in divorce does not terminate parent-child relationship
G. Jurisdictional Aspects Of Adoption
   1. Adoption may take place in
      a. child's domicile
      b. adoptive parent's domicile, or
      c. where both are subject to jurisdiction
H. Abrogation Of Adoption Decrees
   1. Not favored by courts
   2. Adoption will be set aside for
      a. fraud
      b. lack of notice to interested party, or
      c. when in the best welfare of the child
I. Adoption Of Adults
   1. Governed by statute

2. Varies by jurisdiction
3. Main purpose is to act as an inheritance device

J. Inheritance Rights Of Adopted Children—vary by jurisdiction—general principles
  1. Adoptive child may inherit from adoptive parents
  2. Adoptive child may inherit through adoptive parents
  3. Adoptive parents and relatives may inherit from adoptive child

IX. ILLEGITIMACY

A. Common Law Background Of Illegitimacy
  1. Illegitimate child had no inheritance rights
  2. Parents had no duty to support
B. Modern Approach To Illegitimacy
  1. Harsh common law rules abandoned
  2. Illegitimate child has
    a. right to inherit
    b. right to support
  3. Equal Protection Clause of Fourteenth Amendment protects from discrimination
  4. Statutes provide for legitimization
C. Artificial Insemination And Illegitimacy—impregnating a woman with semen of a donor by means other than sexual intercourse
  1. Child legitimate by statute if donor not married to woman
  2. Little case law—conflicting—better rule is that child is legitimate
D. Inheritance Rights Of Illegitimates—intestate inheritance rights
  1. Traditional rule
    a. can inherit from mother
    b. can inherit from father if acknowledged or legitimated
  2. Recent Supreme Court decision—discrimination in intestate inheritance violates Equal Protection Clause (Trimble v. Gordon)

X. TRENDS IN FAMILY LAW

A. Introduction—due process and equal protection clause interpreted to equalize rights of spouses
B. Divorce—enactment of no fault divorce laws in almost all states
C. Property Settlement And Alimony—division of marital property
  1. Contribution of full time housewife recognized and often property divided equally
  2. Types of property found divisible is increasing
  3. Based on need and ability to pay rather than on fault
  4. Rehabilitative alimony awarded
  5. Husbands may now receive alimony
  6. Cohabitation without marriage after divorce may warrant termination of alimony
D. Child Custody And Support
  1. Child custody becoming more common for fathers
  2. Unreasonable discrimination against unwed fathers prohibited
  3. Child support obligations divided between spouses
  4. Federal legislation enacted to enforce child support obligations
    a. locate absent parents
    b. establish paternity
    c. obtain child support from parents
E. Adoption
  1. Religion is valid factor in placing children
  2. Subsidized adoption helps place handicapped children
  3. Adoption records may be divulged if special need shown
  4. Rights of unwed fathers becoming more equal to those of unwed mothers

F. Illegitimacy
  1. Statutory classification of children based upon legitimacy may
     a. violate Equal Protection Clause of Fourteenth Amendment if state statute involved
     b. violate Due Process Clause of Fifth Amendment if federal statute involved
  2. Statute must bear reasonable relationship to legitimate state or federal governmental purpose
G. Marriage, Divorce, And Cohabitation
  1. Freedom to marry is constitutional right—unreasonable restrictions unlawful
  2. Nonmarital relationships—one party may be able to recover from other after break up of relationship based upon
     a. express contract
     b. implied contract or joint venture
     c. quantum meruit or trust
NOTE—Recovery is permitted only for services which are severable from the illicit sexual relationship for which no compensation is allowed.
H. Trends In Rights Of Women
  1. Common law disabilities have been removed
  2. Right of personal privacy recognized
     a. birth control information and contraceptives
     b. abortion
  3. Employment discrimination prohibited
I. Proposed Equal Rights Amendment
  1. If enacted, would prohibit federal, state and local governments from using sex as a factor in determining rights of men and women
J. Rights Of Juveniles In Criminal Law
  1. Common law rules
     a. child under 7—conclusively presumed incapable of committing crime
     b. child between 7 and 14—rebuttable presumption of incapacity
     c. child over 14—rebuttable presumption of capacity
  2. Modern statutes
     a. some establish juvenile courts to protect and rehabilitate children
     b. some give jurisdiction to criminal courts for certain felonies
     c. other states have concurrent jurisdiction of juvenile and criminal courts
  3. Constitutional rights protected
     a. notice of charge
     b. privilege against self-incrimination
     c. right to counsel
     d. confrontation and cross-examination of witnesses
     e. proof beyond reasonable doubt
     f. double jeopardy

I INTRODUCTION AND ANALYSIS

Summary Outline

THE MARRIAGE RELATIONSHIP

1. The principal focal point in the study of family law is the marital relationship. This includes:

   (a) the formation of the marriage,

   (b) the rights and obligations flowing from the marital relationship, and

   (c) termination of the marital relationship.

2. An aspect peculiar to family law is the concern which extends beyond the two immediate parties to the marital relationship. Because of this concern analysis of any family law situation must also include consideration of the interests of:

   (a) any issue of the marriage, and

   (b) the society, at large.

3. Family law concerns itself not only with rights and obligations between parties to a *relationship*, such as husband and wife, but also with rights and obligations flowing from a *status*, such as:

   (a) a married woman,

   (b) a separated spouse,

   (c) a divorced spouse,

   (d) a minor child,

   (e) an adopted child, and

   (f) an illegitimate child.

4. Analysis of the institution of marriage requires consideration of:

   (a) the historical background,

   (b) the nature of the marital relationship,

   (c) the elements of a marriage,

   (d) contracts preventing or promoting marriage, and

   (e) the formalities accompanying the marital relationship.

   See Chapter II.

5. Consideration of the institution of marriage requires consideration of the various ways in which the status of marriage can be achieved:

   (a) ceremonial marriage,

   (b) common law marriage,

   (c) proxy marriage, and

   (d) putative marriage.

   See Chapter III.

6. Some marital relationships may be dissolved, retroactively, to the date of their formation, through the process of annulment. Analysis of such a fact pattern requires consideration of: **ANNULMENT**

(a) jurisdiction to grant the annulment,

(b) grounds for the annulment,

(c) defenses to an action for annulment, and

(d) the rights and obligations of the parties arising from the annulment action.

See Chapter IV.

7. Once the marital relationship has been established, a fact pattern must be analyzed to determine the rights and obligations arising out of family relationships. These include: **FAMILY RELATIONSHIPS**

(a) support obligations,

(b) support actions between members of the family, (husband and wife, one for the other, and parents for children) and

(c) the legal rights, obligations, and special status of minors.

See Chapter V.

8. The process by which the marital relationship is most frequently terminated is divorce. **DIVORCE**

(a) Divorce is effective from the date of the decree and thus is distinguishable from annulment. Any analysis of divorce should take this into account.

(b) Analysis of any divorce fact pattern must include consideration of the following:

　(i) jurisdiction to grant the divorce,

　(ii) grounds for divorce, and

　(iii) defenses to a divorce action.

(c) The divorce action terminates the marital relationship.

(d) The divorce decree determines the property rights of the parties to the divorce and the financial rights and obligations of the parties to the divorce and any children of the marriage.

See Chapter VI.

9. The financial aspects of a divorce include:

(a) division of the marital property, including community property,

    (b) the award of alimony,

       (i)   temporary, and

       (ii) permanent,

    (c) award of custody of minor children of the marriage, and provision for support thereof.

See Chapter VII.

10. The financial aspects of a divorce are generally provided for in a separation agreement entered into between the parties and ultimately incorporated into the court's divorce decree.   See Chapter VII.

11. Regardless of the manner in which the marriage relationship is terminated, the tax implications of the financial aspects of the termination are of prime importance and must be carefully analyzed. See Chapter VII.

ADOPTION AND ILLEGITIMACY

12. Family law deals extensively with the rights of natural children of a valid marriage.   Analysis of a family law fact pattern may thus bring into play two other areas of concern with respect to the parent-child relationship:

    (a) adoption, and

    (b) illegitimacy.

13. Analysis of an adoption matter includes:

    (a) types of placement,

    (b) requisite consent to the adoption,

    (c) termination of the natural parents' rights and duties,

    (d) abrogation of adoption, and

    (e) inheritance rights arising from adoptions of both children and adults.

See Chapter VIII.

14. Analysis of a fact pattern involving illegitimacy involves consideration of:

    (a) specific attention to the laws of the particular jurisdiction involved,

    (b) the identity of the natural parents, and

    (c) the rights and responsibilities of the natural parents, and the illegitimate child itself.

See Chapter IX.

15. Because the subject matter of family law is in a constant state of flux, analysis of any fact pattern must take into account the possible impact of any of the trends of change in the law and forces for social change, which include:

TRENDS IN FAMILY LAW

(a) changes in the law with respect to marriage,

(b) changes in the grounds for and other aspects of the law of divorce, including:

    (i) alimony,

    (ii) child custody, and

    (iii) child support,

(c) changing rights of illegitimate children and their natural parents,

(d) changing law and social attitudes with respect to adoptions,

(e) changing law at state, federal and constitutional levels with respect to women's rights, and

(f) the criminal responsibility and constitutional rights of juveniles.

See Chapter X.

II THE INSTITUTION OF MARRIAGE

Summary Outline

A. Historical Background of Marriage
1. ecclesiastical courts
2. common law (civil) courts

B. Nature of the Marriage Relationship
1. contractual, but with special status as family institution
2. importance to society

C. Elements of a Valid Marriage
1. competency of parties
2. present agreement to become husband and wife
3. compliance with regulations governing marriage

D. Contracts Preventing or Promoting Marriage
1. general restraint usually invalid
2. partial restraint usually valid
3. contracts promoting marriage for profit unenforceable

E. Contracts Made Prior to Marriage
1. statute of frauds requirement of a writing
2. other requirements
3. prohibitions

F. Formalities of the Marriage Relationship

HISTORICAL BACKGROUND OF MARRIAGE

1. Although the law governing marriage in the United States has evolved to its present state through legislative action, this body of law has been influenced greatly by English matrimonial law and traditions. This influence can be seen in three areas:

   (a) the ceremony surrounding the entrance into the marriage contract,

   (b) the guidelines determining the validity of the marriage contract, and

   (c) the instrumentality of the courts to apply their guidelines to the marriage relation.

   See generally, Clark, pp. 32–34; Paulsen, p. 6.

2. The initial step in the Anglo-Saxon marriage customs was the "betrothal", by which the family of the bride agreed to transfer custody of the bride to the groom and the groom agreed to care for, protect and make a settlement upon the bride. Following the betrothal the transfer was accomplished. The settlement involved was the forerunner of "dower." See Clark, p. 32.

3. With the conquest of the Anglo-Saxons by the Normans and the increased influence of Christianity, religion assumed a prominent role in the marriage relationship. The power to regulate such relationship was placed under the jurisdiction of the Church and the ecclesiastical courts.

4. Ecclesiastical courts established certain formalities of a marriage ceremony within the Church which survive today. They include:

   (a) the publishing of the marriage banns (notice of the intended marriage),

   (b) the performance of the wedding ceremony by a priest in a church, and

   (c) the giving of a ring by the groom.

5. Rules with respect to the marriage relationship developed in the English courts.

   (a) The *ecclesiastical* courts prohibited the marriage of relatives of a certain degree of sanguinity and the marriage of children below a certain age.

   (b) The *common law* courts set out civil disabilities that would invalidate a marriage.

6. A distinction developed between void and voidable marriages.

   (a) Civil disabilities, such as a prior marriage, failure to be a required age, fraud, duress and insanity, rendered the marriage void.

   (b) Canonical disabilities, such as marriage of persons within a certain degree of blood relationship and impotence, came from Church law and rendered the marriage voidable.

See Clark, pp. 34–35; Foote, p. 570.

NOTE—At common law there was no necessity for an annulment of a void marriage. An ecclesiastical court could annul a voidable marriage so long as both parties were living.

See generally, Clark, pp. 32–35.

1. Marriage is the civil status or relationship created by the legal union of a man and woman as husband and wife, which imposes certain duties and responsibilities toward each other and society for their joint lives until death or legal termination of the relationship.

NATURE OF THE MARRIAGE RELATIONSHIP

2. Marriage is contractual by nature. However, it is distinguished from other types of contracts in the following manner:

   (a) Marriage creates a *status* as well as imposing rights and duties upon the parties to the marriage contract.

   (b) Marriage is *more restrictive* by nature than other types of contracts due to the limitations imposed upon persons with respect to their capacity to enter into the marriage contract.

   (c) Marriage generally requires a *lesser degree of mental capacity* than many other contractual situations.

   (d) Marriage is *permanent* unless dissolved by a court of competent jurisdiction and, therefore, cannot be revoked at the will of the parties to the marriage contract.

   (e) Marriage creates certain *rights* which *cannot* be *assigned, alienated* or *transferred*.

   (f) *Remedies* for breach of the marriage contract differ from the remedies available to the parties for breach of other types of contracts.

   (g) Marriage does *not* fall within the meaning of the constitutional prohibition against the impairment of contracts by the legislature.

3. The differences between marriage contracts and other types of contracts generally arise from the fact that marriage is an institution upon which the "family", an integral unit in modern society, is based and, therefore, is considered to be of vital importance to the state. Due to the significance of marriage to society and the parties, the state attempts to foster and protect the marriage relationship through its courts. See generally, Paulsen, pp. 8–10.

4. Due to its unique characteristics it can be said that marriage is practically a contract among three parties: the man, the woman and the state.

Case 1 *Ability to understand nature of marriage is sufficient mental capacity*

H suffered mental impairment as a child due to scarlet fever and encephalitis, and was later treated over a period of several years for schizophrenia. Despite those medical problems, H completed three years of high school and found a job as a laborer. When H was 28 years old, he met W whom he married the following year. After three years of marriage H was hospitalized on the advice of a psychiatrist, and subsequently was placed under legal guardianship because of incompetency. His guardian now brings an action to annul H's marriage to W on the ground that H did not have the mental capacity to enter into marriage. Should an annulment be granted?

Answer. No. Absolute inability to enter into contracts, insanity or idiocy renders a marriage void, but mere weakness of mind will not do so unless the party so afflicted mentally does not possess the power to consent. A marriage is valid if the party has sufficient capacity to understand the nature of the contract and the obligations and responsibilities created thereby. Here, the evidence tends to show that at the time of his marriage H had a sufficient understanding of the marriage relationship and consented to it. At the time of his marriage, his illness was not a disabling factor. Therefore, the court should not grant the annulment.

See *Homan v. Homan,* 181 Neb. 259, 147 N.W.2d 630 (1967); *Fischer v. Adams,* 151 Neb. 512, 38 N.W.2d 337 (1949).

Case 2 *Legislative modification of the marriage relationship sustained*

H married W-1, and several children were born of their marriage. H then left W-1, promising to return or send for W-1 and their children. H traveled to the Territory of Oregon where he settled and claimed a parcel of real estate under a congressional act as a married man. A year later the legislature of the Territory of Oregon passed an act which purported to terminate H's marriage to W-1. H then remarried and lived with W-2 on such parcel of real estate until his death. The children of H and W-1 now bring an action to compel the conveyance of the real estate to them, and base their claim on their relationship to W-1, now deceased. Did the act of the legislature constitute a divorce, thereby negating the children's claim?

Answer. Yes. *Marriage is not a contract which falls within the meaning of the constitutional prohibition against the impairment of contractual obligations by legislative action. Marriage is more than a mere contract between two parties which can be modified by agreement of such parties. Marriage can be modified only by legislative authority. Therefore, the act of the legislature constituted a valid divorce, and since W-1 had no valid claim to the real estate, neither did her children who claim through her.*

See Maynard v. Hill, 125 U.S. 190, 8 S.Ct. 723, 31 L.Ed. 654 (1888).

1. There are three essential elements of a valid marriage:

    (a) the *competency of both parties* to the marriage to enter into such marriage,

    (b) the mutual *present agreement* entered into in good faith by the parties to become husband and wife, and

    (c) the *compliance* by the parties *with the regulations* governing their entrance into the marriage relationship.

    See *Formalities of the Marriage Relationship*, below.

2. To be competent to enter into marriage both parties must be free of any legal disabilities which would impede their marriage. See Katz, p. 713.

3. Many states do not consider persons closely related to each other by blood or by an existing marriage competent to marry and prohibit them from entering into a marriage relationship with each other.

    NOTE—It has been uniformly held that the prohibited degrees of consanguinity include persons related by half-blood. See *Grounds for Annulment*, Chapter IV, below. See also People v. Baker, 42 Cal.2d 550, 268 P.2d 705 (1954).

4. Generally, to be competent to enter into marriage both parties must be of a minimum age fixed by law.

    NOTE—Except in jurisdictions having statutes *forbidding* marriage under a certain age, the majority rule holds that where one party is under the age of consent such marriage is voidable, but not void.

5. To be competent to enter into marriage in most jurisdictions both parties must meet certain health standards.

    e.g. Most states forbid the marriage of those persons afflicted with venereal disease.

6. To be competent to enter into marriage both parties must have

ELEMENTS OF A VALID MARRIAGE

sufficient mental ability to understand the nature, effect and consequences of marriage at the time of the marriage.

See *Nature of the Marriage Relationship*, above;   See CASE 2, above.

NOTE—A lesser standard of mental capacity is imposed upon parties to a marriage contract than is imposed upon parties to other contracts.   See Chapter IV, *Grounds for Annulment*, below.

7. To be competent to enter into marriage a party may not be married to another person at the time of such marriage.   Existence of a prior marriage invalidates a successive marriage as well as subjecting such party to criminal prosecution for bigamy.   See *Grounds for Annulment*, Chapter IV, and *Successive Marriages*, Chapter III, below.

8. The parties to a marriage must intend to enter into the complete marriage relationship with all obligations and responsibilities rather than for a limited purpose.

(a) The marriage of A, a citizen of a foreign country, and B, a citizen of the United States, contracted only so that A would be permitted into the United States and entered into without any intention by A and B to live together as husband and wife will not be held to be valid.   Marriage solely for the purpose of immigration where there is lack of intent to assume the "status" of marriage is invalid.

(b) H and W had been sweethearts while they were living in their native Korea.   W immigrated to the United States and became a resident alien.   W came to the United States initially as a business visitor and then as a student.   A year later H and W were married.   W filed a petition on behalf of H to qualify him as the spouse of a resident alien.   Evidence at the hearing showed that H and W quarreled and separated after the marriage, although both H and W testified that they married for love and not to circumvent immigration laws.   The court said: "Petitioner's marriage was a sham if the bride and groom did not intend to establish a life together at the time they were married. . . .   Conduct of the parties after marriage is relevant only to the extent that it bears upon their subjective state of mind at the time they were married. . . .   Evidence that the parties separated after their wedding is relevant in ascertaining whether they intended to establish a life together when they exchanged marriage vows.   But evidence of separation, standing alone, cannot support a finding that a marriage was not bona fide when it was entered."   Thus, it is the intent of the parties at the time of their marriage that determines whether it is valid or a sham.   Evidence of a subsequent separation, without more, does not establish that the marriage was a sham.   See Bark v. Immigration and Naturalization Serv., 511 F.2d 1200 (9th Cir. 1975).

9. Traditional rules have related to marriages of members of the opposite sex.   In recent years homosexuals and lesbians have attempted to marry members of the same sex.   They have challenged state statutes which required the marriage to be between members of the opposite sex.   However, courts have held that it is not a denial of the fundamental right to marry to require that the marriage be between persons of the opposite sex.

e.g.   Two homosexuals were denied a marriage license, and they sought a writ of mandamus to compel issuance of the license. The court interpreted the applicable statute as requiring persons who seek a marriage license to be of the opposite sex.   It concluded that such a requirement did not violate any constitutional right.   The right to be free from invidious sex discrimination under the Equal Protection Clause of the Fourteenth Amendment is not violated by the prohibition of marriage by homosexuals. There is no irrational or invidious discrimination.   The petition for writ of mandamus was denied.   See Baker v. Nelson, 291 Minn. 310, 191 N.W.2d 185 (1971), appeal dismissed 409 U.S. 810, 93 S.Ct. 37, 34 L.Ed.2d 65 (1972).

NOTE 1—Marriage between persons of the same sex has also been prohibited where there was a state Equal Rights Amendment in effect.   The court reasoned that the relationship of marriage has always been the legal union of one man and one woman.   Same sex relationships are outside the proper definition of marriage. The primary purpose of the ERA is to overcome discriminatory legal treatment between men and women "on account of sex." It does not create any new rights or responsibilities such as the right of persons of the same sex to marry each other.   The refusal to issue the marriage license was not a denial based upon sex, but rather a denial based upon the marriage relationship.   Finally, the prohibition of same sex marriage rests upon a reasonable basis, the impossibility of procreation, and therefore, does not violate the Equal Protection Clause of the Fourteenth Amendment.   See Singer v. Hara, 11 Wash.App. 247, 522 P.2d 1187 (1974).

NOTE 2—A marriage between a male and a postoperative transsexual, who surgically changed her external sexual anatomy from male to female, has been upheld.   The court stated: "If such sex reassignment surgery is successful and the postoperative transsexual is, by virtue of medical treatment, thereby possessed of the full capacity to function sexually as a male or female, as the case may be, we perceive no legal barrier, cognizable social taboo, or reason grounded in public policy to prevent that person's identification at least for purposes of marriage to the sex finally indicated."   M. T. v. J. T., 140 N.J.Super. 77, 355 A.2d 204 (1976).

See generally, Clark, pp. 114–118.   See also Chapter X, *Marriage, Divorce and Cohabitation, below.*

CONTRACTS PREVENTING OR PROMOTING MARRIAGE

1. The validity or invalidity of contracts in restraint of marriage is dependent, in most instances, upon whether such restraints are general or partial.

   (a) A *general restraint* which is so complete as to prevent marriage is generally deemed to be invalid.

   (b) The validity of a *partial restraint* which does not prevent marriage completely is dependent upon whether the restraint is beneficial.

   See Clark, pp. 24–27.

2. Contracts which would prevent *remarriage* or contracts regarding conveyances on the condition that no *remarriage* occurs are usually held valid.   See CASE 3, below.   See generally, Clark, pp. 24 and 26.

3. Agreements with a third party which prevent a spouse from performing the obligations of a marriage are illegal and unenforceable.   See Clark, pp. 25–26.

4. Similarly, a contract in which marriage is promoted for profit is unenforceable since it violates the policy that marriage should be entered into freely without the activities of paid third parties.

   e.g.   Contracts in which a broker promotes marriage for profit are unenforceable.   However, many cities have marriage brokers listed in telephone books.   Apparently such services are utilized, and probably the fee is collected in advance.   See Clark, pp. 26–27; Wadlington, p. 110.

Case 3   *All restraints against marriage are not invalid*

H and W were married for over 20 years when W brought an action for separate maintenance since H had had extramarital relations with X.   H and W then entered into a stipulation of their property rights, and W amended her petition to request a divorce, which was granted.   At the same time H and W entered into an agreement which was not filed with the court.   That agreement provided that if either party remarried prior to their youngest child attaining age 20, such party would forfeit the sum of $10,000.00 to the other party.   Within a year H married X.   W now applies to the court for modification of the divorce decree to provide for a judgment against H for $10,000.00. H contends that the contract is void as against public policy and unenforceable because it amounts to a penalty.   Is the contract valid?

Answer. Yes. The jurisdiction in which H and W are domiciled follows the general rule that contracts in general restraint of marriage are against public policy and, therefore, void. A general restraint is construed as a restraint which binds a party from marrying anyone at any time. However, contracts in restraint of marriage, if shown to be reasonable under the circumstances and not general and unlimited, will be held valid. It should be noted that courts are more likely to find restraints against remarriage valid than restraints against first marriages. However, this is probably due to the fact that circumstances surrounding a restraint against remarriage more often prove such restraint to be reasonable and to serve a meritorious purpose. In this case, W feared the effect of X's influence on her children, if H married X. Furthermore, the restraint was not unlimited and appears to be reasonable in view of H's past conduct. Therefore, the contract should be upheld.

See Cowan v. Cowan, 247 Iowa 729, 75 N.W.2d 920 (1956).

Burden of proof on objecting party where competency of other party challenged

Case 4

H and W were married and after two years of marriage W was committed to a mental institution where she still is a patient. After such commitment H learned that W had been committed to a hospital on two previous occasions and had been diagnosed as having schizophrenic tendencies. H now seeks an annulment claiming that W at the time of their marriage was of unsound mind and incapable of understanding the marriage contract. W's guardian states that H has not shown sufficient proof that W was incapable of understanding the nature of the act of marriage. Should H's petition be granted?

Answer. No. Upon presentation of proof of the celebration of a marriage, the validity of such marriage will be presumed and the burden of proof rests with the party objecting thereto to establish the invalidity of such marriage. A definite rule with respect to the mental condition necessary for marriage is difficult to prescribe. It depends upon whether the persons involved could and did act rationally regarding the marriage. However, the parties to a marriage must have sufficient mental capacity to understand the nature of the act. Any proof of lack of such mental capacity must be definite and clear to invalidate a marriage. Here, H did not notice any abnormal behavior on the part of W prior to or at the time of the marriage, and did not present clear evidence that W was mentally incapable of understanding the nature of the marriage contract or consenting to it. Therefore, H did not meet the necessary burden of proof and his petition for annulment should be dismissed.

See Larson v. Larson, 42 Ill.App.2d 467, 192 N.E.2d 594 (1963). See also Ertel v. Ertel, 313 Ill.App. 326, 40 N.E.2d 85 (1942); CASE 16, below.

Case 5   *Failure to meet statutory minimum age will affect competency of parties to a marriage*

W, under age 18, married H in state D although both were domiciled in state N.   The law of state D permits the marriage of females over the age of 16.   The law of state N permits the marriage of females only over the age of 18.   W now brings an action in state N for the annulment of her marriage to H on the ground that she was under 18 at the time the marriage was contracted.   The law of state N permits such an action for annulment where the female has not ratified a marriage after attaining age 18 and where an annulment would be in the best interests of any children born of the marriage. May W's marriage be annulled in state N though it was valid in state D where contracted?

Answer.   Yes.   A marriage may be annulled in the state of domicile though valid where contracted, if it is repugnant to the public policy of the state of domicile.   If H and W had married in state N, the marriage could have been annulled.   Here, the court should not uphold a marriage contracted in another state to evade the law of state N where such marriage is against the public policy of state N. The marriage should be annulled because it is repugnant to the law and public policy of state N, the state of domicile.

See Wilkins v. Zelichowski, 26 N.J. 370, 140 A.2d 65 (1958).

Case 6   *Marriage by person under age—voidable only*

H, without his parents' consent, married W-1 while under the age specified by statute for marriage.   H and W-1 cohabited and then voluntarily separated.   There was no divorce.   H then married W-2. H was arrested and charged with bigamy.   H contends his marriage to W-1 was void because he was under age and, therefore, he was not married to W-1 at the time he married W-2.   Is the marriage of H to W-1 void due to his nonage?

Answer.   No.   The marriage of one under age is not an absolute nullity, but is only annulled from the date fixed by a court in an annulment proceeding.   During the time intervening the marriage is valid.   Here, the first marriage is voidable only, and since no decree of divorce or annulment was obtained, it is still in effect.   Thus, H is guilty of bigamy.

See State v. Cone, 86 Wis. 498, 57 N.W. 50 (1893); State v. Sellers, 140 S.C. 66, 134 S.E. 873 (1926).

CONTRACTS MADE PRIOR TO MARRIAGE

1. A contract made before marriage is called an antenuptial contract.

2. The purpose of an antenuptial contract is to establish the rights of the husband and wife to property owned at the time of the marriage or acquired in the future.

3. The provision in the statute of frauds, which is in effect in most states, requires that a contract made in consideration of marriage or a promise to marry, other than mutual promises to marry, must be in writing and signed by the party against whom it is to be enforced. Thus, where marriage is the entire consideration or only part of the consideration for the contract, the agreement must comply with the statute of frauds. See Clark, pp. 27–28.

e.g. H induced W to come to the United States from Europe and marry him by an oral antenuptial contract. W sued to enforce the agreement, but the court refused enforcement because the requirement of the statute of frauds that the agreement be in writing was not met. See Hutnak v. Hutnak, 78 R.I. 231, 81 A.2d 278 (1951).

NOTE—The fact that the marriage takes place after making an oral antenuptial contract is not sufficient part performance to remove the contract from the statute of frauds. This is so even where there is a change of position.

4. For an antenuptial contract to be valid, there must be:

(a) full disclosure,

(b) fair and reasonable provisions for support, and

(c) valid consideration.

5. "A valid antenuptial agreement contemplates a fair and reasonable provision therein for the wife, or, absent such provision, a full and frank disclosure to the wife, before the signing of the agreement, of the husband's worth, or, absent such disclosure, a general and approximate knowledge by her of the prospective husband's property." Del Vecchio v. Del Vecchio, 143 So.2d 17 (Fla.1962).

6. In weighing the fairness and reasonableness of an antenuptial agreement the courts will consider:

(a) the relative situations of the parties,

(b) their respective ages, health and experience,

(c) their respective properties,

(d) their family ties and connection,

(e) the needs of each party, and

(f) such factors as tend to show whether the agreement was understandingly made.

See Del Vecchio v. Del Vecchio, 143 So.2d 17 (Fla.1962).

7. An antenuptial agreement which is concerned only with the distribution of the property of the spouse upon death is valid where the requirements of numbers 3–6, above, are met. See Le Fevers v. Le Fevers, 240 Ark. 992, 403 S.W.2d 65 (1966), Contra, Watts v. Watts, 390 S.W.2d 30 (Tex.Civ.App.1965).

8. An antenuptial agreement may not regulate marital rights, such as the right to support and maintenance, during the marriage. See Belcher v. Belcher, 271 So.2d 7 (Fla.1972).

9. An antenuptial agreement is void to the extent that it provides for compensation for either spouse for the performance of marital duties. See Garlock v. Garlock, 279 N.Y. 337, 18 N.E.2d 521 (1939).

10. Most states permit suit for breach of promise to marry. The damages which may be recovered in such an action vary widely from state to state.

   e.g. P sued for breach of promise to marry. D moved to dismiss on the ground that the action was contrary to public policy. The suit was dismissed and P appealed. The appellate court noted a number of criticisms to such suits, but concluded that they did not justify abolishment of the action. Since a person will take action based on the mutual promises to marry, injuries which result should not go unanswered merely because the action may be subject to abuses. However, damages for the loss of expected financial and social position should not be allowed because a person generally does not choose a marriage partner for social or financial gain. Evidence of D's wealth or social position should not be permitted because it is immaterial. Damages for mental anguish, loss to reputation, and injury to health may be recovered because the state should afford redress for injuries suffered due to the actions of another. Such injuries are foreseeable at the time the promise is made. P may recover as a quasi-contract, quasi-tort action for foreseeable special and general damages caused by D's breach of promise to marry. See Stanard v. Bolin, 88 Wash.2d 614, 565 P.2d 94 (1977).

11. Suits for breach of promise to marry are termed "heart balm actions" because a person receives "balm" for her or his broken "heart." At least twelve states have abolished suits or limited damages which can be recovered in such actions.

   See generally, Clark, pp. 27–31.

Case 7 *Contract for future separation void as against public policy*

H and W entered into an antenuptial agreement which provided that their forthcoming marriage should continue so long as H and W were satisfied with the arrangement, but that if either party became dissatisfied with the relationship, they would separate. The agreement further provided for the division of property and a monetary settlement for W, if such a separation occurred. W and H married and subsequently separated. At that time W signed a document in which she acknowledged receipt of property and cash in accordance with the terms of the antenuptial agreement and in which she waived future rights against H or his property. H then died and W now sues for a widow's allowance from H's estate. As a defense H's administrator asserts that the antenuptial agreement prevented recovery. Is the antenuptial agreement valid and should such agreement bar W's claim?

*   **Answer.** No. A contract for a future separation of husband and wife is void as against public policy. The marriage relation is so sacred that it cannot be dissolved except in the manner specified by the legislature. It cannot be annulled by contract or at the pleasure of the parties. Here, the antenuptial agreement is a device designed to circumvent the statutes applicable to marriage and, therefore, is void.*

*   See Estate of Duncan, Popham v. Duncan, 87 Colo. 149, 285 P. 757 (1930).*

1. Due to the importance of the marriage relationship to the state, the formalities surrounding the marriage contract are wholly regulated by statute in each of the fifty states in the United States. See F. A. Marriage License, 4 Pa. D. & C.2d 1 (1955).

2. The general rule is that a marriage which is valid where performed is valid everywhere. However, a state may not follow that rule if the marriage is contrary to the public policy of that state. See Clark, pp. 74–77; Case 8, below.

3. In some states, compliance with the statutory requirements regarding marriage is considered "mandatory". If such requirements are not met, a marriage in such states will be held invalid.

4. By contrast, in other states, compliance with the statutory requirements regarding marriage is considered "directory". Failure to meet such requirements in such states, in absence of an expression that a particular requirement is a prerequisite to the validity of a marriage, does not render the marriage invalid. However, such non-compliance may subject the offending parties to criminal sanctions or civil liabilities.

5. Legislatures in all states have enacted statutes governing the formalities of marriage. Such statutes typically regulate the following:

FORMALITIES OF THE MARRIAGE RELATIONSHIP

(a) blood tests,

(b) banns,

(c) licensing,

(d) solemnization,

(e) officiation, and

(f) registration

See generally, Clark, p. 36; Paulsen, pp. 62–69.

6. Most states require that the results of *blood tests* of both parties to the marriage be presented prior to the issuance of a marriage license in order to prove that neither party is afflicted with venereal disease. Such requirement is usually "directory" and consequently the non-compliance with such a requirement *does not ordinarily render a marriage invalid.*

7. Many states, following the English practice of publishing *"banns"* or notice of the prospective marriage, require a waiting period either between the performance of the blood tests and the issuance of the marriage license or between the issuance of the marriage license and the performance of the marriage ceremony. Such statute is usually "directory" and consequently the non-compliance with such a requirement *does not ordinarily render a marriage invalid.*

8. Most states require the issuance of a *marriage license* prior to the performance of the marriage ceremony. The precise provisions governing the circumstances concerning the issuance vary from state to state. Such statutes are "directory" in some states and "mandatory" in other states. Thus, non-compliance with such requirements *in some states does not ordinarily render a marriage invalid, while in other states it does render a marriage void.*

9. Most states require *formal celebration or solemnization* of a marriage, although the precise form that such ceremony takes is not prescribed by statute. While the solemnization itself in some form is required for a *valid ceremonial marriage,* the non-compliance with some requirements concerning the details of such ceremony *does not ordinarily render a marriage invalid,* since such statutes are usually "directory".

10. Most states have enacted legislation with respect to the *persons who may officiate* at a marriage ceremony. This type of legislation generally concerns the qualifications and licensing of such persons and is considered "directory". The performance of a marriage ceremony by a person who does not meet such requirement, therefore, *does not render the marriage invalid.*

NOTE—Some states have enacted statutes which provide that a marriage, entered into in good faith in which the ceremony is performed by an unauthorized person but in which all other aspects comply with the law, *is nevertheless valid.*

11. Most states have enacted legislation governing the recording of marriages. These statutes are "directory" and consequently the noncompliance with such legislation *does not render an otherwise proper marriage invalid.*

Foreign marriage contrary to public policy not recognized   Case 8

H married his niece, W, in Italy. Although such a marriage was prohibited by Italian law, the parties obtained a dispensation in Italy which made the marriage valid. H and W resided in the United States until H's death. W applied for an allowance for support from H's estate under state law. The court denied W's application because the marriage was invalid as incestuous under state law. Was that decision correct?

Answer. Yes. *The general rule is that a marriage valid where performed is valid everywhere. There are, however, certain exceptions to that rule. One such exception regards as invalid an incestuous marriage between persons so closely related that their marriage is contrary to strong public policy of the state of domicile even though it was valid where celebrated. "A state has the authority to declare what marriages of its citizens shall be recognized as valid, regardless of the fact that the marriages may have been entered into in foreign jurisdictions where they were valid." This state has prohibited marriages between uncle and niece for many years and made it a criminal offense. That reflects strong public policy against such marriages. Therefore, W's marriage to H will not be recognized, and W cannot qualify as the surviving spouse of H.*

See *Catalano v. Catalano*, 148 Conn. 288, 170 A.2d 726 (1961).

NOTE—Many states do not follow the rule of the Catalano case, above. One authority suggests that a better rule would be to establish two classes of incest: (a) A marriage between a father and daughter or mother and son would be void. (b) Any other marriage would be merely voidable. Such a rule would avoid the harsh result of the Catalano case. See Clark, p. 74.

Marriage is not void because there were fewer witnesses than   Case 9
required by statute

W, a widow of 50, traveled with H-2 to visit H-2's daughter. W had been under the influence of alcohol for the two months preceding the trip. W remembers only that she awoke the morning after she began the trip with H-2 and was told she married H-2 the previous night. The marriage was performed on the day the marriage license was issued by a minister in the presence of only two witnesses, rather than the three required by statute. A statute of the jurisdiction requires a 72-hour waiting period between the issuance of the license and the performance of the ceremony. W petitions to annul the marriage on the grounds that the ceremony was not performed in accordance with the statutory regulations and that there was lack of consent. Should her petition be granted?

Answer. *No. The statutes providing for the manner and form in which marriages are to be celebrated are merely "directory" and failure to observe them will not make the marriage null and void. Here, despite having only two witnesses to the ceremony which was performed before the 72-hour waiting period had passed, the marriage is valid. This is so since the purpose of such statutes is the prevention of hasty marriages. Furthermore, there was no lack of consent since the minister testified that after speaking with W and H-2 on two occasions he was convinced that they both understood what they were doing and wanted to marry each other. Thus, the petition for annulment will not be granted.*

See Parker v. Saileau, 213 So.2d 190 (La.App.1968).

Case 10   *Marriage performed by an unauthorized party is valid*

H and W were married by a family court judge who was acting outside the geographical limits within which he was authorized to perform marriages. H and W had applied for a license, participated in the ceremony and thereafter lived together as husband and wife. H now seeks to have the marriage annulled on the ground that the judge did not perform a valid marriage. Should an annulment be granted?

Answer. *No. The statute involved pertains only to the form and manner in which marriages are to be celebrated and is merely "directory" in nature. Failure to meet its provisions does not render a marriage void. Furthermore, courts are reluctant to invalidate a marriage unless the law and circumstances indicate clearly that it should be annulled. In this case, it would be contrary to public policy to allow one of the parties to deny the validity of the marriage when a difference has arisen between them and there is no mandatory reason to grant an annulment.*

See Helfond v. Helfond, 53 Misc.2d 974, 280 N.Y.S.2d 990 (1967).

III TYPES OF MARRIAGES

Summary Outline

A. Introduction

B. Common Law Marriages
    1. requirements
    2. no civil or ecclesiastical ceremony

C. Recognition of Common Law Marriages
    1. most states do not recognize
    2. law of parties' domicile controls

D. Proxy Marriages
    1. agent contracts for party
    2. validity depends on state law

E. Putative Marriages
    1. rights of spouse who "married" in good faith

F. Successive Marriages
    1. second marriage void if first spouse is still living and undivorced
    2. Enoch Arden statutes

INTRODUCTION
1. The status of marriage can be achieved in a variety of ways, the principal two of which are:

   (a) ceremonial marriage, and

   (b) common law marriage.

2. Ceremonial marriages are provided for under the laws of all of the states. By contrast, common law marriages are recognized in only one-quarter of the jurisdictions.

3. In the law of marriage, occasionally the concept of proxy marriage is encountered.

4. In civil law jurisdictions, putative marriage is the analogue to common law marriage.

5. The sections which follow explore the definitions and implications of these terms.

COMMON LAW MARRIAGES
1. A common law marriage is an agreement between a man and a woman to enter into the marital relationship without benefit of a civil or ecclesiastical ceremony.

   CAVEAT—If the parties to a valid common law marriage separate, they must obtain a divorce before either may contract a later marriage.

2. Where common law marriages are recognized, courts reason that marriage is a civil contract and no specific ceremony is required.

3. Historically, a common law contract of marriage made *per verba de praesenti* (by words of the present [tense]) was a valid marriage. It is an express contract of marriage. See Voorhees v. Voorhees, Ex'rs 46 N.J.Eq. 411, 19 A. 172 (1890).

   e.g. Each party says: "I agree to take you as my husband (or wife) and live with you as husband and wife." These words, spoken by both parties, are sufficient to establish a common law marriage.

4. If the future tense is used, there would only be a promise to marry. e.g. "I will take you for my husband" would create an engagement. No marriage would occur at that time.

5. Under present law, courts look to the actions of the parties rather than to specific words used. The elements of a valid common law marriage include:

   (a) *consent* or *agreement* by the parties to enter into the marriage relationship, which may be implied from conduct,

   (b) *representation* by the parties to the public that they are husband and wife, and

(c) *cohabitation* by the parties as husband and wife.

e.g. M and W told a few persons they were married although they never had a ceremonial marriage. M and W had sexual relations, but did not live together and observed great secrecy with respect to their relationship. M and W do not have a valid common law marriage because:

    (i) they did not enter into a present agreement to marry,

    (ii) they did not hold themselves out to all persons that they are husband and wife, and

    (iii) they did not cohabit.

See Ex parte Threet, 160 Tex. 482, 333 S.W.2d 361 (1960).

RECOGNITION OF COMMON LAW MARRIAGES

1. Common law marriages are recognized in approximately one-fourth of the jurisdictions in the United States. See Clark, p. 45.

2. In the majority of the remaining jurisdictions statutes have been enacted which require all marriages to conform with certain prescribed regulations as to the ceremony, license and other aspects of the marriage. Such statutes, therefore, bar common law marriages since they lack licensing and requisite ceremonies.

   CAVEAT—Some cases in jurisdictions which require all marriages to conform with certain formalities have held those statutes to be "merely directory." In the interest of public policy, which encourages marriage, those courts have found non-conforming marriages, such as common law marriages, to be valid. Those cases, however, are in the minority. See Meister v. Moore, 96 U.S. 76, 24 L.Ed. 826 (1877). See also *Formalities of the Marriage Relationship*, Chapter II, above.

3. Other jurisdictions have found common law marriages to be invalid through case law.

4. "Habit and repute" appears to be the most important determining factor in deciding the existence of a valid common law marriage. In fact, in many instances where the parties have not entered into an express agreement to be husband and wife, the majority of courts nevertheless have found that an inference of an agreement can be made from "habit and repute". See Chaachou v. Chaachou, 73 So.2d 830 (Fla.1954).

   CAVEAT—A hard and fast rule concerning evidentiary proof sufficient to find the existence of a common law marriage cannot be stated due to the reluctance of many courts to validate common law marriages.

e.g.   M and W lived together and held themselves out as husband and wife for twenty-five years.   Upon M's death W makes claims as his widow.   The court did not find a valid common law marriage since there was no proof that M and W had entered into an express agreement to be husband and wife.   See In re Erickson's Estate, 75 S.D. 345, 64 N.W.2d 316 (1954).

5.   The law of the parties' domicile controls common law marriage status.

(a)   H and W lived together and held themselves out as husband and wife in State A in which common law marriages were not recognized.   H and his brother purchased a farm in State B in which common law marriages were recognized.   H and W made short visits to the farm, but continued to reside in State A.   When H died W filed suit to obtain a share of H's estate.   The court denied W's claim based upon a common law marriage because brief visits to State B did not make H and W residents of that state.   Thus, there was no common law marriage for State A to recognize.   See Kennedy v. Damron, 268 S.W.2d 22 (Ky.1954).

(b)   H and W lived together and held themselves out as husband and wife in a state in which common law marriages were not recognized.   They moved to a second state in which common law marriages were recognized.   H and W continued to hold themselves out as husband and wife and lived there until H's death.   The court held that a valid common law marriage existed in the second state.   See Travers v. Reinhardt, 205 U.S. 423, 27 S.Ct. 563, 51 L.Ed. 865 (1906).

(c)   Where parties live together and hold themselves out as husband and wife in a state in which common law marriages are recognized and then move to a state in which common law marriages are *not* recognized, a valid common law marriage will be found under the Full Faith and Credit Clause of the United States Constitution.   See Boltz v. Boltz, 325 Mass. 726, 92 N.E.2d 365 (1950).

6.   When an impediment to a valid common law marriage is removed while the parties are living together as husband and wife in a jurisdiction in which common law marriages are recognized, a valid common law marriage will result as of the time the impediment is removed.   See CASE 11, below.

See generally Clark, pp. 45–58.

Case 11   *Removal of an impediment to a common law marriage validates such marriage*

M and W lived together as husband and wife in a jurisdiction which recognized common law marriages for twenty-two years until M's death. M and W never participated in a formal marriage ceremony, but did hold themselves out as being married to each other. W had married H prior to living with M and did not obtain a divorce from H before cohabiting with M. H, however, did divorce W after she had lived with M for sixteen years. Thus W was married to H until six years before M's death at which time she was legally free to remarry. At M's death, W claims certain death benefits as M's surviving common law wife. Is W entitled to such benefits?

***Answer.** Yes. If parties agree to be husband and wife regardless of the existence of an impediment to their lawful marriage, and such impediment is later removed while they are still cohabiting, a valid common law marriage will result at the time the impediment was removed. It is not to be expected that parties once having agreed to be married will deem it necessary to agree to do so again when an impediment to marriage is removed. In this case, M and W agreed to marry before an impediment was removed and lived together as husband and wife after the impediment was removed, giving rise, therefore, to a valid common law marriage which was established at the time H obtained the divorce from W. Therefore, W is entitled to death benefits as M's surviving spouse.*

See Matthews v. Britton, 112 U.S.App.D.C. 397, 303 F.2d 408 (1962).

1. A proxy marriage is a marriage contracted or celebrated by one or more agents rather than by both parties themselves.

2. The validity of a proxy marriage is dependent upon the regulatory statutes governing marriage procedures in a particular jurisdiction.

   (a) If such statutes require the actual presence of both parties to obtain a marriage license and/or at the marriage ceremony, a proxy marriage will be held invalid.

   (b) If such statutes are silent with respect to the presence of both parties to obtain a marriage license and at the marriage ceremony, such statutes may be construed as allowing proxy marriages. See Barrons v. U. S., 191 F.2d 92 (9th Cir. 1951).

3. If a proxy marriage is performed in a jurisdiction in which proxy marriages are valid, other jurisdictions, including the domicile of the parties will recognize the proxy marriage as valid under the Full Faith and Credit Clause of the United States Constitution. See Hardin v. Davis, 30 Ohio Op. 524, 16 Ohio Supp. 19 (Hamilton County C.P.1945).

4. Proxy marriages are not prevalent. Such marriages are found mainly in times of war in order to:

PROXY MARRIAGES

(a) enable a person in the armed services to marry, and

(b) legitimize children.

See Clark, p. 58.

PUTATIVE   **1.** A putative marriage is a marriage contracted in good faith and in
MARRIAGES   ignorance of some existing impediment on the part of at least one
of the contracting parties.

See U.S. Fidelity & Guaranty Co. v. Henderson, 53 S.W.2d 811
(Tex.Cir.Ct.App.1932); Succession of Marinoni, 183 La. 776, 164
So. 797 (1935).

2. The concept of putative marriage comes from the Napoleonic Code
and is recognized only in a few states with a civil law tradition.

e.g. Texas, Louisiana and California recognize putative marriages. In addition, the state of Wisconsin has a statute similar
to the putative marriage doctrine. See Smith v. Smith, 52 Wis.2d
262, 190 N.W.2d 174 (1971).

3. Putative marriage is the device utilized in such civil law jurisdictions to reach results analogous to those reached in the jurisdictions which recognize common law marriages. See Clark, p. 54.

4. Putative marriage is more restrictive than common law marriage
since in putative marriages good faith of at least one participant
is required, whereas in a common law marriage both parties may
be and usually are fully aware that ceremonial requirements have
not been met.

5. In an action based on the existence of a putative marriage, the
party asserting a claim must prove lack of knowledge of the impediment to a valid marriage. See Smith v. Smith, 1 Tex. 621
(1846).

NOTE—The benefits applicable to the putative spouse terminate
when that spouse learns that the marriage is invalid. See Hager
v. Hager, 553 P.2d 919 (Alaska, 1976).

6. If a putative marriage is found to exist, then the spouse who entered into such marriage in good faith can:

(a) claim interest in community property,

(b) inherit from the other spouse, and

(c) sue for the wrongful death of the other spouse.

See CASE 12, below.

Case 12   *Putative wife inherits as if she were lawful wife*

*H married W-1 and departed for an overseas assignment the following
year. W-1 did not accompany H, but remained in Texas. H then*

married W-2 in Singapore. H told W-2 that he had been married, but that he had been divorced. In fact, H had never been divorced from W-1. Subsequently, H was killed in a shipwreck at sea. Approximately one month after H's death both W-1 and W-2 gave birth to daughters. Suit was brought to determine a proper division of proceeds from H's insurance policy and wages due H. Is W-2 entitled to part of H's estate even though H never divorced W-1?

Answer. Yes. Where there are successive marriages there is a presumption that the second marriage is valid. Applying that presumption to the present case W-2 would be considered H's widow. However, the evidence showed that there had been no divorce between H and W-1 in any place where H might reasonably have pursued such an action. That evidence is sufficient to rebut the presumption. Thus, W-1 is the lawful widow of H. W-2 showed that her marriage fulfilled all formal requirements, and that W-2 and H lived as wife and husband for two years thereafter. The facts also demonstrated that W-2 married H in good faith believing that he had been divorced. These facts establish that W-2 is H's putative wife, and is entitled the same right to H's property as if she were a lawful wife. In this case it is one-half. With regard to the children, the evidence demonstrated the impossibility of access between H and W-1 during the time the child might have been conceived. Thus, the daughter of W-1 could not have been H's child, and may not inherit from him. The balance of H's estate was divided equally between W-1 and the daughter of W-2.

See *Davis v. Davis,* 521 S.W.2d 603 (Tex.1975).

1. Under case law and statutory law a person may have only one spouse at a time. Thus, in circumstances where there are successive marriages, the later marriage will be held null and void, if one party to that marriage has a spouse of a previous marriage still living and undivorced.

   NOTE—Such a rule is applicable even when the first marriage is a common law marriage and the second marriage is one that meets all legal requirements with respect to a marriage license and ceremony. This is so because a common law marriage constitutes a valid marriage where permitted by law and must be dissolved before remarriage. See Beaudin v. Suarez, 365 Mich. 534, 113 N.W.2d 818 (1962).

2. The underlying principle governing successive marriages is the concept of "monogamy", marriage to but one person at a time. Violation of the requirement of monogamy will subject a person to criminal prosecution. A person "married" to two spouses will be charged with the crime of bigamy, and a person "married" to more than two spouses will be charged with the crime of polygamy. See Clark, p. 61.

SUCCESSIVE MARRIAGES

NOTE—Bigamy and polygamy are punishable even though committed due to religious beliefs and practices. See CASE 13, below.

3. A polygamous marriage will not be recognized in the United States even for matrimonial remedies, such as divorce, even if the marriage is contracted in a country permitting such a practice. It will, however, be recognized for the purposes of the legitimization of children born of such a marriage or the barring of a successive marriage. See In re Dalip Singh Bir's Estate, 83 Cal.App.2d 256, 188 P.2d 499 (1948); Application of Sood, 208 Misc. 819, 142 N.Y.S.2d 591 (1955).

4. Many states have enacted statutes exculpating from criminal prosecution a person who marries for a second time after the spouse of the first marriage has been missing for a certain period of time.

    (a) Such statutes absolve a person from only criminal charges of bigamy and do not validate the second marriage.

    (b) Such statutes are designed to relieve the hardships occurring in so-called "Enoch Arden" cases which concern a second marriage following a long, unexplained absence of a spouse of the first marriage.

    NOTE—The term "Enoch Arden" is derived from the name of a sailor memorialized in Tennyson's poem, who returned home after a ten-year absence due to a shipwreck only to find that his wife remarried, believing him to be dead. The law at such time provided no relief to her for the bigamous second marriage.

5. In an effort to provide more complete relief in an "Enoch Arden" case to the spouse who desires to remarry some states have enacted more far-reaching statutes:

    (a) Some statutes permit a court to issue a decree of dissolution of a marriage where a spouse has disappeared for a certain length of time and is not known to be alive. Such statutes, therefore, free a deserted spouse to remarry, if such a dissolution is obtained.

    (b) Some statutes permit a court to find the absent spouse of an applicant for a marriage license to be declared dead after notice of publication. This type of statute is more effective since it prevents an Enoch Arden case from occurring.

6. In the case of successive marriages, there is a presumption that the latest of such marriages is valid. This presumption arises since the law presumes matrimony, morality and legitimacy, rather than concubinage, immorality and bastardy.

7. Because of the presumption that the most recent marriage is valid, the burden of proof is on the spouse of the previous marriage who

is attacking the latest marriage to prove, by conclusive evidence, the validity and the continuity of such previous marriage.

See CASE 14, below.

NOTE—It is the majority view that the presumption of the validity of the latest marriage may be based on a valid common law marriage as well as a valid ceremonial marriage. See generally, Clark, p. 68. See also Anderson-Tully Co. v. Wilson, 221 Miss. 656, 74 So.2d 735 (1954).

Freedom to practice religion does not include bigamy   Case 13

H married W-1. While still married to W-1 H married W-2. H was indicted and convicted under a federal statute for the crime of bigamy. H's defense was that such marriages were in conformance of the practices of his religion and protected by the First Amendment as part of his religious belief. Is the statute prohibiting bigamy a violation of the constitutional prohibition against laws restricting the exercise of freedom of religion?

Answer. No. Laws are made to govern actions. Although laws may not interfere with religious worship, beliefs and opinions, they may interfere with practices. To permit such a defense would make religious belief superior to law and "permit every citizen to become a law unto himself." Polygamy and bigamy are and have been considered offenses against society among nations of Northern and Western Europe and America. Therefore, the statute prohibiting bigamy and making it a criminal offense was a valid exercise of the legislative power, and H may be prosecuted for the bigamous practice.

See Reynolds v. United States, 98 U.S. 145, 25 L.Ed. 244 (1878).

NOTE—It has been suggested that the rationale above distinguishing between religious beliefs and practices is an unsatisfactory distinction and that the true basis of the decision is simply that certain marriage customs are at such odds with the widely accepted morals of society that they cannot be tolerated. See generally, Clark, p. 62.

Presumption of the validity of the latest marriage means first wife has burden of showing second marriage invalid   Case 14

W-2 filed a claim for compensation as the surviving spouse of H-1, to whom she was married on June 2, 1948. Subsequently W-1 appeared and filed a claim as the surviving spouse of H-1, stating that she had married H-1 in 1923; that nine children were born of such marriage; that she and H-1 had separated in 1936; and that W-1 then had married and lived with H-2. A hearing was held during which W-2 proved that she was married to H-1 and evidence was given that H-1 had been previously married and had not divorced his prior spouse. In absence of proof that there was no divorce terminating the first marriage, is there a presumption in favor of the validity of the second marriage?

Answer. Yes. Where two marriages of the same person are proved, the second marriage is presumed to be the valid marriage. Such a presumption is stronger than the presumption of the continuance of the first marriage. A person attacking the second marriage, therefore, has the burden of producing evidence with respect to its invalidity. Where both parties to the first marriage are living at the time of the second marriage, it is presumed that the first marriage was terminated by divorce. Since W-2's marriage to H-1 was proved, W-1 had the burden of producing evidence of its invalidity. W-1 offered no proof that there had been no divorce and since H-1, under oath, in the procurement of a marriage license with W-2, stated he was divorced, there is insufficient evidence to support W-1's claim.

See Parker v. American Lumber Corp., 190 Va. 181, 56 S.E.2d 214 (1949). See also CASE 12, above.

NOTE 1—The presumption that the second marriage is valid still applies where it is a common law marriage. See Warner v. Warner, 76 Idaho 399, 283 P.2d 931 (1955); Anderson-Tully Co. v. Wilson, 221 Miss. 656, 74 So.2d 735 (1954); Texas Employers' Ins. Ass'n. v. Elder, 155 Tex. 27, 282 S.W.2d 371 (1955).

NOTE 2—Courts often state that the presumption that the second marriage is valid is based on probabilities. However, a better reason may be that in many cases the parties act upon the assumption that the second marriage is valid.

IV ANNULMENT

Summary Outline

A. Historical Background of Annulment

B. Annulment as Distinguished From Divorce
   1. annulment results from invalid marriage
   2. annulment terminates marriage from date of inception
   3. grounds must have existed at time of marriage
   4. usually no permanent alimony is granted

C. Jurisdiction in Annulment Actions
   1. normally based on domicile of one or both spouses
   2. conflict of laws rules for annulment

D. Grounds for Annulment
   1. similar to grounds for divorce
   2. general grounds

E. Defenses to an Annulment Action
   1. ratification
   2. clean hands
   3. antenuptial knowledge
   4. res judicata
   5. statute of limitations

F. Property Settlements in Annulment Actions
   1. temporary alimony may be awarded
   2. permanent alimony traditionally not awarded

HISTORICAL BACKGROUND OF ANNULMENT

1. An annulment of a marriage is the legal process by which a marriage is invalidated retroactively to the date of the inception of the marriage.

2. Annulment in the United States, unlike other aspects of matrimonial law, does not have strong roots reaching back to English law. It is purely a statutory creation developed by state legislatures.

3. Until 1857 only ecclesiastical courts in England had jurisdiction to annul marriages. The procedure, called "divorce a vinculo matrimonii", provided the sole method of dissolving a marriage. It was based upon conditions existent at the time of the marriage which would render such marriage invalid.

4. In the northeastern section of the American Colonies annulment was authorized by statute and granted by courts and legislatures. In the southern colonies and New York, however, English traditions prevailed and since there was no ecclesiastical courts as were found in England, annulment pleadings were not heard. After 1776 diverse rulings with respect to annulment were handed down, some of which stated that only statutory law could confer authority to grant annulments; others stated that only equity could annul marriages on the grounds of fraud, duress or insanity. See Burtis v. Burtis, 1 Hopk. Ch. 557 (N.Y.1825); Brown v. Westbrook, 27 Ga. 102 (1859).

5. In the nineteenth and twentieth centuries, however, an increasing number of states passed legislation authorizing and governing annulment proceedings.

6. Today most states have a statute which sets forth the grounds for annulment. In states which have not enacted such a statute, a court may nevertheless annul a marriage based upon its equitable powers.

   CAVEAT—The ground for annulment must have existed at the time of the marriage.

   e.g. Mental incapacity at the time of the marriage is a ground for annulment because the afflicted party was incapable of consent. If the mental incapacity occurs after the marriage ceremony, no annulment may be granted, but a divorce may be possible.

ANNULMENT AS DISTINGUISHED FROM DIVORCE

1. Distinctions between annulment and divorce have developed through legislative and judicial actions. See CHART **I**, below.

2. For purposes of annulment, there are two types of invalid marriages:

   (a) a *void* marriage is one which is invalid for any purpose at any time,

(b) a *voidable* marriage is one which is valid for all civil purposes until and unless attacked by one of the parties to such marriage.

NOTE—Where a marriage is only voidable, it is effective until a decree of annulment is obtained. However, the effect of the decree is retroactive to the time of the marriage ceremony. Nevertheless, children born of an annuled marriage are usually deemed to be legitimate.

3. As a method for terminating the marriage relation, annulment is not utilized as frequently as divorce since the grounds for annulment are not present in most discordant marriages.

Differences in grounds between annulment and divorce   Case 15

W and H were married for a year. W sued H for divorce due to H's cruelty towards her. H counterclaimed for an annulment because W refused to stop taking birth control pills and have children. W and H agreed upon their marriage to have children but to postpone having them for awhile and to have W take birth control pills. W refused to cease taking such pills due to H's cruel behavior. W was granted a divorce and H appeals, claiming he should have been granted an annulment. Should H have been granted an annulment?

Answer. *No. A representation to have children goes to the essentials of a marriage. However, in order to grant an annulment for the falsity of a representation to have children the party defrauded must show that the other party did not intend to have children at the time of the marriage. Here, H did not show that W at the time of*

CHART I. DIFFERENCES BETWEEN DIVORCE AND ANNULMENT

DIVORCE	ANNULMENT
1. Predicated on a valid marriage.	1. Predicated on an invalid marriage.
2. Terminates marriage as of the date of such decree.	2. Terminates a void or voidable marriage retroactively to the date of its supposed inception.
3. Grounds arise *after* the marriage.	3. Grounds exist *prior to* the marriage.
4. Alimony is generally granted in a divorce action.	4. Unless state statutes provide otherwise, alimony is not granted after issuance of the annulment decree.

See generally, Clark, pp. 121–143.

marriage did not intend to have children, but merely showed that W thereafter changed her mind. H's annulment action should not be sustained.

See Heup v. Heup, 45 Wis.2d 71, 172 N.W.2d 334 (1969).

JURISDICTION IN ANNULMENT ACTIONS

1. Jurisdiction in an annulment action is based on the domicile of the parties since the domicile has the primary governmental interest in the marital relationship of its residents.

2. Domicile of one or both parties is the basis for jurisdiction in annulment proceedings.

   (a) If *both* parties are domiciled in state X, then the court in state X *has jurisdiction* to grant an annulment.

   (b) If *neither* party is domiciled in state X, even though both parties are in court, the court in state X *has no jurisdiction* to grant an annulment, the interest of such state being minimal.

   (c) If *one* party is domiciled in state X, then the court in state X has jurisdiction to grant an annulment. See Perlstein v. Perlstein, 152 Conn. 152, 204 A.2d 909 (1964). See generally *Smith's Review, Conflict of Laws*, Chapter XIV, *The Law Governing Domestic Relations*.

   CAVEAT—The general principle of number 2(b), above, is not followed in all states. A California court held that the interests of the state where the marriage occurred, and the interests of the state of domicile of either party, do not preclude a court in another state from granting an annulment if it has personal jurisdiction over both parties. The crucial question is whether there are sufficient factors to justify the exercise of jurisdiction by a court. See Whealton v. Whealton, 67 Cal.2d 656, 63 Cal.Rptr. 291, 432 P.2d 979 (1967).

3. The court of the state having jurisdiction to annul a marriage will, under its conflict of laws rule, refer to and apply the law of the state which determined the validity of the marriage.

   (a) By the law of state R a "common law" marriage, created by mere consent and living together as man and wife, is invalid. By the law of state M such a marriage is valid. H and W enter into a "common law" marriage in state R and cohabit as man and wife. W leaves H and establishes her domicile in state M. W sues for a decree of annulment in state M. May the court grant the decree? *Ans.* Yes. First, because W has her domicile in state M, that particular state's interest in W's marital status is present in the state. Hence, the state has jurisdiction over the status of the marriage and over W. Second, the court will look to and apply the law of the place where the marriage took place when the ground for annulment is that of the validity of the ceremony or lack of it. Here, the "common law" marriage was void in state R. Therefore, the parties not having lived together as man and wife in state M, the court in state M will apply the law of state R and declare the marriage void ab initio.

(b) By the law of state R first cousins may marry. By the law of state M such a marriage is void. H and W are first cousins domiciled in state M. To evade the laws of state M these cousins go to and are married in state R. Later H establishes his domicile in state N and sues W for a decree of annulment in state N. May the court grant the decree, and if so what law should be applied? *Ans.* The court may grant the decree and the law of state M should be applied. The fact that H is now domiciled in state N gives the court in state N jurisdiction to grant the decree. The law which ultimately determined the validity of the marriage between H and W was that of the state of their domicile, state M. By the law of that state there was a strong public policy against the incestuous marriage of first cousins which H and W could not evade by leaving that state and marrying in another. Hence, the court in state N, under its conflict of laws rule, should refer to and apply the law of state M, which originally determined the validity of the marriage of its domiciliaries, and decree the marriage null and void ab initio.

See Goodrich, pp. 226–243. See also *Smith's Review, Conflict of Laws* Chapter XIV, "The Law Governing Domestic Relations."

4. The Restatement, Second, Conflict of Laws, § 283(1) states that the "validity of a marriage is to be determined by the local law of the state which, with respect to the particular issue, has the most significant relationship to the spouses and the marriage."

5. The following factors are considered in determining which state has "the most significant relationship to the spouses and the marriage:"

"(a) the needs of the interstate and international systems,

"(b) the relevant policies of the forum,

"(c) the relevant policies of other interested states and the relative interests of those states in the determination of the particular issue,

"(d) the protection of justified expectations,

"(e) the basic policies underlying the particular field of law,

"(f) certainty, predictability and uniformity of result, and

"(g) ease in the determination and application of the law to be applied."

Restatement, Second, Conflict of Laws, § 6.

6. In addition to the principles of numbers 4 and 5, above, the following principle is also applicable where there is a conflict of laws question:

(a) "A marriage which satisfies the requirements of the state where the marriage was contracted will everywhere be recognized as valid unless it violates the strong public policy of another state which has the most significant relationship to the spouses and the marriage." Restatement, Second, Conflict of Laws, § 283(2). See CASE 8, above.

(b) H, an officer in the Polish army, and W, a Polish refugee, were married by an army chaplain while they were in Italy. The marriage ceremony did not comply with either Italian or Polish law. H and W subsequently moved to England where they lived for several years, but they never became British citizens. In a suit for annulment, the court held the marriage valid because all the requirements of a common law marriage were met. See Taczanowska (orse. Roth) v. Taczanowski, 2 All Eng.Rep. 563 (1957).

NOTE—The court in the Taczanowska case protected the justified expectations of H and W in order to uphold the marriage. Thus, this factor was given controlling importance over others listed in the Restatement, § 6, number 5, above.

GROUNDS FOR ANNULMENT

1. Grounds in annulment actions are similar to the grounds in divorce actions. However, sometimes a divorce may be sought instead of an annulment in order to obtain alimony. See Chapter VI, *Fault Oriented Grounds for Divorce*, below.

2. Generally, grounds on which an annulment will be granted include the following:

(a) impotency,

(b) fraud,

(c) dare or jest,

(d) prior existing marriage,

(e) mental incapacity, and

(f) duress.

NOTE—Despite an overlapping of grounds in divorce and annulment, the time at which such grounds arise determines which action to choose. See *Annulment as Distinguished from Divorce,* above.

3. A marriage will be declared invalid on the ground of mental incapacity, if the afflicted party was incapable of consent at the time of marriage.

4. Impotency is grounds upon which a marriage will be declared voidable.

   e.g. A marriage in which one spouse is impotent is a valid marriage until attacked by the other spouse, at which point it becomes voidable. See T. v. M., 100 N.J.Super. 530, 242 A.2d 670 (1968).

5. Fraud relating to the essentials of marriage constitutes grounds for annulment. This is known as the doctrine of essentials. It includes:

   (a) misrepresentation of pregnancy by a wife where the husband is *not* the father of the child, and

   (b) misrepresentation of a willingness to engage in sexual relations and to have children.

   See CASE 18, below.

   CAVEAT—Misrepresentation of the existence of pregnancy where the husband *is* the alleged father will generally *not* warrant an annulment, even though the wife is not pregnant by anyone. See Levy v. Levy, 309 Mass. 230, 34 N.E.2d 650 (1941).

6. Some courts permit an annulment based upon a material misrepresentation of character, status or past life where the marriage would not have been entered into had the true fact been known. See CASE 19, below.

   e.g. The concealment of heroin addiction has been held to be a fraud going to the essentials of the marriage. Thus, an annulment was granted where W learned of H's addiction five weeks after the marriage and immediately left H. See Costello v. Porzelt, 116 N.J.Super. 380, 282 A.2d 432 (1971).

   CAVEAT—Policy considerations may influence a court in determining whether to grant an annulment. Where children of an annuled marriage would be considered illegitimate, a court would be less likely to grant an annulment than where a statute makes the offspring legitimate. See Bove v. Pinciotti, 46 D.&C.

159 (Pa.1942); Schibi v. Schibi, 136 Conn. 196, 69 A.2d 831 (1949).

7. Misrepresentation or concealment of infirmities at the time of the marriage will sometimes be a ground for annulment. Conditions for which an annulment will be granted for health reasons are:

(a) sterility,

(b) venereal disease, or

(c) mental illness.

8. An annulment will be granted where marriage was entered into on a dare or in jest.

9. A marriage is voidable, if one party has not obtained a valid divorce from his previous spouse.

10. Duress may be grounds for an annulment depending on the particular pressure brought against the spouse.

(a) The threat or use of force constitutes duress and is grounds for annulment.

(b) The threat of legal action for seduction, fornication or bastardy would not normally be grounds for annulment.

See CASE 21, below.

NOTE—Today most courts hold that a marriage entered into under duress is voidable and not void ab initio. Thus, the rights and duties of the marriage bind both parties until the marriage is formally annulled. See Clark, p. 100.

11. A misrepresentation as to the love and affection for one's spouse at the time of marriage, by itself, is not grounds for annulment. However, lack of love and affection may be relevant as evidence to show another misrepresentation which is grounds for annulment, such as:

(a) intent to defraud spouse of property and then desert, see Robert v. Robert, 87 Misc. 629, 150 N.Y.S. 366 (1914),

(b) intent to marry for the sole purpose of obtaining an immigration visa, see Ernst v. Ernst, 263 A.D. 844, 32 N.Y.S.2d 795 (1943), or

(c) intent to continue an illicit relationship with another person, see United States v. Rubenstein, 151 F.2d 915 (2d Cir. 1945), cert. denied 326 U.S. 766, 66 S.Ct. 168, 90 L.Ed. 462.

See generally, Foote, pp. 173–179.

Annulment of marriage for mental incapacity

Case 16

C, H's child from H's first marriage, seeks to have H's second marriage annulled on the ground that H was insane at the time of the marriage and thus incapable of consent. H at the time of his second marriage was elderly. After the death of H's first wife, H's appearance and health declined. He became slovenly, confused mentally and partially paralyzed due to a stroke. The woman who eventually became H's second wife attended H after his stroke and he improved. H then married her. Should the marriage be annulled?

Answer. No. A marriage contract will not be annulled on the ground of mental incapacity unless there existed at the time of the marriage such a lack of understanding as to render a party incapable of consenting to the contract. The condition at the time of the marriage must govern the question of capacity. If a party is cognizant of the nature and obligations of the marriage contract, an annulment decree will not be issued. Here, the circumstances did not warrant that an annulment be granted.

See Fischer v. Adams, 151 Neb. 512, 38 N.W.2d 337 (1949). See also Ertel v. Ertel, 313 Ill.App. 326, 40 N.E.2d 85 (1942); and CASE 4, above.

Annulment of marriage for impotency

Case 17

H and W married. W seeks an annulment on the ground that H is impotent due to psychological reasons rather than physical reasons. Should an annulment be granted?

Answer. Yes. Although the statute involved appears to be limited to impotency caused by physical reasons, it must be ruled that the intention of the legislature is to include physical incapacity caused by psychological reasons. Hence, the fact that H's impotence was caused by psychological rather than physical reasons is irrelevant when the question of W's right to an annulment for physical incapacity is at issue.

See Rickards v. Rickards, 53 Del. 134, 166 A.2d 425 (1960).

Doctrine of essentials in annulment actions—bride's unknown pregnancy grounds for annulment

Case 18

H, age 17, married W, age 30, after knowing her six weeks due to W's representation that she was chaste when in fact she was pregnant by another man. Upon learning of W's condition, H filed for an annulment. Should an annulment be granted?

Answer. Yes. In order to invalidate a marriage due to fraud, under the doctrine of essentials any misrepresentation must go to the *essentials of the marriage. Misrepresentations with respect to fortune, temper or character will not qualify as such misrepresentations. By contrast, such an essential misrepresentation occurred here since W was already bearing another man's child and could not execute the marriage contract with H which entails sexual relations and child bearing.*

See Reynolds v. Reynolds, 85 Mass. (3 Allen) 605 (1862).

NOTE 1—The trend since CASE 18, above, has been to enlarge the types of fraud for which an annulment will be granted. Nevertheless, most states continue to pay lip service to the doctrine of essentials, that is, the fraud must go to the essentials of marriage for an annulment to be granted. See Clark, p. 105.

NOTE 2—W induced H to marry her by representing to H that she was pregnant with his child. After the marriage H learned that W was not pregnant, and sued for an annulment. The court granted the annulment. It reasoned that since H would not have married W absent the false representation, it was material and a ground for annulment. See Masters v. Masters, 13 Wis.2d 332, 108 N.W.2d 674 (1961). Most courts would not grant the annulment in this situation. See CAVEAT after number 5, above. See also Clark, p. 110.

Case 19   *Annulment of marriage based on fraud—sustained*

W married H who concealed from her that he had been an officer in the German Army during World War II and was fanatically anti-Semitic. After their marriage, H required W to stop socializing with all Jewish friends. W now brings an annulment action against H. Should an annulment be granted?

Answer. *Yes. The misrepresentation upon which an annulment action is based need not go to what is commonly called the essentials of the marriage relation, the duties and rights concerning cohabitation and consortium. Fraud is sufficient ground for annulment if it is material. H's concealed sentiments made the marriage intolerable. W should be granted an annulment since had she been aware of H's concealed sentiments prior to the marriage, she would not have married him.*

See Kober v. Kober, 16 N.Y.2d 191, 264 N.Y.S.2d 364, 211 N.E.2d 817 (1965).

Case 20   *Annulment of marriage based upon claimed fraud—denied*

W, who was very wealthy, married H, who was a poor Russian nobleman, on the representation that H worked and was a socially prominent U.S. citizen. In reality H never worked; received money from other women; was without social position; and had lived in South America for such a long period of time that his U.S. citizenship was revocable. W sued for an annulment on the ground of fraud. Should W's petition be granted?

Answer. *No. An annulment will not be granted for every type of fraud. Only frauds which go to matters essential to the marriage relationship are grounds for annulment. Here, H did not promise to support W and a promise to find a job is not vital to the marriage. H did not enter into any fraud with respect to his American citizenship. H's representation with respect to money from other women likewise does not go to the essentials of the marriage. Thus, fraud vital to the marriage relationship is not proved and W's petition for annulment should not be granted.*

See *Woronzoff-Daschkoff v. Woronzoff-Daschkoff*, 303 N.Y. 506, 104 N.E.2d 877 (1952).

CAVEAT—This view obviously goes beyond the doctrine of essentials. The New York courts in an effort to circumvent the New York divorce statute in effect at that time may have liberalized annulment holdings. However, the New York courts in Woronzoff-Daschkoff retreated from an earlier liberal position taken in the Shonfeld v. Shonfeld, 260 N.Y. 477, 184 N.E. 60 (1933), only to revert back to the liberal position in the Kober case, CASE 19, above.

See Paulsen, p. 181.

NOTE—It would appear that the standard of fraud required for annulment in cases of unconsummated marriages is lower than in cases of consummated marriages.

Annulment granted where fear or duress vitiate consent to marriage

Case 21

H was domiciled in England. He was employed by the British government in Malta. As H was preparing to leave Malta he was arrested and charged with corrupting W, a minor, and H's passport was confiscated. H had dated W a few times, but they did not have sexual intercourse. A solicitor was appointed to represent H. The solicitor told H that it was not uncommon for British personnel to seduce Maltese women and then return to England before they could be prosecuted. That fact was resented by the Maltese people and it was certain that H would be convicted. Therefore, even though H said he was innocent, he could expect to be sentenced to prison unless he married W. H asked his British supervisor who confirmed the advice of the solicitor. To avoid what appeared to be a certain prison sentence H married W. Subsequently, H returned to England and sought an annulment of the marriage. Did the unjustified threat of a prison sentence invalidate H's consent to the marriage?

Answer. *Yes. "In the absence of consent there can be no valid marriage; and fear may vitiate consent." H was placed in fear by the unfounded charge against him. That fear was strengthened by the advice of H's appointed solicitor and H's work supervisor. H believed that he had to choose between marriage and prison. Further, H's fears were reasonably entertained and arose from circumstances for which H was not responsible. Therefore, H's fears were genuine and sufficient to negative his consent to the marriage. The marriage ceremony was void.*

See Buckland v. Buckland, 2 All E.R. 300 (1965).

NOTE—The duress must be present at the time of the marriage. The test for duress is subjective rather than objective. That is, was the person seeking the annulment prevented from freely assenting to the marriage, rather than was the fear reasonable in light of all the circumstances. See Clark, p. 100.

DEFENSES TO AN ANNULMENT ACTION

1. Among the defenses to an annulment action are the following:

    (a) ratification,

    (b) clean hands,

    (c) antenuptial knowledge,

    (d) res judicata, and

    (e) statute of limitations.

    See Clark, p. 130.

2. If a married couple continues to live together after one spouse learns of valid grounds for annulment, that may be considered ratification and used as a defense.

3. The equitable defense of clean hands may be asserted in some jurisdictions. In those jurisdictions inequitable conduct or bad faith by the plaintiff may be a valid defense to the suit for annulment.

4. Antenuptial knowledge is a valid defense in some states. It may be asserted by the defendant when the person seeking the annulment knew of the marital defect before the marriage.

5. All courts agree on the principle that where two parties have fully litigated a particular claim, and a *final judgment* has resulted, that claim may not later be relitigated by the loser. This is the doctrine of *res judicata*.

6. All courts similarly are in agreement that if a particular finding of fact has been made in the course of a lawsuit between two parties, that issue of fact may not later be retried by the loser,

even though the cause of action is different in the second suit. This is the doctrine of collateral estoppel.

NOTE—The term "res judicata" is sometimes used loosely to refer to both the rule preventing relitigation of claims and that preventing relitigation of findings of fact. Usually, however, the term refers only to the former. See generally, *Smith's Review, Civil Procedure*, Chapter XI, "Former Adjudication."

7. Collateral estoppel should be distinguished from res judicata. There are two primary differences:

   (a) Whereas res judicata applies only where the cause of action in the second action is the same as the one adjudicated in the first action, collateral estoppel applies so long as any issue of fact is the same, even though the causes of action are different.

   (b) Whereas res judicata prevents the second suit altogether, collateral estoppel does not prevent suit, but merely compels the court to make the same finding of fact on the identical factual issue that the first court made. Sometimes, of course, this will as a practical matter bar suit, as in the example below.

   > e.g. H sued W for a separation which was granted based upon abandonment. In the litigation W admitted the validity of the marriage. Subsequently, W brought an action against H to annul the marriage because H was validly married when he married W. W's suit was dismissed. The court reasoned that the court decree in H's suit for a separation determined that the marriage between H and W was valid, even though that question was not actually litigated. To annul the marriage would undermine the factual basis of the prior judgment. Thus, the defense of res judicata may be asserted by H. See Statter v. Statter, 2 N.Y.2d 668, 163 N.Y.S.2d 13, 143 N.E.2d 10 (1957), See also Foster, Domestic Relations and Something About Res Judicata, 22 U.Pitts.L.Rev. 313 (1960).

8. Many states have a statute of limitations for each specific ground upon which an annulment may be sought. Other states apply the general statute of limitations and some states permit the equitable defense of laches. See Clark, pp. 130–131.

9. Whether or not an annulment action can be brought *after* the death of a spouse depends upon whether the marriage was "void" or "voidable".

   (a) If the marriage was *void*, an annulment action can be brought and the marriage attacked collaterally.

(b) If the marriage was *"voidable"*, an annulment action cannot be brought.

10. If a party to a *void* marriage under attack by an annulment action dies during the annulment action before the decision is issued, the action may continue. If a party to a *voidable* marriage under attack by an annulment action dies during the action, the action abates. See Dibble v. Meyer, 203 Or. 541, 278 P.2d 901 (1955). See also Clark, p. 129.

Case 22   *Defenses in annulment action rejected where plaintiff was below statutory age at time of marriage*

M, mother of W who was age 17 and below the statutory age of consent, filed an action for a divorce on behalf of W against H. There were two children of the marriage. A temporary support order was issued by the court. Upon reaching eighteen, W amends the complaint and files for an annulment on the ground of nonage. H excepted on the ground of election of remedies, estoppel, clean hands and confirmation of the marriage. Should H's exceptions be sustained?

Answer. No. In order to confirm the marriage, a party must perform some unequivocal, voluntary act confirming the marriage upon reaching the age of consent. Cohabitation would fulfill such a requirement. Moreover, acceptance of temporary support is neither an act of confirmation or an election of remedies. Clean hands is not conclusive in annulment proceedings, and since the legitimacy of the children of a voidable marriage is not affected, the defenses of estoppel, election of remedies and clean hands should be overruled in this case.

See Powell v. Powell, 97 N.H. 301, 86 A.2d 331 (1952).

Case 23   *Collateral attack on voidable marriage—after death of one spouse not allowed*

W and H married. W died leaving H, a surviving spouse, and X, Y and Z, collateral relatives, as heirs. Due to the inheritance they would receive if H were not W's husband, X, Y and Z now file a suit to have the marriage of H and W annulled on the ground that W was gravely ill at the time of the marriage. Such a condition renders such marriage voidable under the laws of the jurisdiction involved. May a "voidable" marriage be attacked collaterally by others after the death of one of the parties thereto?

Answer. No. Where a marriage is merely voidable, rather than void, it cannot be attacked by a third party after the death of one of the parties to the marriage. A marriage entered into through fraud and misrepresentation is classified as "voidable" rather than "void".

Thus, here, X, Y and Z could not collaterally attack the marriage of H and W after W's death since their attack on the marriage was based on fraud. X's, Y's and Z's petition should be dismissed.

See Patey v. Peaslee, 99 N.H. 335, 111 A.2d 194 (1955).

1. In addition to ruling a marriage to be invalid, a court also may settle the property rights of the parties in an annulment action.

PROPERTY SETTLEMENTS IN ANNULMENT ACTIONS

2. Alimony may only be awarded in annulment actions as follows:

(a) Temporary alimony during the pendency of the suit may be awarded by the court to the defendant-spouse, if such spouse does not admit the invalidity of the marriage.

(b) Temporary alimony during the pendency of the suit will not be awarded to a defendant-spouse who admits the invalidity of the marriage, since there is no support owing a person who is not a spouse.

(c) Temporary alimony during the pendency of the suit will not be awarded to a plaintiff-spouse who is attacking the validity of the marriage, since this would be an inconsistent position.

(d) Permanent alimony at the end of the action will generally not be granted in absence of statutory authorization.

See Clark, pp. 135–137.

3. Many states, however, have passed legislation expanding the use of alimony by awarding alimony in annulment actions.

(a) Some states have attempted to provide for alimony by including grounds for annulment in the divorce statutes.

(b) Some states have specifically provided that alimony may be granted in annulment cases in the court's discretion.

(c) Some states have provided that alimony may only be awarded to an innocent spouse in an annulment action.

See Clark, pp. 135–137.

4. To avoid the situation in which one spouse would be left penniless due to lack of legislation authorizing alimony in annulment actions some courts may order one spouse to pay the other spouse fair compensation for services rendered during their invalid marriage. See CASE 24, below.

Annulment—equitable division of property

Case 24

W-2 entered into a common law marriage with H not knowing that H was already married to W-1 from whom he had not obtained a divorce. W-2 and H lived together as husband and wife for 6 years during which time the parties accumulated real estate, household furnishings and equipment. W-2 filed for a divorce from H, which was denied due to the fact that H was married already to W-1. However, the court granted an annulment of the later marriage. W-2 then filed a complaint asking for the value of her services as a housekeeper and the reimbursement of the amounts she had contributed towards the real estate, household furnishings and equipment. Should the court hear such action and grant such sums?

Answer. Yes. Equity has jurisdiction to adjudicate the property rights between persons whose marriage has been declared void. In this case W-2 entered into a supposedly valid marital relationship in good faith, and such marriage would be valid except for the incapacity of H. Since W-2, the innocent party, contributed to such marriage materially, she should recover the proportion of property accumulated during the relationship as would be just and equitable.

See Walker v. Walker, 330 Mich. 332, 47 N.W.2d 633 (1951); Sclamberg v. Sclamberg, 220 Ind. 209, 41 N.E.2d 801 (1942).

FAMILY RELATIONSHIPS

Summary Outline

A. Introduction

B. Support Obligations in a Family
1. types of statutes which impose obligations
2. support always includes necessities
3. support includes all expenses in some states
4. Uniform Reciprocal Support Act

C. Intra-family Immunities in Tort Actions
1. common law
2. recent trends

D. Legal Disabilities Affecting Minors
1. areas of legal disabilities
2. reasons underlying disabilities

E. Contracts and Minors
1. voidable at minor's option
2. minor's liability for necessaries

F. Responsibility of Minors for Torts
1. test less strict than for adults
2. test for adults—where applicable

G. Special Rules Governing Minors

INTRODUCTION 1. Analysis of family law problems frequently focuses on two aspects of the individuals involved:

(a) their *status*, and

(b) their *relationships* to one another.

2. Obligations of support of one spouse for the other arise out of the marital relationship.

3. The obligation of parents to support their children arises out of the parent-child relationship.

4. The husband-wife relationship and the parent-child relationship may alter what would otherwise be causes of action as between individuals who were unrelated.

e.g. H was driving an automobile with his wife and child as passengers. There was an accident due to H's negligence and his wife and child were injured. Under the common law rule H would be immune from suit by his wife and child. This rule has been changed to allow suit against H in some jurisdictions. See *Intra-family Immunities in Tort Actions,* below.

5. The relationship of husband and wife, without more, does not create an agency. If the parties intend that one shall act for the other in a transaction, a principal-agent relationship arises. See Express Publishing Co. v. Levenson, 282 S.W.2d 357 (Tex.1956).

e.g. W purchased several articles from X Department Store for her own use, and charged them by signing her own name. W did not pay the bill and X sued H, W's husband for the amount due. The court said that neither a husband or a wife has the power to act as agent for the other merely because of their relationship as husband and wife. To hold H liable it would be required that X show that H was an undisclosed principal or that the articles purchased were necessities which H had the duty to provide W. In the case of necessities H is only obligated to pay once. Thus, if H gave W money for necessities he is not responsible if W charged the goods and failed to pay for them. The articles involved in the present case were not necessities and there was no evidence that H was an undisclosed principal. Therefore, H is not liable for the articles charged by W. See Saks & Co. v. Bennett, 12 N.J.Super. 316, 79 A.2d 479 (1951).

6. The rights of individuals who are minors may be affected in many ways by their age. These include:

(a) capacity to enter into contracts,

(b) liability for torts,

(c) property ownership,

(d) will execution,

(e) agency and partnership relationships,

(f) criminal liability,

(g) ability to bring civil suits,

(h) voting,

(i) right to be employed, and

(j) compulsory school attendance.

7. The sections which follow explore the rights and remedies of individuals as they are affected by these statutes and these particular relationships.

SUPPORT OBLIGATIONS IN A FAMILY

1. There are three types of statutes which impose familial support obligations:

   (a) Statutes which obligate a husband to support his wife. These statutes are patterned after the common law.

   (b) Statutes which render the expenses of the family chargeable against the property of both the husband and the wife. These statutes are commonly termed "Family Expense Acts".

   (c) Statutes which place a duty to support the husband on the wife, if he is infirm or unable to support himself. These statutes are commonly termed "Family Responsibility Acts".

   NOTE—Number 1(a) is the traditional rule. The trend of recent statutes is to equalize the duty of support, but that is a minority view.

   See generally, Clark, pp. 181–187.

2. What constitutes support is dependent upon the statutes of each jurisdiction.

   (a) Some statutes impose liability only for necessaries.

   (b) Other statutes impose liability for all expenses.

   See CASE 25, below. See also Clark, pp. 185–186.

3. Most statutes which impose support obligations on the wife or the property of the wife do not release the husband of his obligation of support. Unless an intention of a gift from the wife to the husband is shown, a wife is entitled to be reimbursed by her husband for payment by her of his obligations of support. See Clark, p. 187.

   CAVEAT—Such rule is not valid in Iowa where neither spouse may receive reimbursement for support from the other in the absence of a specific agreement. See Truax v. Ellett, 234 Iowa 1217, 15 N.W.2d 361 (1944).

4. Enforcement of a support obligation against an individual, usually the husband or father, can be achieved by the wife or child through the following methods:

    (a) buying necessaries for which the father or husband will be held liable,

    (b) bringing a suit against the father or husband for support, or

    (c) utilizing the sanctions under the Uniform Reciprocal Enforcement of Support Act.

    See Clark, pp. 187–189.

5. Statutes imposing the duty on a father and husband to provide necessaries for his family find their bases in the common law "doctrine of necessaries".

6. The "doctrine of necessaries" is based on the principles of restitution and quasi-contract rather than agency. See Clark, p. 18.

    NOTE—The two bases of liability in number 6 make it unnecessary to prove that the wife was the authorized agent of the husband because marriage by itself does not render a wife an agent of her husband.

7. Under the "doctrine of necessaries" a merchant sells goods to a wife or child and charges the husband or father directly for such items.

    See CASES 26 and 27, below.

8. The "doctrine of necessaries" is not an extremely effective tool in the imposition of support because:

    (a) merchants do not want to rely on it since it requires them to make a decision whether or not an item is a necessary, and

    (b) the persons who are in need of such a law do not generally have credit extended to them.

    CAVEAT—Generally, so long as necessaries are provided the duty of support is satisfied. Courts will not settle family budget disputes and direct that money be expended to raise the standard of living of one spouse when the couple is living together and there is no ground for divorce or separation. See CASE 28, below.

9. If the husband fails to meet his obligations of support to his wife or children he may be subject to criminal sanctions in addition to any civil relief which may be available to his wife or children against him. See CASE 29, below.

10. The Uniform Reciprocal Enforcement of Support Act is a civil statute which allows reciprocity between states in order to provide support for members of a family.　See CHART II, below.

11. The Uniform Reciprocal Enforcement of Support Act is generally utilized by a wife and children whose husband and father has moved to another state, or vice versa, and who refuses to support them.　See Chapter VII, *Determination of Child Support*, and CASE 62, below.

12. The principles relating to the support of a wife are generally applicable to support of children.　However, a child must submit to reasonable parental regulations in return for maintenance and support.　See CASE 31, below.

CHART II.　PROCEDURAL OUTLINE OF AN ACTION UNDER THE REVISED UNIFORM RECIPROCAL ENFORCEMENT OF SUPPORT ACT (1968)

Step 1—Filing of a complaint by the plaintiff, usually a wife or child, which sets forth the names of the parties and their addresses as well as the facts on which the action is based.　Such complaint is filed with a court of competent jurisdiction in the plaintiff's domicile.

Step 2—The court then ascertains if the complaint sets forth facts from which the duty of support may be imposed on the defendant and a court in another state ("the responding state") may obtain jurisdiction over the defendant.

Step 3—If the court can so ascertain, then it certifies such a decision and transmits three copies of the complaint with such certification to an appropriate court in the responding state.

Step 4—The court in the responding state then dockets the case and attempts to obtain jurisdiction over the defendant or his property, usually through service of summons.

Step 5—If jurisdiction is obtained, a trial is then held.　The defendant may raise defenses, which may pose procedural problems since the plaintiff is usually not present.　A counter-claim for divorce cannot be made by the defendant since the Act covers support only and public officials, who usually represent the plaintiff, cannot litigate a divorce.

Step 6—The responding state may order the defendant to furnish support if it finds such a duty.

Step 7—If an order of support is issued, the defendant pays the amount due under such order to the court in the responding state which forwards it to the court in the plaintiff's domicile.

See Revised Uniform Reciprocal Enforcement of Support Act (1968), §§ 11–14, 18–29.　See also CASES 30 and 62.

13. The state has an interest in the education, health and safety of children, and may impose reasonable regulations on parents in such matters.   See CASES 32 and 33, below.

14. Support obligations in a family is an area which should change in the future with the changing economic status of women and increasing numbers of employed women.   See Chapter X, *Trends in Rights of Women*, below.

Case 25   *Husband is liable for support of wife who abandons him*

H and W were married for sixteen years when W left H with no explanation.   Almost a year later W requested H to leave the apartment in which they had lived since W regarded it as still belonging to her.   H complied with W's request and had no further contact with W until she instituted a suit for support.   W claimed that H should support her since she is still his wife.   W is currently receiving public assistance.   H contends that he is not liable for W's support by reason of W's abandonment of him.   Is a husband responsible for the support of a wife who has deserted him and who is a public charge?

Answer.   Yes.   The wife's abandonment of her husband is not sufficient reason to relieve him of his duty of support if she is or liable to become a public charge.   The statute of the jurisdiction pertaining to support provides for the spouse of a recipient of public assistance to be responsible for the support of such person.   There is no exculpatory language concerning desertion.   Thus, the statute is mandatory and a court cannot alter obligations of a legally responsible spouse.   Therefore H is responsible for W's support by virtue of W's status as H's wife and the language of the statute.

See *Campas v. Campas*, 61 Misc.2d 49, 304 N.Y.S.2d 876 (1969).

Case 26   *Husband is liable for necessaries of separated wife*

W and H were married and had two minor children when H left W. W's mother and brother, M and B, provided W and her children with lodging and board.   M and B now sue H for such lodging and board. Is H liable for the support of his estranged family which he voluntarily left?

Answer.   Yes.   A husband must support his wife in a manner in keeping with his circumstances and his wife's needs.   When the parties are separated due to the husband's fault, the wife can pledge his credit for her support.   When the separation is due to the wife's fault, the wife forfeits her right to support and a third person cannot hold H liable for necessaries furnished to her.   The burden of proof rests with the third person asserting a claim with respect to fault.   Thus, M and B may recover from H, if they meet such burden of proof.

See *Mihalcoe v. Holub*, 130 Va. 425, 107 S.E. 704 (1921).

Husband may not be required to pay twice to provide necessaries

H and W, husband and wife, were sued by a department store, S, for goods sold to W. The trial court awarded several judgments in favor of S against H totaling $344.00 and against W totaling $27.00. H appeals the judgments against him, claiming that he had already supplied W with necessaries to which their station in life entitled her, or with sufficient funds to purchase them. Must H be obligated to pay bills for necessaries supplied to W when he had already once supplied them?

Answer. No. In the purchase of articles for domestic use, the law regards the wife as her husband's agent. When the wife procures on credit such articles that can be classified for domestic use and for her personal use suitable to the style to which they live, the husband is prima facie liable. The husband, however, may have a good defense if he has already provided for such articles. The store, at its own risk, must inquire into the circumstances of the parties in order to ascertain whether the husband will be liable for goods purchased by his wife. Here, there was no evidence that H authorized W to buy the articles that are the subject of S's claim. Moreover, H proved that he gave W $167.00 for baby items for W's granddaughter who did not reside with H and W and who was not H's granddaughter. W charged such items instead of paying cash. Moreover, H gave W an adequate amount of cash for her personal use and supplied W with a house, a car, a maid and food. Thus, H did properly support W and had already supplied W with sufficient money to enable her to buy necessaries as well as articles in keeping with their style of living. "The tradesman must, at his peril, inquire into the circumstances in order to ascertain whether the husband will be liable when his wife goes shopping." H is under no obligation to pay twice. The judgments against H, therefore, are reversed.

See Saks & Co. v. Bennett, 12 N.J.Super. 316, 79 A.2d 479 (1951).

Grounds for separation or divorce required for support decree

H and W were married and lived together on a farm. H was extremely frugal and did not inform W of his finances. H did not give W any money for furniture or household necessities as H made all purchases he believed necessary. The house had no inside toilet and the kitchen had no sink, water being obtained from a well outside. H never took W to social events. H gave W only small amounts of money although he had over $100,000 in bank accounts and bonds. W obtained funds for her personal needs by selling farm products, but at the time suit was filed she was no longer able to do that because of her health and age. W has some rental income from property she owned before marrying H. W filed suit against H for suitable maintenance, although she continued to live with H. At trial W was not able to show grounds for divorce under state law, but the court ordered H to give W a personal allowance, make certain house repairs, purchase a new automobile, and pay W's travel expenses to visit her daughters. H appealed, contending that W had no grounds for separation or divorce and she was not entitled to an order for support. Was H obligated to support W in the manner which his financial circumstances permitted?

Answer. No. Living standards are a matter of concern to the household and not for the courts to determine so long as H provided W with necessaries and there were no valid grounds for separation or divorce under state law. H maintained their house, although not well, and W continued to live there. There was no proof of extreme cruelty as alleged in W's petition. H was legally supporting his wife, and W was not entitled to a decree compelling H to support her according to H's wealth and circumstance.

See *McGuire v. McGuire*, 157 Neb. 226, 59 N.W.2d 336 (1953).

NOTE—The basis for the decision in the McGuire case was public policy. Courts are not equipped to settle the countless number of family budget disputes which could be brought into court if the decision were otherwise. Furthermore, there is no assurance that courts could settle family budget disputes justly or better than the parties themselves.

Case 29   *Conviction of husband for willful neglect to support his wife*

H and W were married for twenty-eight years, during which time H adequately supported W. W then filed a suit for divorce and later had the proceedings dismissed. During the period of divorce negotiations H became unemployed. H gave W no support. W later went to the State Attorney's office to compel H to support her. At the trial W testified that she had only $2,000.00. H testified that he had only $100.00 and was living on borrowed funds. H was convicted of failure to support his wife and the matter was referred to the probation department. Upon investigation, the probation department found that W had $10,000.00. H now moves to strike the trial court's judgment due to W's false testimony. Should his motion be upheld?

Answer. No. Statutes in almost every state have made it a crime for a husband to fail to support his wife. To be guilty under such type of statute the husband must wilfully and without cause fail to provide for his wife. Here, the possession of money by W does not bar the state from convicting H for failure to support W. The evidence tended to show that H had the ability to provide for W and could have found employment, if he desired it. Therefore, even though H had little money and no job, since H was capable of earning a living *and had chosen not to do so, the trial court's conviction of H was upheld.*

See Ewell v. State, 207 Md. 288, 144 A.2d 66 (1955).

Uniform Reciprocal Enforcement of Support Act—scope of responding state's role

Case 30

W filed a complaint under the Uniform Reciprocal Enforcement of Support Act in Pennsylvania which was transmitted to the proper court in New Jersey. The court in New Jersey thereupon ordered H to pay W a specified amount of support after determining that W was the wife of H. H appeals claiming that W deserted him while they were living in New Jersey, and no support is due W. W did not appear or offer any evidence to the New Jersey court on the issue of desertion. Is the court of the responding state limited to a determination of whether W is the wife of H?

Answer. No. Under the statute the court in the initiating state has the obligation only to decide if the complaint contains facts from which it may be determined that H owes W the duty of support. It is then the responsibility of the court in the responding state to determine whether or not H is under a duty to support W. Such a determination can only be made by the latter court upon the evidence and depositions before such court. Here, the trial court in the responding state (New Jersey) did not have enough evidence concerning the desertion to render a decision. The case was remanded so that W could testify in person on the issue or, if that was not feasible, W's deposition could be taken. The decision was reversed and the case remanded for further proceedings.

See Pfueller v. Pfueller, 37 N.J.Super. 106, 117 A.2d 30 (1955).

Child's right to support and duty to submit to reasonable parental regulations

Case 31

X was the 20 year old daughter of F. F permitted X to attend college out of state and provided ample support for her. X moved out of the college dormitory contrary to her father's instructions and without his knowledge. X lived with a female classmate in an apartment, experimented with drugs, and did poorly in college. When F discovered that X was living off campus he directed her to return home and attend school there. X refused, and F stopped all further support. Subsequently, a family court ordered F to pay X's tuition and other expenses until she reached the age of 21. F appealed, contending that he had no obligation to support X since she abandoned F's home for the purpose of avoiding reasonable parental control. Should the appeal succeed?

Answer. Yes. Parents are charged with the discipline and support of their children. If a child merely disobeys her parent or becomes delinquent the duty of support generally continues. However, a parent may impose reasonable regulations for his child in return for maintenance and support. If a child voluntarily abandons the parent's home to seek her fortune in the world to avoid parental discipline and restraint, the child forfeits her claim to support. In this case F did not cast his daughter out into the world forcing her to fend for herself, or make arbitrary demands upon her. F made reasonable demands of X, which was his right. X could elect not to comply with F's demands, but where she did and abandoned her home, she may not enlist the aid of the court in frustrating parental authority and require F to underwrite her chosen lifestyle. X by her actions has forfeited her right to be supported by her father.

See Roe v. Doe, 29 N.Y.2d 188, 324 N.Y.S.2d 71, 272 N.E.2d 567 (1971).

Case 32 *Parents' decision regarding education of children protected by religious beliefs*

State law required all children to attend school until age sixteen. Parents, who are members of the Amish Church, refused to send their children to school beyond the eighth grade. This meant that the children did not attend approximately two years of high school. They viewed secondary school education as an impermissible exposure of their children to "worldly" influence which conflicted with their religious beliefs. The parents were prosecuted and convicted of violating the compulsory education law. They appealed, contending that their actions were an integral part of their religious beliefs and protected by the First Amendment. Should the appeal succeed?

Answer. Yes. State laws regulating education must not impinge upon religious freedom unless it is necessary to promote a compelling state interest. The state attempted to justify the law because education is necessary to prepare citizens to participate in our political system and to be self-sufficient participants in society. However, the Court concluded that those reasons did not justify encroachment upon the religious beliefs of the Amish that such schooling would cause the children and their parents to risk their salvation. The Amish sect has existed for three hundred years, and it has been a successful and self-reliant part of society. In addition, Amish children receive vocational training in their own community after the eighth grade, which substantially achieved the state educational goals. The purpose of the law cannot justify the harm it would do to traditional Amish religious values and, therefore, it is unconstitutional.

See Wisconsin v. Yoder, 406 U.S. 205, 92 S.Ct. 1526, 32 L.Ed.2d 15 (1972).

Refusal of court to order medical treatment of minor upheld   Case 33

X was a 16 year old boy suffering from paralytic scoliosis (94% curvature of the spine). Because of this condition X was unable to stand, and if there were no corrective surgery, X could become a bed patient. X's doctors recommended a spinal fusion, but that was a dangerous type of operation. X's mother was a Jehovah's Witness, and her religious beliefs prohibited her from consenting to blood transfusions which would be necessary for the operation. Otherwise, she had no objection to the operation. While the operation, if successful, would be beneficial, X's life was not in immediate danger and there was no need for the operation to be performed immediately. The director of a hospital filed a petition for appointment of a guardian for X who would consent to the corrective surgery. Should a state interfere with parental control of a child to enhance the child's physical well-being when life is not in danger and the proposed action conflicts with the religious beliefs of the parent?

Answer. No. It is well settled that a state may not interfere with religious beliefs and opinions, but it may interfere with religious practices where the state's interest is of sufficient magnitude. As between a parent and the state, the state does not have an interest outweighing a parent's religious beliefs when the child's life is not immediately imperiled by his physical condition. However, the inquiry does not end at that point. The preference of X, who is intelligent and of sufficient maturity, should be considered by the court. Since the record did not reflect X's wishes, or even if his religious beliefs, the case was remanded for further proceedings.

See In re Green, 448 Pa. 338, 292 A.2d 387 (1972).

NOTE 1—At the subsequent hearing X stated that he did not want the operation. His decision was not based on religious beliefs alone, but also because he had been hospitalized for a long period, and there was no assurance that the operation would be successful.

NOTE 2—If X had stated that he wanted the operation, the court may well have ordered the surgery. Such a decision would be consistent with the Supreme Court's holding that a minor female has a right to an abortion, and a state cannot require parental consent prior to the abortion. See CASE 88, below.

NOTE 3—The court cited Wisconsin v. Yoder, CASE 32, above, to support its position. Actually, the Yoder case can be distinguished from the Green case: (a) the parental decision in Yoder did not involve the health of the children, and (b) there was evidence in the Yoder case that requiring Amish children to attend public school could lead eventually to the disappearance of the Amish religion. There was no threat to the existence of Jehovah's Witnesses if the boy in the Green case were given blood transfusions.

INTRA-FAMILY IMMUNITIES IN TORT ACTIONS

1. An "immunity" denotes the absence of civil liability for what would otherwise be tortious conduct if it were not for a special status, position, or relation between the parties.

   e.g.   husband and wife or parent and child.

   NOTE—Where immunity is conferred the tort is not eliminated, but the liability for the otherwise tortious conduct is avoided insofar as the tort occurs within the limits of the immunity.

2. The basic rule, at common law, was that no action for personal torts could be maintained between husband and wife.

3. The rule has been sustained traditionally on two grounds:

   (a) the "legal identity" of husband and wife at common law, and

   (b) the idea that litigation between spouses would destroy the peace, harmony and unity of the family.   See, e.g., Lyons v. Lyons, 2 Ohio St.2d 243, 208 N.E.2d 533 (1965).

4. Some courts have drawn a distinction between "personal" torts and "property" torts.   They have allowed recovery by one spouse for tortious property damage inflicted by the other spouse.

5. Other courts have drawn a distinction between intentional torts and negligent torts.   They have been more inclined to permit recovery for intentional torts than for negligent torts.   The negligent torts in question generally involve automobile accidents in which insurance companies, and not the other spouse, are actually paying the damages.   In other cases, involving members of the same family, the presence of liability insurance has served as the basis for *imposing* liability.

6. One rationale for allowing recovery for intentional torts between spouses is that "the peace and harmony of the home has been so damaged that there is little danger that it will be further impaired." Prosser, p. 863.   The court sustained a cause of action on behalf of a wife against her former husband for a rape committed upon her three weeks before they were divorced, because there was "no domestic harmony left to be disrupted."   See Goode v. Martinis, 58 Wash.2d 229, 361 P.2d 941 (1961).

7. The trend of recent decisions is to permit intra-family suits for all personal torts, whether negligent or intentional.   See Gelb-

man v. Gelbman, 23 N.Y.2d 434, 297 N.Y.S.2d 529, 245 N.E.2d 192 (1969); MacDonald v. MacDonald, 412 A.2d 71 (Me. 1980).

CAVEAT—Intrafamily Offense Acts have been enacted in at least thirty states. Such statutes provide civil and criminal remedies to victims of domestic violence. Intrafamily offenses may include: threats of physical harm, assault and battery, burglary, sexual abuse, false imprisonment, kidnapping, child stealing, and damage to property. Civil remedies may include: money damages, moving expenses, medical expenses, and restitution.

8. Under the traditional rule a husband could not rape his wife. The reason for the rule was that marriage implied consent to sexual relations. Recent legal developments have changed that rule.

    (a) Some states permit a man to be prosecuted for rape where the couple is legally separated.

    (b) A few states have completely eliminated marriage as a defense to rape even when the couple is cohabiting.

9. The refusal to allow actions for personal torts between parent and child was first enunciated in 1891 in the case of Hewlett v. George, 68 Miss. 703, 9 So. 885 (1891). The rule was justified on the following grounds:

    (a) preserving domestic tranquility,

    (b) parental control and discipline, and

    (c) danger of fraud.

10. A retreat, however, from a hard and fast stance against actions between parent and child for personal torts has been developing in case law. Such retreat has resulted in a series of exceptions to such refusal:

    (a) in cases where the child has been emancipated due to the parent's surrender of parental control and the parent has given up any claim to the child's earnings or services,

    (b) in cases where intentional injuries are inflicted, and

    (c) in cases where the parent-child relation is severed due to the death of one of the parties.

See Prosser, pp. 866–867.

NOTE—Wisconsin has abolished parent-child tort immunity with the exception of cases concerning the exercise of parental control and parental discretion with respect to food and care. See Goller v. White, 20 Wis.2d 402, 122 N.W.2d 193 (1963). See also Zelinger v. State Sand & Gravel Co., 38 Wis.2d 98, 156 N.W.2d 466 (1968).

11. Other courts have allowed recovery for injuries to children arising out of the parents' business or employment, in contrast to injuries arising from the discharge of parental duties. See Dunlap v. Dunlap, 84 N.H. 352, 150 A. 905 (1930); Briere v. Briere, 107 N.H. 432, 224 A.2d 588 (1966).

12. Parental immunity has not barred suits between parents and children with respect to property torts. See Prosser, p. 861.

13. The major exception to the basic rule of intra-family immunity is that which permits one sibling to sue another. See Emery v. Emery, 45 Cal.2d 421, 289 P.2d 218 (1955).

LEGAL DISABILITIES AFFECTING MINORS

1. The age of majority is the age at which a person achieves full legal capacity.

2. The age of majority at common law was 21 years, and that age was adopted in the United States.

3. The modern trend is to reduce the common law age of majority from 21 years to 18 years of age. This has been accomplished by statute in many jurisdictions. This reduction in age conforms to the standard for enlistment in the military service and the age requirement for making a will in many states.

4. A person under the age of majority is considered to be a minor or infant and subject to certain legal disabilities.

5. There are two reasons underlying the legal disabilities of a minor:

   (a) *protection* of a minor from the consequences of his own lack of judgment,

   e.g. ability of a minor to disaffirm contracts made while under the age of majority,

   (b) *prevention* of a minor from acting in situations where he does not have enough maturity,

   e.g. prohibition from holding some public offices. See Clark, p. 230.

6. Legal disabilities affect minors with respect to the following:

   (a) contracts,

   (b) torts,

   (c) property ownership,

   (d) will execution,

   (e) agency and partnership,

(f) criminal activity,

(g) litigation,

(h) voting,

(i) employment, and

(j) school attendance.

See Clark, pp. 231–234.

CONTRACTS AND MINORS

1. A minor may enter into a contract, but may disaffirm the contract before attaining the age of majority or within a reasonable period thereafter. Such a contract is said to be "voidable."

2. A "voidable contract" is one as to which one or more of the parties has the power:

   (a) to avoid the legal relations created by the contract by a manifestation of election to do so, or

   (b) to ratify the contract and thereby extinguish the power of avoidance. See Restatement, Contracts, § 13.

3. A contract made by an infant is, although voidable, valid and enforceable unless it is disaffirmed by the infant.

   (a) D, a student who was a minor, leased a room from P for 40 weeks, but moved after thirteen weeks. D paid the rent due for the thirteen weeks he occupied the room. P sued for the balance of the rent. May D avoid the contract? Ans. Yes. D is only liable for rent during the period he occupied the room. D is not liable on the lease after he disaffirmed the contract and ceased to use the room. See Gregory v. Lee, 64 Conn. 407, 30 A. 53 (1894).

   (b) An infant sold land to D. During the year after the infant reached her majority, she observed D build a dairy, a barn, and make other improvements on the land. One year after reaching majority the emancipated infant then conveyed the property to P, who sued to eject D from the land. Is P entitled to possession? Ans. No. An infant may disaffirm a contract within a reasonable time after reaching majority. A reasonable time is determined by the circumstances. Here equity for D required the contract be disaffirmed promptly. Failure to disaffirm for a year while the land was being improved is regarded as an affirmance of the contract, so D could keep the land. See Jellings v. Pioneer Mill Co., Ltd., 30 Haw. 184 (1927).

   NOTE—Where both parties to a contract are minors, either party may disaffirm the contract.

4. If a minor disaffirms the contract and sues for restitution of the money or goods he gave, the minor must restore any consideration which he received, if he still has it. The burden of proof is on the minor to show that he squandered or otherwise disposed of the consideration he received so that it cannot be returned. See Whitman v. Allen, 123 Me. 1, 121 A. 160 (1923).

5. The general rule shields minors from liability on contracts made by them and subsequently disaffirmed. However, there are certain exceptions which impose liability on the minor for his contractual obligations.

6. An infant is bound by and cannot disaffirm an obligation imposed by law. Therefore, a minor who as part of a sales transaction, deposits money to be used in payment of obligations imposed by law, cannot recover such expended funds upon a disaffirmance of the contract. These include:

   (a) funds expended for sales taxes, for certificate of title to a motor vehicle, for transfer of plates,

   (b) a recognizance in a felony case,

   (c) rules and regulations of a bank with regard to a minor's funds are as binding on a minor as if he were of legal age,

   (d) contracts of enlistment in the military service by an infant, which have been held to be valid, and

   (e) necessaries furnished to the minor, his spouse or his children. This is also true of obligations imposed by statute. See CASE 34, below. See also Calamari & Perillo, pp. 212–215.

7. Necessaries include those things reasonably needed for subsistence, health, comfort or education.

8. Although a contract of a minor may be voidable, such person may still be liable in quasi-contract to avoid unjust enrichment, for the reasonable value of the goods or services furnished.

   See generally, *Smith's Review, Contracts,* Chapter V, "Capacity of Parties."

Case 34   *Recovery of payments made during minority*

M and W were married and purchased a home from S. In order to finance such home purchase, M, an emancipated minor, lied to L about his age. L lent M the money and M gave L a note and a mortgage on the house. M and W separated and M now sues L to recover payments made on the mortgage. L counterclaims to foreclose on the mortgage. Will M, who has lied about his age in order to obtain money for a necessity, be held to a contract which enabled him to obtain the necessity?

Answer. Yes. Under certain circumstances, age, maturity, fraud, estoppel, lack of restitution, emancipation and necessity will combine to preclude an infant from disaffirming a contract entered into while a minor. Emancipation does not, by itself, operate to make an infant sui juris. It is, however, of practical importance in deciding questions under the law of necessaries. Here, the combination of facts are such that M should be held to the performance of the contract entered into while a minor. Thus, he may not recover amounts paid under the mortgage.

See Merrick v. Stephens, 337 S.W.2d 713 (Mo.App.1960).

Contracts of infants—power of disaffirmance

Case 35

D, an infant of the age of 19, buys a new automobile from P, on a conditional sales contract. At the time of the transaction, D represents to P that he, D, is 23 years of age and he appears to be that old. The contract is for $3100, of which D pays in cash the sum of $100. The following day D negligently drives the car against a telephone pole and damages it. He calls P on the telephone and asks him to tow the car to P's garage. This is done. D then tells P his true age and disaffirms the contract. P sues D, setting forth two counts in the complaint: (1) for damages for breach of the conditional sales contract, and (2) for damages for deceit in tort. May P recover on either count?

Answer. (1) P may not recover on the first count. (2) P may recover on the second count. (1) This is an executory contract. The general rule is that an infant may disaffirm his contracts and plead his infancy as a defense in a suit thereon. Such plea is a protection which the law throws around an infant to shield him during his tender years because of undeveloped judgment and inexperience. With such view it may be said that an adult contracts with an infant at his peril with respect to the right of the infant to disaffirm. Of course such right is wholly personal to the infant. Thus, as to P's count for breach of the contract, D's defense of infancy is valid and prevents P's recovery thereon. (2) An infant is liable for his torts. No doubt the deceit of D in misrepresenting his age to P caused P to make the contract with D and resulted in D's getting possession of the car. For such tortious conduct the infant D should be held liable in damages, and the better considered cases so hold. Other cases, however, take the view that P's second count is merely a change in theory and that through the tort cause of action he is trying indirectly to recover on the contract, and to deprive the infant of his proper legal protection. Such view denies recovery against the infant and in effect permits the defense of infancy to be used not as a shield, but as a sword.

See Simpson, pp. 228–234.

Case 36   *Infants—limit on power to disaffirm—estoppel exception*

D, an infant 20 years of age, buys from P a new automobile and pays $2500 cash for it.   Within 6 months he has driven the car more than 50,000 miles.   This has transformed the new car into a virtually worthless wreck.   D, having reached the age of 21, returns the car in its terrible condition to P and demands the return to him of $2500. May D recover from P?

> **Answer.**   No.   Of course, from a strictly legal standpoint and following the general rule which is designed to protect the infant, D would be able to recover.   However, a few better considered recent cases on this typical set of facts, deny recovery on the ground that D is estopped to take advantage of his infancy, and that to permit recovery would clearly amount to injustice.   Here D has bought the car at age 20, has received full value for his money, has kept and substantially "consumed" the subject matter, and now demands a return of all the money paid.   The power to disaffirm afforded the infant is intended as a shield for his protection.   It is not intended as a sword for the purpose of injuring others affirmatively.   Here D is using infancy as a weapon of aggression.   Justice requires that recovery be denied in such a case.

RESPONSIBILITY OF MINORS FOR TORTS

1. A minor is liable for his torts.   However, the law applies less strict standards to him than it applies to adults.   See generally, Prosser, pp. 1024–1027.

2. *The test for children is primarily subjective, dealing with the capacity of a particular child to recognize and avoid risk and harm, taking into consideration this child's age, his intelligence and his experience.*   This test recognizes that children develop at different rates even in the same age group, and acquire capacity individually, and not in conformity to any presupposed pattern.   See Kuhns v. Brugger, 390 Pa. 331, 135 A.2d 395 (1957). See also, Restatement, Second, Torts §§ 283A, 464.

3. When children engage in activities normally pursued only by adults, such as driving a car or flying an airplane, they are held to the same standard as an adult.   If they are acting in an adult world, they should be held to adult standards of care.   In addition, the policy is to relieve adults of the continuing responsibility of determining whether the individual in such cases is a child or an adult.   See CASE 37, below.

4. If a minor employs other persons, he will be liable for the torts of his employees under the theory of *respondeat superior* if an employee's act or omission is within the scope of the employment and in furtherance of the minor's (employer's) business.   See *Smith's Review, Agency and Partnership*, Chapter VIII, "Relation Between Principal and Third Person in Tort."

Standard of care applied to minors—traditional rule   Case 37

D, age 17, while driving an automobile struck and killed P's three year old son. P sued D for damages for negligence. The court instructed the jury that if they found that the defendant, D, exercised the care and caution of a reasonable, prudent person, taking into consideration the defendant's age, intelligence and experience, under the circumstances then surrounding the defendant, then they should find for the defendant. The jury found for the defendant. The plaintiff appealed contending that the court should have treated any youth who is permitted by law to drive an automobile exactly the same as an adult. Was there error?

Answer. No. The instruction given is a proper statement of the law. The test for determining the proper conduct of an adult in the field of negligence is objective. It is that of the reasonable, prudent man under the circumstances. The age factor is ignored and all adults must meet the standard or be liable for falling short of it. However, it would be highly prejudicial to children if their conduct were judged by the same standard which is applied to a mature person. In some jurisdictions children who have attained the age of 14 or over are treated as adults. In other states every child is required to act according to the standard conduct of a child of his own age. In still others the courts arbitrarily hold a child of 17, 18, 19 or 20, to the same standard of conduct as an adult. Each of these tests is arbitrary, inflexible and objective. The fundamental fault is that any such test presupposes that children develop uniformly in point of age or time which simply is not true. The test applied to children should be uniform and primarily subjective. It should allow for varying degrees of development of children of different ages and also for those of the same age. The instruction given by the court in this case permitted the jury to consider not only the care and caution of a "reasonable, prudent person" (not limited to a man or adult), but also the "defendant's age, intelligence and experience", under the circumstances. To the extent that the infant is treated as a "reasonable, prudent person" the test may be said to be objective. To the extent that the particular child's age, intelligence and experience, may be taken into consideration, the test is subjective. On the whole, such a standard laid down by the court to the jury in this case, is fair and just to the infant and seems a proper protection for society. Thus, the standard may be said to be correct and the court was without error.

See *Charbonneau v. MacRury,* 84 N.H. 501, 153 A. 457 (1931).

NOTE—The trend of more recent decisions is to treat minors as adults when they engage in some activity, such as operating a car or motorcycle, which is normally done only by adults. See *Daniels v. Evans,* 107 N.H. 407, 224 A.2d 63 (1966).

SPECIAL RULES GOVERNING MINORS

1. A minor may own property, real or personal. However, any contracts involving such property may be disaffirmed.

2. To avoid the disaffirmance of contracts by a minor with respect to property and to manage a minor's property in an orderly, legal fashion, a custodian or guardian may be appointed.

3. Testamentary capacity is strictly governed by state statutes. In some jurisdictions minors of eighteen may make a will, while in others they may not.

4. Any person may act as an agent so long as he is able to perform the task of the agency. The fact that the agent might not have sufficient capacity to perform the act for himself is not controlling because the agent does not act for himself, but for his principal.

   e.g. A minor, or person mentally incompetent, may act as an agent if properly authorized. However, the lack of capacity of the agent may leave the principal without the usual remedies for breach of fiduciary duty by the agent. In such a case the principal may obtain restitution from the agent for unjust enrichment.

5. A minor is competent to be a principal although he has the power to disaffirm contractual obligations during minority or within a reasonable time after reaching majority. See Goldfinger v. Doherty, 153 Misc. 826, 276 N.Y.S. 289 (1934).

6. Any natural person who has the capacity to contract has capacity to become a partner in a partnership.

   e.g. A, *an infant*, agrees with adult, B, to become B's partner. A contributes $500 to the capital assets of the firm. The firm becomes indebted to creditor C. C sues "A and B, co-partners doing business as A and B Co." What are A's rights? Ans. The defense of infancy is personal to the infant and only A can set up that defense. The infant's contract is not void but only voidable. As to C, the infant, A, may disaffirm his personal liability to C on the partnership debt. However, the assets of the firm, including A's contribution, may be taken by C to satisfy the debt. With respect to B, the infant can disaffirm the partnership agreement, although it is valid until disaffirmed and avoided by A.

7. In approximately one-half of the jurisdictions a minor of the age of sixteen or eighteen years old, depending on the jurisdiction, may be treated as an adult if he is charged with a crime. A minor below such ages who commits a crime is considered a juvenile delinquent. There are specific statutes in each jurisdiction concerning the treatment of juvenile delinquents. See Clark, pp. 233–234.

8. In the remaining jurisdictions the judge has the discretion to decide whether or not to treat a minor as an adult or as a juvenile delinquent in criminal cases. See Clark, p. 234.

9. A minor must be represented by a guardian if he is suing or being sued. See Clark, p. 233.

10. The 1970 Voting Rights Act fixed the voting age at 18 for state and federal elections. The Supreme Court held that provisions fixing the voting age at 18 are constitutional with respect to congressional, senatorial, vice presidential, and presidential elections, but are unconstitutional with respect to state and local elections. The Court based its decision on the power of Congress to supervise congressional elections by virtue of the Necessary and Proper Clause and the provision in Article I, Section 4 allowing Congress to make or alter the states' regulations for the times, places, and manner of holding elections for senators and representatives. See Oregon v. Mitchell, 400 U.S. 112, 91 S.Ct. 260, 27 L.Ed.2d 272 (1970).

11. Following the result in Oregon v. Mitchell, Congress proposed, and the states ratified, the Twenty-Sixth Amendment. The Amendment provides as follows:

"Section 1. The right of citizens of the United States, who are eighteen years of age or older, to vote shall not be denied or abridged by the United States or by any State on account of age.

"Section 2. The Congress shall have power to enforce this article by appropriate legislation."

12. Employment of minors is governed by the Fair Labor Standards Act and specific state statutes. See Clark, p. 234.

13. A minor generally must attend school until attaining age sixteen. See generally, Paulsen, p. 903.

VI PROCEDURAL ASPECTS OF DIVORCE

Summary Outline

A. Introduction

B. General Principles of Jurisdiction

C. Application of General Principles
    1. domicile of either spouse may terminate marriage
    2. personal jurisdiction
    3. full faith and credit clause
    4. minimum residency requirement

D. Fault Oriented Grounds for Divorce
    1. based on statute
    2. fault oriented grounds

E. Traditional Defenses to Divorce Actions

F. No Fault Divorce
    1. traditional divorce contrasted
    2. grounds determined by state statute

INTRODUCTORY NOTE—PROCEDURES.   This Chapter deals with a number of issues which affect the granting and enforcing of divorce decrees, including the legal incidents related to the termination of the marriage.   The first series of sections highlights the most important substantive areas treated in the balance of this Chapter and in the following Chapter.   The student should be alert to the following important basic areas:

(a) historical development of divorce law and important definitions,

(b) financial aspects of separation and divorce,

(c) jurisdictional and procedural aspects of obtaining and enforcing divorce, alimony and child support decrees, and

(d) contrasts between traditional fault oriented divorces and modern no-fault divorces.

INTRODUCTION   1. Divorce procedures in the United States are a curious blending of:

(a) English law,

(b) equity law,

(c) statutory law, and

(d) all are subject to an overlay of federal constitutional law.

See Clark, p. 379.

2. A divorce dissolves the marriage relationship as of the date of the divorce decree.

3. A legal separation is a partial suspension of the marriage relationship.   Older cases refer to this as a "divorce from bed and board."

4. A divorce may involve payment of alimony.   A legal separation may involve payment of separate maintenance.   See *Chapter VII, Financial and Other Aspects of Divorce*, below.

5. A state has jurisdiction to grant a divorce where:

(a) at least one spouse is domiciled in that state, and

(b) a minimum residency requirement is met.

6. Article IV, Section 1 of the United States Constitution provides: "Full faith and credit shall be given in each state to the public acts, records, and judicial proceedings of every other state."

7. The Full Faith and Credit Clause requires all states to recognize divorce decrees of the forum state where the forum state had

jurisdiction on the basis of bona fide domicile and the decree was otherwise valid, that is, free from extrinsic fraud.

CAVEAT—There are situations where a divorce decree may not be challenged because of estoppel which must be differentiated from situations where it may be attacked collaterally. These cases are analyzed in the sections which follow. See, for example, CASE 41, below.

8. The procedures for divorce are determined by the applicable state statute. They vary widely from state to state.

   (a) In some states the divorce decree is final when issued.

   (b) In some states an interlocutory decree is issued which does not immediately dissolve the marriage; the parties must wait a specified period. At the end of that period the divorce becomes final at the request of either party.

   (c) Some states prohibit remarriage for a certain period of time after the divorce is granted.

9. Traditionally, legislatures and courts attributed the failure of a marriage to the fault of one or both spouses. Consequently, there were only fault oriented grounds for divorce.

10. In recent years a new type of divorce has evolved: no fault divorce. No fault divorce is strictly a product of social change, which rejects the procedures and underlying philosophy of historical divorce law.

    CAVEAT—Where the divorce is contested, the spouse petitioning for the divorce may be required to show an irretrievable breakdown of the marriage through fault oriented criteria even in no fault jurisdictions. Fault or misconduct of one spouse may also be important in determining custody of children.

INTRODUCTORY NOTE—JURISDICTION IN DIVORCES

1. The basic fact pattern in a divorce involves a situation in which both parties are:

   (a) domiciled and resident in the jurisdiction in which the divorce action is instituted; and

   (b) before the court at the time of the hearing with personal service having been made upon the defendant and with the court having jurisdiction over the issue of the marriage.

2. Over the years questions have arisen as to the extent to which this fact pattern can be altered and the contacts with the forum jurisdiction "watered down" with the divorce decree and/or custody

decree yet maintaining vitality and being assured of protection of the full faith and credit clause.

3. The ultimate fact pattern in such watering down is the so-called "Mexican divorce" where neither party appears in the Mexican court or has any contact whatsoever with the court or the jurisdiction. The various steps between these two ends of the spectrum are reviewed in the sections which follow and *Application of General Principles*, below.

GENERAL PRINCIPLES OF JURISDICTION

1. A divorce action is an action to terminate the marital status of the parties. Such status is found to be a res or thing which "exists" and thus serves as a basis of jurisdiction, in the state of the domicile of either party. See CASE 38, below.

2. The general rules regarding the jurisdictional aspects of divorce are as follows:

   (a) A state in which *either* spouse is domiciled has jurisdiction through its courts to terminate the marriage by divorce.

   (b) A state in which *neither* spouse is domiciled has no jurisdiction to terminate the marriage even though both parties are before the court and consent to the decree.

   e.g. H and W are domiciled in state R. While they are on a trip to state M, a suit for divorce is brought by W against H in state M and personal service is made on H personally in state M. H moves to dismiss the suit on the grounds that the court has no jurisdiction over the action. H's motion is sustained since the marriage status of H and W constitutes a relationship in which State R, their domicile, has an interest and without that interest as a res being before the court in State M, State M has no jurisdiction to terminate the relationship. See *Smith's Review, Conflict of Laws*, Chapter XIV, "The Law Governing Domestic Relations."

3. The Restatement, Conflict of Laws, Second, in §§ 70–72 elaborates on three rules with respect to jurisdiction to grant a divorce:

   (a) "A state has power to exercise judicial jurisdiction to dissolve the marriage of spouses, *both* of whom are domiciled in the state."

   (b) "A state has power to exercise judicial jurisdiction to dissolve the marriage of spouses, *one* of whom is domiciled in the state."

   (c) "A state may not exercise judicial jurisdiction to dissolve the marriage of spouses if neither spouse is domiciled in the state and neither has such other relationship to the state as would make it reasonable for the state to dissolve the marriage."

4. A valid divorce decree, terminating the marital relationship, may be obtained without personal jurisdiction over the defendant spouse. However, it is necessary for a court to have personal jurisdiction over the parties to settle property rights such as support payments. See CASE 59, below.

5. Because personal jurisdiction is required to settle property rights, but not to dissolve the marriage itself, the concept of a divisible divorce was developed. Under this concept a valid ex parte divorce dissolves the marriage, but may not affect the property rights of the spouse who did not appear in the proceedings. See CASES 60 and 59 below.

e.g. H obtained a divorce from W in Nevada. W received notice, but did not participate in the litigation. The divorce was granted, but no provision for W's support was made. Subsequently, H moved to Rhode Island where W commenced an action for support. The court determined that although the Nevada divorce was valid, a continuing marital relationship between H and W was not required for W to be entitled to support. The reason for the rule lies in applying traditional notions of due process to domestic relations. The divorce-granting state which lacks personal jurisdiction over W cannot adjudicate the property rights of W to support. Thus, W's right to support survived the Nevada divorce decree, and she is entitled to have her claim for support determined by the Rhode Island court. See Rymanowski v. Rymanowski, 105 R.I. 89, 249 A.2d 407 (1969).

1. The general principles relating to court jurisdiction to grant a divorce decree must be applied in the following situations:

   (a) recognition of divorces in other states,

   (b) divorces of servicemen and servicewomen who have no permanent residence, and

   (c) divorces obtained in foreign countries.

   NOTE—All petitions for divorce are handled by state courts. Federal courts have no jurisdiction to grant divorces.

2. A decree of divorce granted by a court having jurisdiction of the plaintiff spouse who is a bona fide resident (meaning domiciliary) of the state, is entitled to full faith and credit in every other state. See CASE 38, below.

3. The court of the forum may decide for itself whether a court in another state had jurisdiction to grant a divorce. Where the divorce-granting court had no jurisdiction because the plaintiff seeking the divorce had not established a bona fide domicile in that state, the court of the forum need give no faith and credit to the divorce decree. See CASES 38 and 39, below.

APPLICATION OF GENERAL PRINCIPLES

4. If a defendant spouse makes an appearance in a divorce action in which the jurisdictional fact of domicile is properly at issue, and the court finds it has jurisdiction, such determination becomes res judicata. By virtue of the Full Faith and Credit Clause under Article IV of the United States Constitution, neither spouse can raise the issue of jurisdiction at a later time in another jurisdiction.

5. A state may impose minimum residency requirements before entertaining a petition for divorce. See CASE 40, below.

6. One who procures a void divorce decree or who uses a void divorce decree to his or her advantage by remarrying is estopped from attacking such decree. See CASE 42, below.

7. A party will also be estopped from later attacking a divorce decree if:

    (a) such attack is inconsistent with the position taken by such party at the time of the divorce,

    (b) the party upholding the divorce has relied upon the decree, or

    (c) the party upholding the divorce in reliance on such divorce has acted in such a way so as to treat the marriage as ended.

    See Clark, p. 304.

8. The jurisdictional rules pertaining to divorce do not always apply to "divorce from bed and board". A state has jurisdiction through its courts to grant a decree of divorce from bed and board if the parties are before the court, even though neither party is domiciled in the state. Such a "divorce" does not terminate the marital status of the parties. It only terminates their personal rights and obligations to one another, and allows them to live apart.

    e.g. H and W are domiciled in state C. W sues H in state M seeking a decree permitting her to live separate and apart from H, but not an absolute divorce decree. Service of process is made on H personally in state M. H's defense to such action that neither party is domiciled in state M is not valid.

    CAVEAT—Local statutes, however, often do in fact require the plaintiff to be domiciled in the state to maintain such an action.

9. Many states have passed statutes for the benefit of servicemen or women which permit a local divorce based on a serviceman or woman having been stationed in the state for a significant period of time, such as six or twelve months even though legally domiciled elsewhere. Thus, although such statutes do not take domicile into account, they have been held valid since more than

"presence" is required. See Wood v. Wood, 159 Tex. 350, 320 S.W.2d 807 (1959); Wallace v. Wallace, 63 N.M. 414, 320 P.2d 1020 (1958).

NOTE—For servicemen and servicewomen in many cases "domicile" is not relevant due to the transient nature of their vocation. Therefore, these statutes do not change domicile of servicemen, but constitute an exception to normal jurisdictional requirements.

10. In some circumstances the rule concerning domicile of either spouse is further reduced. The most important of such reductions are "Mexican divorces" which comprise an even further step in the watering down of requirements for out-of-state divorce jurisdiction than suggested in Restatement, Conflict of Laws, Second, §§ 70–72. See *General Principles of Jurisdiction*, above.

(a) One type of Mexican divorce is a "paper divorce" in which neither spouse makes an appearance in Mexico. This type of divorce will not be recognized in the United States.

(b) A second type of Mexican divorce is one in which both spouses make an appearance in Mexico. It is unclear whether this type of divorce will be recognized in the United States.

(c) A third type of Mexican divorce is one in which one or both spouses actually live in Mexico for a short period of time. If the time period is long enough to obtain a Mexican domicile, the divorce will be held valid in the United States. If it is not long enough to do so, the divorce will *not* be valid. See Clark, p. 294.

CAVEAT—The law concerning the validity of Mexican divorces is scanty and even if one does find a case, it is not clear that the holding will be followed in other jurisdictions.

e.g. H and W, who resided in New York, obtained a Mexican divorce. Mexican jurisdiction was based on the plaintiff's having met the Mexican formalities of establishing residence by a one-day presence and on the defendant's filing of a pleading along with an appearance by his Mexican attorney. The divorce was recognized because H established residence and W was represented by counsel, thus giving the Mexican court jurisdiction over the marital res. The court reasoned that to disallow such divorces where jurisdictional requirements were met would be inconsistent with the recognition of divorces obtained in other states for similar grounds. See Rosensteil v. Rosensteil, 16 N.Y.2d 64, 262 N.Y.S.2d 86, 209 N.E.2d 709 (1965).

NOTE—Since a state is not required to recognize a divorce obtained in a foreign country, the Full Faith and Credit Clause does not apply to such decrees, and a state may ignore such a divorce decree in order to follow its own policies. The holding in the Rosensteil case has received much criticism, and it would appear that many, if not most, jurisdictions would not follow it. See Leflar, "Conflicts of Law," 1966 Annual Survey of American Law, p. 20.

Case 38   *Application of full faith and credit doctrine to divorce*

H and W, husband and wife, and M and F, also husband and wife, were domiciled in North Carolina. W and M went to Nevada, lived there six weeks, and began actions for divorce against H and F respectively. Service of process was made on H by publication and on F by a sheriff in North Carolina. Neither H nor F made a personal appearance in the proceeding. The Nevada court found that W and M had established a bona fide residence there and granted each a decree of divorce. W then married M and they returned to North Carolina. W and M were prosecuted for bigamy in North Carolina, and in defense they raised the divorce decree. They were convicted and appealed. Did the Full Faith and Credit Clause of the Constitution require North Carolina to honor the Nevada divorce decree where Nevada had jurisdiction?

Answer. Yes. *A divorce action is one in rem and not in personam. It is an action to terminate the marital status. This status is held to exist (and have a situs) wherever one of the spouses has a bona fide domicile. When a court in one state, having proper jurisdiction and acting in accord with the requirements of procedural due process, alters the marital status of one domiciled in that state by granting a divorce from an absent spouse, the decree must be honored by other states under the Full Faith and Credit Clause of the Constitution of the United States. The Court assumed for purpose of its decision that W and M had bona fide domiciles in Nevada. In those circumstances the Nevada court had jurisdiction to grant the divorce regardless of where H and F were domiciled at the time of the divorce. Every other state is required to give full faith and credit to such decree. The case was remanded for further proceedings consistent with the Court's opinion.*

See Williams v. North Carolina, 317 U.S. 287, 63 S.Ct. 207, 87 L.Ed. 279 (1942), which overruled Haddock v. Haddock, 201 U.S. 562, 26 S.Ct. 525, 50 L.Ed. 867 (1906). See also Goodrich, pp. 264–265.

CAVEAT—In reaching its decision the Supreme Court assumed that the Nevada court had jurisdiction to grant the divorces. The issue of whether the jurisdiction of the Nevada court could be attacked in North Carolina when jurisdiction had not been litigated in Nevada was not ruled upon. However, that was the issue in a subsequent case involving the same parties and the same facts. See CASE 39, below.

Jurisdiction—limitation to application of full faith and credit doctrine to divorce

Case 39

After the decision in CASE 38, above, W and M were retried for bigamy in North Carolina. The facts were the same in the second trial, but the prosecution contended that the divorces which W and M obtained in Nevada were invalid because they never established a bona fide domicile in Nevada. That issue was litigated, and the jury concluded that no domicile had been established in Nevada, and W and M were convicted and appealed. May North Carolina refuse to give full faith and credit to a Nevada divorce decree where the North Carolina court finds, contrary to the findings of the Nevada court, that the Nevada court lacked jurisdiction because no bona fide domicile was acquired in Nevada?

Answer. Yes. If there were a bona fide domicile in Nevada, then the Nevada decree must be given full faith and credit in every other state under the Constitution. However, the issue of domicile of the parties was never litigated in the original proceedings in Nevada, and there was no personal jurisdiction over H and F in the Nevada proceedings. To compel North Carolina to admit that W and M established a bona fide domicile in Nevada would be to compel North Carolina to submit to the governing of its internal affairs by the state of Nevada with respect to a marital status in which North Carolina has a vital interest. Therefore, North Carolina can find that W and M were still domiciliaries of North Carolina and still subject to the government of North Carolina. In such event the North Carolina court could find that W and M had not established a bona fide domicile in Nevada, and that the court in Nevada had no jurisdiction over the marital status of H and W and M and F. Having found as a fact that W and M were not bona fide residents of Nevada, but always residents of North Carolina, North Carolina need not give full faith and credit to the Nevada divorce decree. Since the divorce was not recognized in North Carolina, the convictions were upheld.

See *Williams v. North Carolina*, 325 U.S. 226, 65 S.Ct. 1092, 89 L.Ed. 1577 (1945).

NOTE 1—In the first Williams v. North Carolina case, CASE 38, (N.C.1942) above, the existence of the domicile of the plaintiff spouse in the divorce action was NOT questioned. Thus, *assuming domicile*, the Supreme Court precluded collateral attack. However, on remand the domicile was successfully attacked. See Goodrich, pp. 37, 49, 256, 259, and 264–265.

NOTE 2—At the second trial the defense of former jeopardy was raised, but rejected. Since the defendants were tried and convicted in the first case on an unsound principal of law, the state followed its usual procedure and ordered a new trial using the law of the case established by the Williams I decision. See State v. Williams, 224 N.C. 183, 29 S.E.2d 744 (1944). The prohibition of double jeopardy in the Fifth Amendment of the Federal Constitution had not then been made applicable to the states through the Fourteenth Amendment, so only the state law was applied. However, even if federal constitutional law were applied, there would be no double jeopardy because the convictions were set aside on defendants' appeal, thus allowing a second trial. See *Smith's Review, Constitutional Law,* Chapter X, "Double Jeopardy Clause."

Case 40 *State durational residency requirement for divorce upheld*

H and W were married and lived in New York. They separated and W moved to Iowa. A month later W filed for divorce. H, who was served when he traveled to Iowa to visit his children, made a special appearance to contest jurisdiction of the Iowa court. W's petition was dismissed because Iowa law required residence of one year before filing for divorce. W appealed, contending that the residency requirement placed an unconstitutional burden on the right of interstate travel and violated her due process right of access to divorce courts. Is W's contention valid?

Answer. No. A divorce decree is of concern to both spouses as well as to the state. It may include a settlement of property rights and provisions for the custody of minor children and their support. "With consequences of such moment riding on a divorce decree issued by its courts, Iowa may insist that one seeking to initiate such a proceding have the modicum of attachment to the State required here." The durational residency requirement furthers the state's interest in avoiding intermeddling in matters in which another state has a paramount interest, and in decreasing the chance that its own divorce decrees will be subject to collateral attack. "A State such as Iowa may quite reasonably decide that it does not wish to become a divorce mill for unhappy spouses who have lived there as short a time as [W] had when she commenced her action in the state court after having long resided elsewhere. Until such time as Iowa is convinced that [W] intends to remain in the State, it lacks the 'nexus between person and place of such permanence as to control the creation of legal relations and responsibilities of the utmost significance.' " citing CASE 39, above. Jurisdiction to grant a divorce is based on domicile. A state which is asked to grant a divorce may insist that the plaintiff satisfy something more than the bare minimum of constitutional requirements. The fact that other states may establish a *constitutionally permissible shorter period does not compel Iowa to do the same. Finally, it should be noted that the residency requirement did not deny W access to Iowa courts, but only delayed it. The residency requirement did not violate the Constitution, and it was proper to dismiss W's petition for divorce.*

See Sosna v. Iowa, 419 U.S. 393, 95 S.Ct. 553, 42 L.Ed.2d 532 (1975).

Failure to raise domicile issue in a divorce action— issue foreclosed

Case 41

H and W have their matrimonial domicile in Massachusetts. W went to Florida and after the requisite period of time to establish residence in Florida W sued H in Florida for a divorce. H entered a general appearance in the case and contested the divorce. The general appearance and contest of the divorce afforded him an opportunity to raise the question of W's domicile, but he did not do so. A divorce decree was entered in W's favor. Some time later in Massachusetts, H served W and attacked the decree on the ground that W was not domiciled in Florida at the time of the divorce. May H collaterally attack the decree granted in Florida?

Answer. No. When H entered a general appearance in the case in Florida the question of W's domicile was a proper issue to be raised, and even though it was not raised and litigated, it became res judicata when the decree in Florida was issued because of the opportunity to do so. H was present, represented by counsel, and had the opportunity to litigate all issues, including domicile, fully. There is no evidence that the Florida court did not evaluate the issues fairly. Under the Full Faith and Credit Clause a state must recognize the decree of another state where all the issues of the case were contested and decided or where there was full opportunity to do so. Thus, H's petition should be dismissed.

See Sherrer v. Sherrer, 334 U.S. 343, 68 S.Ct. 1087, 92 L.Ed. 1429 (1948); Coe v. Coe, 334 U.S. 378, 68 S.Ct. 1094, 92 L.Ed. 1451 (1948).

NOTE 1—In the initial litigation in Florida, H made a general appearance and he had the opportunity to contest the jurisdiction of the court by questioning W's domicile. If he does not do so, and the divorce is ultimately granted to W, the court, in so doing, implicitly finds W's domicile to be as she alleges. The rule in Sheerer is that this procedural circumstance precludes H from colaterally attacking the jurisdiction of the first court, in proceedings in a second court, where he had the opportunity to do so in the initial proceedings, but chose not to do so. In other words, the parties to the divorce are estopped from challenging the divorce in another state in these circumstances.

NOTE 2—The state of domicile has a vital interest in the marital status of the couple seeking a divorce in another state. However, the interests or justified expectations of the couple who obtain a divorce in another state are considered more important, and may be a reason for the decision in the Sherrer case.

NOTE 3—The general rule concerning the application of res judicata to jurisdictional questions is that where they could have been litigated in an earlier proceeding but were not raised, such jurisdictional questions may not be raised in a subsequent action. See Chicot County Drainage Dist. v. Baxter State Bank, 308 U.S. 371, 60 S.Ct. 317, 84 L.Ed. 329 (1940).

Case 42   *Invalid divorce decree—estoppel to deny jurisdiction subsequently*

H-1 and W are husband and wife domiciled in state A. H becomes totally and permanently disabled. W procures a "paper Mexican divorce" through a Mexican court. She makes no appearance in Mexico and no service of process is made on H-1. W then marries H-2. Upon H-1's death, W seeks letters of administration in H-1's estate and claims part of the estate as H-1's widow. Will her claim be sustained?

    Answer. *No. The Mexican divorce is void and, therefore, H-1 and W were still husband and wife at H-1's death. Because of that fact W's marriage to H-2 was bigamous. However, when W procured the Mexican divorce and then remarried on the strength of such divorce, W was estopped later to claim that the divorce was valid for some purposes and invalid for others.*

    See Rediker v. Rediker, 35 Cal.2d 796, 221 P.2d 1 (1950); Restatement, Conflict of Laws, Second, § 112.

NOTE—In a Mexican divorce proceeding W appeared personally and H appeared by an attorney. The divorce decree awarded custody of their child to H. Subsequently, W petitioned for divorce from H in the District Court of the Virgin Islands and sought custody of their child. H contended that because of the prior Mexican divorce there was no existing marriage for the court to dissolve. W contended that the Mexican divorce was invalid because neither W nor H were domiciled in Mexico at the time of the divorce. The court dismissed W's petition, reasoning that W may not collaterally attack the validity of the Mexican divorce since she was the spouse who sought and obtained the divorce. W obtained the divorce by representing to the Mexican court that she resided in Mexico. Under these circumstances W may not later deny the validity of the Mexican divorce decree. Court jurisdiction to award custody of the children of a marriage arises when the court dissolves the marriage or declares it void. Since W's marriage was dissolved by the Mexican decree, no marriage remained to give the court jurisdiction over the custody proceeding. Thus, H retained custody of their child. See Perrin v. Perrin, 408 F.2d 107 (3d Cir. 1969). See also *Smith's Review, Constitutional Law,* Chapter V, "Full Faith and Credit Clause."

1. Due to the interest of a state in the marital status of its residents, all state legislatures have passed laws governing the grounds on which a divorce will be granted.

   FAULT ORIENTED GROUNDS FOR DIVORCE

   CAVEAT—If the action which forms the basis of the complaint for the divorce *does not* constitute a ground under the divorce statute of that jurisdiction, the divorce will not be granted. This is so since divorce is controlled strictly by statute.

2. Grounds on which a divorce will be granted are enumerated separately in the statutes of each jurisdiction. Typically, they include the following:

   (a) adultery,

   (b) desertion,

   (c) habitual drunkenness,

   (d) non-support,

   (e) insanity,

   (f) criminal conviction, and

   (g) drug addiction.

3. In addition to the rather specific grounds outlined in number 2, above, many statutes contain the more general grounds of:

   (a) physical cruelty,

   (b) mental cruelty, or

   (c) gross neglect.

   NOTE—Some court decisions use only the word "cruelty" without distinguishing between physical cruelty and mental cruelty.

4. Originally, physical cruelty involved some danger to life, limb or health. This ground was often used when the parties desired to obtain a collusive consent divorce. As divorce laws became more liberal, mental cruelty was the more common ground used to obtain a divorce.

5. The terms mental or physical cruelty or gross neglect allow the court to hear evidence as to a wide variety of conduct, and the interpretation of these words varies widely from state to state.

(a) W sought a divorce from H on the ground of extreme cruelty. H was addicted to heroin and refused all aid in overcoming the habit. As a result there was an attrition of H's sexual powers and he refused to have intercourse with W. The court said: "Rejection of sex, however it may be accomplished, can turn marriage from a benediction and a fulfillment into a nightmare of frustration, despair and decay. That has been plaintiff's tormented experience. . . . The touchstone of extreme cruelty is its impact upon the victim." In this case the denial of sexual relations was more than transitory, and W has shown its detrimental effect on her physical and mental health. Therefore, W is entitled to a divorce. See Melia v. Melia, 94 N.J.Super. 47, 226 A.2d 745 (1967).

(b) Courts in some states have ruled that homosexual conduct of one spouse constituted cruelty, and is grounds for divorce. See H. v. H., 59 N.J.Super. 227, 157 A.2d 721 (1959).

See also CASES 45 and 46, below.

6. The degree of proof as to the kinds of behavior which constitute "physical cruelty", "mental cruelty" or "gross neglect" also varies depending on whether the divorce is contested or uncontested.

(a) In a *contested* action the issues are sharply joined and the court is faced with specific decisions as to whether or not certain kinds of conduct fall within the statutory definition.

(b) By contrast, in an *uncontested* divorce where there is no adversary aspect to the proceeding, generally, the plaintiff's statement with respect to the defendant's conduct, unassailed, and unquestioned, presents no factual or legal issue in terms of whether or not it falls within the statutory definition.

7. In some jurisdictions a divorce will also be granted for grounds that are the same as those for an annulment. These grounds include:

(a) bigamy,

(b) fraud,

(c) duress, or

(d) impotence.

NOTE—Often divorces will be petitioned for and granted in cases where an annulment action would be in order. Such a procedure is followed to prevent a financial hardship for the wife. If an annulment is granted, the marriage terminates retroactively and the wife is not entitled to alimony. By contrast, if a divorce is granted, the marriage is terminated as of the date of the decree and alimony may be awarded. See Chapter VII, *Permanent Alimony.*

8. In circumstances involving more than one state the law of the domicile of the plaintiff at the time the divorce action is commenced determines the grounds available for a divorce.

e.g. H and W are husband and wife domiciled in state B where mental cruelty is *not* a ground for divorce. W moves to state C where she establishes residence and sues for divorce from H on the ground of mental cruelty committed by H in state B. Mental cruelty is a ground for divorce in state C at the time the action is commenced. W is, and should be, granted the divorce since she is a bona fide resident of state C and has grounds for divorce under the law of state C. *It is immaterial where the cause of action arose.* See Restatement, Second, Conflict of Laws, § 285.

Willful desertion as a ground for divorce   Case 43

H and W are Hungarians who were married in Budapest. After their marriage H became involved in revolutionary activities, and due to such involvement was forced to flee from Hungary. H eventually came to the United States and asked W to join him. W refused to do so. H now sues in the United States for divorce on the ground of willful desertion. Should H be granted a divorce?

Answer. *Yes. Desertion as a ground for divorce may be actual or constructive. Constructive desertion exists when cohabitation is terminated by the misconduct of one of the parties to a marriage. Such misconduct may be the natural result of certain acts as well as acts committed with the intent of forcing the other party from the home. Under the statutes of the jurisdiction in which H brought the suit, willful desertion is a ground of divorce if such desertion has existed for three years. A husband may choose and fix the domicile of himself and his wife, and her refusal to follow him constitutes desertion. In this case, W stated that she would not follow H and preferred to remain in Hungary even though H could not return in safety to Hungary. Thus, H should be granted a divorce.*

See Toth v. Toth, 23 Conn.Supp. 161, 178 A.2d 542 (1962).

Constructive desertion as a ground for divorce   Case 44

H and W are husband and wife. W became intoxicated frequently and would quarrel with H, insulting H in public and private by calling him a homosexual. H now brings an action for divorce on the ground of desertion. Should his petition be granted?

Answer. *Yes. A pattern of behavior which is persistent and intolerable to the other party of the marriage will warrant a finding of constructive desertion. Here, W's persistent behavior was detrimental to H's health, and her accusations were so demeaning that they amount to constructive desertion. H should be granted a divorce.*

See *Liccini v. Liccini*, 255 Md. 462, 258 A.2d 198 (1969).

Case 45   *Cruelty as a ground for divorce*

W brought a divorce action against H, her husband, and was granted a default judgment on the ground of cruelty. W gave evidence that H treated her cruelly, stayed away from home, used abusive language to her and visited another woman's apartment. Such evidence was corroborated. H now brings a motion to vacate the judgment, contending that the evidence was insufficient to support a decree of divorce on the ground of cruelty. Should H's motion be denied?

Answer. Yes. Under the applicable law mere incompatibility is not sufficient to warrant a divorce. However, the evidence here showed more than mere incompatibility. H's conduct was a long continued course of ill-treatment which resulted in injury to W's health. Such conduct constitutes cruelty even though there was no actual or threatened violence. W's evidence which was corroborated was sufficient to justify the granting of a divorce decree and H's motion should be denied.

See *Swenson v. Swenson*, 257 Minn. 431, 101 N.W.2d 914 (1960); but compare to CASE 46, below.

NOTE—Cruelty is a ground for divorce in almost all jurisdictions, but what constitutes cruelty differs from jurisdiction to jurisdiction and depends to a great extent upon whether the action is contested or uncontested. The determining criteria are:

(a) the acts and conduct of the defendant,

(b) the motivation of the defendant, and

(c) the effect of such acts and conduct on the plaintiff.

Case 46   *Extent of cruelty in a divorce action—traditional rule*

H and W had been married for 12 years when W brought an action for divorce on the ground of cruelty. W alleges that H is sullen, morose and tyrannical and that she is mild and tender. H alleges the opposite is true. Should W's petition for divorce be granted?

Answer. No. A party to a marriage may be released from the duty of cohabitation by the cruelty of the other party. However, that cruelty must be of such character that the duties of married life cannot be discharged. No such duties can be discharged in a state of personal danger, but acts that fall short of constituting such danger must be reviewed carefully. In some instances, the wounding of mental feelings constitutes cruelty and will justify the granting of a divorce decree. However, the denial of little indulgences and accommodation does not constitute cruelty. In this case there is no proof of *reasonable apprehension of bodily harm or severe mental cruelty. Therefore, the complaint should be dismissed.*

See *Evans v. Evans,* 161 Eng.Rep. 466 (1790).

NOTE—The holding and reasoning in the above case are often quoted in modern cases regarding the subject of cruelty in divorce situations. See Clark, p. 341.

1. Defenses generally available in fault oriented jurisdictions include the following:

TRADITIONAL DEFENSES TO DIVORCE ACTIONS

(a) collusion,

(b) condonation,

(c) connivance,

(d) recrimination,

(e) laches, and

(f) provocation.

See generally, Paulsen, pp. 452–472.

NOTE—These defenses are not available in no fault jurisdictions.

2. *Collusion* is a defense to divorce recognized in all jurisdictions in the United States. It is an *agreement* between the parties to a marriage that one of them will appear to commit an act that will constitute grounds for a divorce in order to obtain a divorce, but the act will not actually be committed. See Clark, p. 363.

3. *Condonation* is the *voluntary resumption of the marital relationship* between spouses, one of whom had committed an act that constituted grounds for a divorce and the other of whom had knowledge of such act.

4. There are two aspects to condonation:

(a) forgiveness, and

(b) restoration of the marital relationship.

5. The various jurisdictions are divided with respect to the necessity of *both* aspects in condonation.

(a) In some jurisdictions, *either* forgiveness or the resumption of sexual relations constitutes condonation.

(b) In some jurisdictions, only the marital relationship must be resumed in order to find condonation.

(c) In some jurisdictions, both forgiveness and the resumption of sexual relations constitute condonation.

See Clark, pp. 365–370.

NOTE—Condonation is a *factual* issue to be determined at trial.

6. *Connivance* is defined as the consent of one of the parties to a marriage to an act by the other party that will constitute grounds for a divorce, and such act is committed.

NOTE—Connivance is usually found only in divorce actions based on adultery.   See CASE 48, below.

7. *Recrimination* is the barring of a divorce to either spouse where both spouses have committed acts which constitute grounds for a divorce.   However, states have passed legislation or developed special doctrines permitting divorces in cases of fault on the part of both spouses.

(a) In some jurisdictions the spouse committing the less serious act is granted the divorce.   This is known as the doctrine of *comparative rectitude*.   See Paulsen, pp. 462–463.

(b) Other jurisdictions have granted a *dual divorce* where both spouses were at fault.   A *dual divorce* grants a divorce to each party.

e.g.   H petitioned for a divorce from W because of cruel and inhuman treatment.   W filed a counterclaim seeking a divorce on the same grounds.   The court did not determine whether H or W was ultimately at fault for the breakdown of the marriage.   Instead, the court found that both H and W had grounds for divorce, and granted a divorce to each spouse.   See John W. S. v. Jeanne F. S., 48 A.D.2d 30, 367 N.Y.S.2d 814 (1975).

NOTE—The decision above is important because: (a) traditional policy considerations of preserving a marriage which was no longer viable were rejected, and (b) the difficulty or impossibility of determining which spouse was ultimately at fault for the breakdown of the marriage was recognized.

Case 47   *Element of intent necessary for connivance*

H and W are husband and wife.   W had been guilty of habitual drunkenness for over two years when H sued for divorce on the ground of habitual drunkenness.   W now seeks to bar the divorce by raising the defense of connivance.   W states that H, knowing of her problem, made liquor available to her.   Specifically, H brought liquor home, took W to social affairs where liquor was served and drank with her. H often cautioned W against overindulgence.   Should W's defense prevail?

Answer.   *No.   An essential element of connivance is the corrupt (deliberately wrongful) intent on the part of the spouse bringing the* divorce action that the other spouse committed the act forming the basis of the action. Here, the evidence does not tend to show that H had the corrupt intent that W acquire a confirmed habit and inability to control her appetite for liquor. Undoubtedly, H could have taken precautions to protect W from her own weaknesses, but as a matter of law he is not obligated to forego his own pleasures at the risk of being charged with the corrupt intent to make W a habitual drunkard. The divorce was granted.

See Muir v. Muir, 46 Del. 578, 86 A.2d 857 (1952).

Connivance as a defense—implied from conduct   Case 48

H and W are husband and wife. H, however, wants a divorce since he believes W to be unfaithful. H hires a detective agency that sends an agent to entertain W. The agent takes W drinking and dining and then proceeds to have sexual relations with W. H now brings a suit for divorce and W raises the defense of connivance. Is her defense good?

Answer. *Yes. If a wronged party hires detectives or other persons as agents to lure his spouse into acts of infidelity, such wronged party's acts amount to connivance. Mere acquiescence does not constitute connivance. Here, H is not entitled to a divorce since connivance may be implied from his acts which in a positive manner tended to bring about W's adultery and which amounted to H's consent thereto.*

See McAllister v. McAllister, 137 N.Y.S. 833 (Sup.Ct.1912); Rademacher v. Rademacher, 74 N.J.Eq. 570, 70 Atl. 687 (1908).

Element of knowledge necessary for condonation   Case 49

H and W were husband and wife when W committed adultery. H learned of the incident, but forgave W and cohabited with her when she promised to be faithful. Subsequent to such promise W committed adultery on several additional occasions. H cohabited with W afterwards, but he was unaware of W's adultery at that time. H now brings a suit for divorce on the ground of adultery, and W raises the defense of condonation. Should W's position be upheld?

Answer. *No. One cannot condone acts of adultery of which one is unaware. Here, H had no knowledge of W's subsequent acts of adultery, and, therefore, could not have condoned them. Condonation of specific past acts of adultery does not affect subsequent acts of adultery. The divorce was granted.*

See McKee v. McKee, 206 Va. 527, 145 S.E.2d 163 (1965).

Case 50   *Element of fraud necessary for collusion*

H and W are husband and wife. While H was in the Army, W lived with A and had a child by him. W informed H of the situation and H agreed to a divorce so that W could marry A. Upon returning from the military, H filed for divorce on the grounds of adultery and abandonment. W filed an answer, entering an appearance and requesting that the divorce be granted. The lower court then dismissed the suit holding it to be collusive. On appeal, should the lower court's decision be upheld?

     Answer. No. The lower court's judgment should be reversed and remanded with instructions that H be granted a divorce. Collusion is an agreement to defraud or to obtain an object otherwise forbidden by law. Here, W merely stated that she had no objection to the divorce since she had no defense to the action. There was no collusion and the divorce should be granted.

     See Conyers v. Conyers, 311 Ky. 468, 224 S.W.2d 688 (1949).

Case 51   *Recrimination as a bar to divorce*

W and H were married for a period of three years before W brought a suit for divorce against H. H denied the allegations and filed a cross-complaint for divorce. The lower court heard evidence that H had physically injured W on various occasions, that H was often intoxicated, and that he boasted of sexual relations with other women. The evidence also showed that W wrote letters to different persons falsely accusing H of homosexuality. The court denied a divorce to either party on the ground of recrimination. The court reasoned that although H's actions were grounds for divorce, W's actions should bar her from obtaining a divorce. W appealed the denial of her divorce petition. Should the lower court's decision be upheld?

     Answer. No. Whether or not mutual cruelty is a bar to an action for divorce depends on the circumstances of the case, including: (a) the comparative fault of the parties, (b) the prospects of reconciliation, and (c) the effect of the marital strife upon the parties, their children and the community. Although there is no precise formula to determine whether mutual cruelty results in recrimination, the lower court did not look at all the facts of the case. The decision was reversed and remanded to the lower court for further consideration.

     See DeBurgh v. DeBurgh, 39 Cal.2d 858, 250 P.2d 598 (1952).

NO FAULT DIVORCE   **1.** Traditionally, fault has been the basis upon which divorce has been granted. That is, one spouse committed some wrongful act which, under a state statute was grounds for the other party to obtain a divorce.

2. The concept of no fault divorce developed because of:

   (a) recognition that divorces based solely upon fault failed to prevent the break-up of marriages and,

   (b) fault oriented grounds for divorces encouraged perjury to obtain a divorce.

3. As this Review goes to press all states but two have some form of no fault divorce statute.

4. In states where it is not necessary to show fault in divorce proceedings, the issue is what evidence is required to show that there has been a marital breakdown.

   e.g. The no fault divorce statute in California requires "irreconcilable differences, which have caused the irremediable breakdown of the marriage." Cal. Civ. Code § 4506 (1970). A case interpreting that section stated that it meant "substantial marital problems which have so impaired the marriage relationship that the legitimate objects of matrimony have been destroyed and as to which there is no reasonable possibility of elimination, correction or resolution." In re Marriage of Walton, 28 Cal.App.3d 108, 104 Cal.Rptr. 472 (1972). See CASE 52, below.

5. A Delaware statute provides for divorce where the marriage is "irretrievably broken." This may be shown by:

   (a) voluntary separation,

   (b) separation caused by mental illness,

   (c) separation caused by misconduct of one spouse, or

   (d) separation caused by incompatibility where reconciliation is improbable.

6. The Uniform Marriage and Divorce Act provides, in Section 302, for the granting of a divorce if:

   "(2) the court finds that the marriage is irretrievably broken, if the finding is supported by evidence that (i) the parties have lived separate and apart for a period of more than 180 days next preceding the commencement of the proceeding, or (ii) there is serious marital discord adversely affecting the attitude of one or both of the parties toward the marriage;

   "(3) the court finds that the conciliation provisions of Section 305 either do not apply or have been met;

   *   *   *

"Section 305.

"(a) If both of the parties by petition or otherwise have stated under oath or affirmation that the marriage is irretrievably broken, or one of the parties has so stated and the other has not denied it, the court, after hearing, shall make a finding whether the marriage is irretrievably broken.

"(b) If one of the parties has denied under oath or affirmation that the marriage is irretrievably broken, the court shall consider all relevant factors, including the circumstances that gave rise to filing the petition and the prospect of reconciliation, and shall:

"(1) make a finding whether the marriage is irretrievably broken; or

"(2) continue the matter for further hearing not fewer than 30 nor more than 60 days later, . . . and may suggest to the parties that they seek counseling. The court, at the request of either party shall, or on its own motion may, order a conciliation conference. At the adjourned hearing the court shall make a finding whether the marriage is irretrievably broken.

"(c) A finding of irretrievable breakdown is a determination that there is no reasonable prospect of reconciliation."

NOTE—Statutory criteria for no fault divorce are intentionally broad in most states. The purpose is to give much discretion to the court which decides whether to grant the divorce. Such statutes have been held constitutional. See CASE 53, below.

Case 52   *No fault divorce granted when marriage irretrievably broken*

H petitioned for divorce on the ground that his marriage to W was irretrievably broken. W denied H's allegations and asked for a jury trial on the issue of whether the marriage was irretrievably broken. H moved for summary judgment, and submitted an affidavit stating that H and W's present separation was permanent. H stated that he was unwilling to live with W at any time in the future, and that there was no possibility of a reconciliation ever taking place. W opposed the motion, and submitted an affidavit which denied that the marriage was irretrievably broken, and stated her willingness to reconcile and continue the marriage. Should H's motion be granted?

Answer. Yes. It takes two consenting parties to make a contract, and it takes two consenting parties to make a reconciliation. Just as one party cannot make a contract, one party cannot make a marriage or a reconciliation. There is no issue of fact as to the irretrievable brokenness of the marriage. H refuses to cohabit with W, and the fact that W desires a reconciliation will not support a finding by the trier of fact that there are prospects for a reconciliation. Since H has shown that the marriage is irretrievably broken, his motion for summary judgment should be granted, and the divorce decree issued.

See Manning v. Manning, 237 Ga. 746, 229 S.E.2d 611 (1976).

No fault divorce statute held constitutional   Case 53

A Florida statute provided that the sole grounds for divorce were irretrievable breakdown or insanity. In a suit under the statute, its constitutionality was challenged on the following grounds: (a) it impaired the rights and obligations of the parties to the marriage contract, (b) it was unconstitutionally vague and uncertain, and (c) it operated retroactively to marriages entered into before its enactment. Is the statute constitutional?

Answer. Yes. (a) The federal and state constitutions prohibit statutes which impair contract obligations. That applies to contracts which provide certain, definite and fixed private property rights which are vested in the contract. Rights of dower and curtesy are statutory; they are not vested. Potential alimony or equitable interest in property are not vested rights. They arise upon judicial determination at the termination of the marriage contract. Thus, these rights are not property rights contemplated by the constitutional prohibition. (b) The phrase "irretrievably broken" is not unconstitutionally vague. It is not necessary for the legislature to enumerate every circumstance under which a marriage could be dissolved. A petition for divorce need only allege the ultimate fact that the marriage is irretrievably broken. The trial court will then determine whether the particular facts of a case meet that standard based upon the evidence presented. (c) The authority to regulate marriages and provide for their dissolutions is vested in the legislature. There is no denial of due process in the no fault divorce law even though it applies retroactively to marriages contracted before its enactment. The new law does not deprive the parties of any rights enjoyed under the former, fault oriented statute. Only the procedure for obtaining a divorce has been changed, and that is a "remedy" which is the prerogative of the legislature. The new law represents a change of philosophy in the approach to the dissolution of marriage which is within the province of the legislature. Thus, the law is constitutional.

See Ryan v. Ryan, 277 So.2d 266 (Fla.1973).

VII

FINANCIAL AND OTHER ASPECTS OF DIVORCE

Summary Outline

A. Introduction

B. Property Division in Divorce
   1. "just and reasonable" standard
   2. community property state standard

C. Historical Background of Alimony

D. Temporary Alimony

E. Permanent Alimony

F. Enforcement of Alimony and Support Decrees

G. Termination of Duty to Pay Alimony

H. Determination of Child Custody

I. Child Support

J. Federal Legislation and Child Support

K. Separation Agreements

L. Background of Community Property Law

M. Basic Principles of Community Property Law

N. Community Property Management and Control

O. Community Property and Divorce

P. Tax Aspects of Divorce

INTRODUCTION

1. Generally, a divorce decree does more than terminate the marriage status of the parties. It does the following:

   (a) grants the divorce to one of the parties,

   (b) divides the marital property,

   (c) awards alimony,

   (d) awards custody of the minor children of the marriage, and

   (e) awards child support.

2. In many instances the financial aspects of a divorce constitute the focal point of the controversy between the parties.

3. For both parties the financial aspects have emotional and practical implications.

   (a) The husband often attempts to evade or at least to minimize his support responsibilities in order to show contempt for his wife and to retain as much of his income as he can for his new life.

   (b) Similarly, the wife may use the divorce proceedings as a device to vent her emotions as well as seeking legal redress for wrongs to her, and she may seek to secure ample resources for her new life.

4. During the 1970s a number of United States Supreme Court decisions have applied the Equal Protection Clause of the Fourteenth Amendment to traditional Family Law concepts. This has brought about many changes, some of which are:

   (a) men are entitled to alimony in appropriate cases,

   (b) the age of majority for child support purposes must be the same for males and females,

   (c) fathers have gained rights comparable with women in child custody and related matters, and

   (d) discrimination against illegitimate children in public welfare programs and elsewhere has been reduced.

5. Community property laws are being modernized to avoid discrimination against women.

6. Federal legislation has affected child support.

   e.g. The Social Security Act was amended in 1935 to create a program of Aid to Families with Dependent Children (AFDC). Subsequent expansion of the program now ensures public assistance to aid in the support of minor children and to provide a mechanism for collection of child support and alimony.

1. Upon divorce, most state statutes provide that property of the spouses should be divided according to what is "just and reasonable."

   (a) In community property states each spouse has an equal and undivided vested interest in all property acquired by his or her spouse during the marriage. See *Background of Community Property Law*, below.

   (b) In other states, in the absence of specific statutory guidance, the contribution of money or services by each spouse must be evaluated.

2. Where the grounds for the divorce are fault oriented, the misconduct of the one spouse may be taken into account in establishing the value of the contribution of the other, innocent spouse.

3. Recent cases view the services of a full time housewife as a substantial contribution to the marriage and often divide the property equally regardless of which spouse earned the money to buy the property. That policy is consistent with the reasons for no fault divorce. See DiFlorido v. DiFlorido, 459 Pa. 641, 331 A.2d 174 (1975); In re Marriage of Dietz, 19 Or.App. 334, 527 P.2d 427 (1974).

4. The marital property which some courts have found to be divisible in divorce proceedings is increasing.

   e.g. One court held that the "good will" of a physician's practice was an asset capable of evaluation and division upon divorce. See In re Marriage of Lukens, 16 Wash.App. 481, 558 P.2d 279 (1976).

PROPERTY DIVISION IN DIVORCE

1. Alimony is the legally imposed allowance paid to one spouse (or former spouse) by the other spouse for maintenance and support.

2. The prerequisite to the granting of alimony is the existence of a marriage.

   (a) *Temporary* alimony, if the financial conditions of the parties so warrant, may be awarded to a spouse who does not admit the invalidity of the marriage because the existence of the marriage is still in controversy. It is awarded while the litigation is pending.

   (b) *Permanent* alimony may be awarded at the conclusion of the litigation. However, it will not be awarded, in absence of statutory authorization, in annulment actions since the existence of a marriage had been adjudicated and denied.

HISTORICAL BACKGROUND OF ALIMONY

See Chapter IV, *Property Settlements in Annulment Actions,* above.

3. Alimony in the United States has been influenced by English law. In England alimony was utilized to provide support for wives living apart from their husbands. In the United States the concept of alimony has been expanded so that historically, it was utilized in the following:

   (a) as a continuation, after divorce, of the support which a wife received during marriage,

   (b) as a measure of damages for breach of the marriage contract, and

   (c) as a penalty levied upon a guilty husband.

   See Clark, pp. 420–422; Paulsen, pp. 529–531.

   NOTE—In England alimony was awarded to a wife who was separated from her husband but nevertheless still married to him. By contrast, in the United States alimony is awarded both to the wife who is separated from her husband and yet still married *and also to the wife who is divorced.*

4. Today, alimony awards are generally based upon the needs and abilities of each party. The following factors are considered:

   (a) age of the parties,

   (b) health and physical condition of the parties,

   (c) the earning capacity of the parties,

   (d) present income of the parties, and

   (e) in some jurisdictions, the duration of the marriage.

5. When divorce statutes were fault oriented, there were two additional factors which courts considered in awarding alimony:

   (a) The degree of fault of one spouse in causing the breakdown of the marriage was considered. Courts reasoned that the party at fault should be punished, and the innocent party should be compensated for the wrong done to him or her. See Melny v. Melny, 90 Cal.App.2d 672, 203 P.2d 588 (1949).

   (b) The wife should be permitted to continue the lifestyle which she had during the marriage. This criterion was justified by the husband's continuing duty to support his wife. See Radandt v. Radandt, 30 Wis.2d 108, 140 N.W.2d 293 (1965).

   NOTE—Although the reasons for the criteria above may be somewhat inconsistent with the theory of no fault divorce, some courts continue to apply them in no fault cases. See Magruder

v. Magruder, 190 Neb. 573, 209 N.W.2d 585 (1965); contra, In re Marriage of Williams, 198 Iowa 513, 199 N.W.2d 339 (1972).

6. Rehabilitative alimony is defined as alimony to support the spouse during a period of retraining or re-education for entry into the work force, and to enable such spouse to become self supporting. In contrast to traditional alimony, which imposes the burden of support on the defendant spouse, rehabilitative alimony assumes that the spouse is ultimately responsible for her own support, but needs temporary assistance in becoming able to do so.

7. The award of rehabilitative alimony has been allowed in recent court decisions where the wife had the potential to earn a livelihood, but required support from the time of the divorce to the realization of her potential as a wage earner. See Dakin v. Dakin, 62 Wash.2d 687, 384 P.2d 639 (1963); Morgan v. Morgan, 81 Misc.2d 616, 366 N.Y.S.2d 977 (1975).

8. The basic rationale for rehabilitative alimony is that support should be provided until one spouse is able to become self-supporting.

    e.g. W obtained a divorce and an award of alimony for three years. The state statute limited alimony awards to a three year period where there were no minor children involved, but permitted an extension of the period if justice so required. When W petitioned for an extension beyond the three years, the court said that the purpose of alimony was "not to provide . . . a life-time profit-sharing plan" for one spouse, but rather to provide support for a limited period until the spouse could obtain employment and become self-supporting. The court placed the burden of proof on W to show that justice required an extension of the alimony period. See Calderwood v. Calderwood, 114 N.H. 651, 327 A.2d 704 (1974).

9. The answer to the question of whether alimony may be awarded to a husband has changed over the years.

    (a) Prior to 1970 most states did not permit an award of alimony to the husband.

    (b) Most state laws were changed in the 1970s so that husbands could be awarded alimony in appropriate cases. See Pfohl v. Pfohl, 345 So.2d 371 (Fla.App.1977).

    (c) In 1979 the United States Supreme Court held that a state law which provided that a husband, but not a wife, could be required to pay alimony deprived men of equal protection of the law, thus violating the Equal Protection Clause of the Fourteenth Amendment. See CASE 54, below.

10. A number of courts have been sympathetic to alimony awards or property settlements where an unmarried couple separated after living together. See Chapter X, *Marriage, Divorce and Cohabitation*, and CASE 86, below.

Case 54   *Gender-based alimony statute unconstitutional*

H and W were granted a divorce, and H was ordered to make certain alimony payments to W. The applicable state law provided that husbands, but not wives, may be required to pay alimony. Two years later W filed a petition seeking to have H held in contempt for failure to maintain alimony payments. At the hearing on W's petition, H contended that the statute under which he was required to pay alimony was unconstitutional because its gender-based classification violated the Equal Protection Clause of the Fourteenth Amendment. Was the statute constitutional?

   Answer. *No. In authorizing the imposition of alimony only on husbands the statute established a sex-based classification which was subject to scrutiny under the Equal Protection Clause. In such a case the classification by gender must serve important government objectives and must be substantially related to achievement of those objectives. The statute effectively announces the state's intention to allocate family responsibilities so that the wife plays a dependent role. However, the "old notion" that "generally it is the man's primary responsibility to provide a home and its essentials," cannot justify a statute which discriminates on the basis of sex. A wife is no longer destined solely for the home and the rearing of a family, with her husband alone working to support the family unit. Likewise, the argument that the statute is designed to assist the wife of a broken marriage who needs financial assistance is insufficient. A statute which provides only for women either uses the female sex as the equivalent of need or attempts to compensate women for discrimination against them during the marriage which assertedly has left them unprepared to fend for themselves in the working world after divorce.*

   The statute provides for individualized hearings at which the parties' relative financial circumstances are considered and where only the needs of the wife are taken into account. This unconstitutional aspect of the statute can be rectified in the future at a hearing where the needs of both females and males can be determined. Similarly, the hearing can determine which women are unprepared to work or have been discriminated against in some way during the marriage. Those family units which are contrary to the stereotype because the husband is dependent on the wife can be identified. Thus, a hearing can determine and provide for the needs of each spouse with little or no additional expense to the state. Furthermore, the challenged statute gives an advantage only to a financially secure wife whose husband is in need. Such a wife might be required to pay alimony under a gender-neutral statute. However, the financially independent wife is the least likely female to have been the victim of discrimination which the statute seeks to remedy. For those reasons the statute does not withstand judicial scrutiny. The gender-based distinction of the statute was not related to the achievement of important governmental objectives, and violated the Equal Protection Clause of the Fourteenth Amendment. The case was remanded to the lower court to determine whether there were other grounds, besides the unconstitutional alimony statute, which would require H to continue his alimony payments.

See *Orr v. Orr*, 440 U.S. 268, 99 S.Ct. 1102, 59 L.Ed.2d 306 (1979).

TEMPORARY ALIMONY

1. A decree for temporary alimony, or alimony pendente lite, is a decree in personam, and consequently, it must be based upon personal service within the jurisdiction or on a personal appearance of the defendant.

2. The right to enforce an award of temporary alimony expires when the divorce action, upon which it is based, terminates.

3. The award or denial of temporary alimony lies within the discretion of the court. The amount, absent a statute, depends upon the circumstances of each situation. See CASE 55, below.

4. The amount of temporary alimony awarded is subject to modification as the circumstances of the parties change.

Criteria in an award of temporary alimony

Case 55

W and H marry and go on a four day honeymoon after which H takes W to the hotel where she lived before their marriage and leaves her. H is a wealthy man with assets totaling over $1,000,000. W worked prior to her marriage to H and earned $180 per month. After being left at the hotel for six days, W forcefully entered H's home and refused to vacate it. While in the home she has use of H's Cadillac and now refuses to give it up, claiming it is a gift. In an action for divorce and temporary alimony instituted by W, H maintains that he should pay only $200 a month temporary alimony; he should receive the return of his car; and W should vacate his home. W claims that she should receive sufficient temporary alimony to enable her to live according to the station of life of the parties. The trial court awarded W temporary alimony of $750 a month; attorney's fees; use and control of the car; and enjoined H from disposing of his other property during the litigation, except as necessary to maintain himself. H received sole possession of his home. H appeals, claiming that *the award to W was excessive and that the trial court abused its discretion in making such award.   Is his contention correct?*

Answer.   *No.   The amount of temporary alimony to be awarded is in the discretion of the court, which must look to the facts of the case.   Where the wife has no separate means of her own, temporary alimony should furnish the wife with means of support consistent with the husband's means and the station in life of the parties during the marriage relationship.   In determining the ability of the husband to pay, not only his income, but also property of all types must be considered.   The amount awarded for attorney's fees is also in the court's discretion and the same factors that are applied in the award of temporary alimony should be applied in determining the amount awarded for such fees.   Voluntary litigation by the parties to a marriage of their respective property rights without objection places the issue before the court and allows the court to determine the question raised irrespective of whether or not the court would have otherwise had jurisdiction to do so.   Here, the trial court did not abuse its discretion.*

See *Hempel v. Hempel,* 225 Minn. 287, 30 N.W.2d 594 (1948).

PERMANENT ALIMONY

1. Permanent alimony may be awarded to a spouse after a divorce. It can take different forms:

   (a) periodic payments,

   (b) lump-sum payment,

   (c) annuity purchase, and

   (d) alimony trusts.

   See Clark, p. 447.

2. The periodic payments of alimony which allow a spouse to discharge alimony over a period of time provide:

   (a) a spouse the means by which to pay a generally large sum over a period of time,

   (b) a spouse receiving such payments support over a time span, and

   (c) the court continuing jurisdiction over the decree to prevent hardship on either spouse.

3. The lump-sum payment of alimony permits:

   (a) a spouse to discharge his obligation totally and not contend with a continuing liability, and

   (b) a spouse receiving such payment to have a large sum with which to plan a new life.

4. Annuities and alimony trusts provide security and flexibility to both spouses.

5. The particular form that alimony takes is dependent upon:

    (a) the circumstances and needs of the parties,

    (b) the statutes of the jurisdiction,

    (c) the negotiations between the parties, and

    (d) the discretion of the court.

6. The broad discretion which rests with the trial judge in dividing marital property, determining alimony and establishing child support is illustrated by one statute, the Ohio Revised Code, which provides:

"§ 3105.18 Alimony.

"(A) In a divorce, dissolution of marriage, or alimony proceedings, the court of common pleas may allow alimony as it deems reasonable to either party.

   "The alimony may be allowed in real or personal property, or both, or by decreeing a sum of money, payable either in gross or by installments, as the court deems equitable.

"(B) In determining whether alimony is necessary, and in determining the nature, amount, and manner of payment of alimony, the court shall consider all relevant factors, including:

"(1) The relative earning abilities of the parties;

"(2) The ages, and the physical and emotional conditions of the parties;

"(3) The retirement benefits of the parties;

"(4) The expectancies and inheritances of the parties;

"(5) The duration of the marriage;

"(6) The extent to which it would be inappropriate for a party, because he will be custodian of a minor child of the marriage, to seek employment outside the home;

"(7) The standard of living of the parties established during the marriage;

"(8) The relative extent of education of the parties;

"(9) The relative assets and liabilities of the parties;

"(10) The property brought to the marriage by either party;

"(11) The contribution of a spouse as homemaker.

"(C) In an action brought solely for an order for alimony under section 3105.17 of the Revised Code, any continuing order for periodic payments of money entered pursuant to this section is subject to further order of the court upon changed circumstances of either party."

"§ 3109.05 Child support; visitation rights.

In a divorce, dissolution of marriage, alimony, or child support proceedings, the court may order either or both parents to support or help support their children, without regard to marital misconduct. In determining the amount reasonable or necessary for child support, the court shall consider all relevant factors including:

"(A) The financial resources of the child;

"(B) The financial resources and needs of the custodial parent;

"(C) The standard of living the child would have enjoyed had the marriage continued;

"(D) The physical and emotional conditions of the child, and his educational needs;

"(E) The financial resources and needs of the noncustodial parent;

"(F) The educational needs of the child and the educational opportunities which would have been available to him had the circumstances requiring a court order for his support not arisen.

"The court may make any just and reasonable order or decree permitting the parent who is deprived of the care, custody, and control of the children to visit them at *the* time and under *the* conditions as the court may direct. The court may, upon notice and hearing, make such modification as it determines just in an order of support of a child or an award of alimony upon proof that the party subject to *the* order has been continuously or repeatedly prevented from exercising a right to visit *the* child established by an order of court. In the discretion of the court, reasonable companionship or visitation rights may be granted to any other person having an interest in the welfare of the child. The juvenile court shall have exclusive jurisdiction to enter *the* orders in any case certified to it from another court."

"§ 3105.21 [Care of dependent children.]

"(A) Upon satisfactory proof of the causes in the complaint for divorce, annulment, or alimony, the court of common pleas shall make an order for the disposition, care, and maintenance of the children of the marriage, as is in their best interests, and in accordance with section 3109.04 of the Revised Code.

"(B) Upon the failure of proof of the causes in the complaint, the court may make the order for the disposition, care, and maintenance of any dependent child of the marriage as is in the child's best interest, and in accordance with section 3109.04 of the Revised Code."

NOTE—One judge has attempted to reduce the above factors to a mathematical formula to provide consistency of decisions. Since total needs of the wife and children, if there are any, are taken into account in establishing child support and alimony, the formula deals with the *inter-relationship* of both, as they relate to the assets and earnings of both spouses. See Milligan, "Guidelines in Alimony and Support For Ohio," Vol. 14, West's Ohio Practice.

ENFORCEMENT OF ALIMONY AND SUPPORT DECREES

1. Where a final alimony decree of one state is based on jurisdiction over the subject matter of the action and personal jurisdiction over the defendant spouse, it must be recognized by the courts of other states under the Full Faith and Credit Clause of the Constitution. See Sistare v. Sistare, 218 U.S. 1, 30 S.Ct. 682, 54 L.Ed. 905 (1909).

2. An alimony decree may be enforced by contempt proceedings if it has been merged into the divorce decree and is part of the court's judgment. However, if a former spouse is not financially able to make payments, contempt proceedings and jail will not provide the other spouse with the needed support. See Appendix, Question 1.

3. The amount of permanent alimony awarded may be modified by the court if there is a change of circumstances of either party. See *Termination of Duty to Pay Alimony*, below. See also Appendix, Question 5.

4. The traditional rule, under the Full Faith and Credit Clause, is that a judgment rendered by one state need not be recognized or enforced in a sister state, so long as it remains subject to modification in the rendering state, either as to sums that have accrued and are unpaid, or as to sums that will accrue in the future. See Restatement, Second, Conflict of Laws, § 109. This Rule has been applied, traditionally, to alimony and support decrees.

5. Although traditionally there has been no constitutional mandate binding upon a sister state requiring it to enforce a modifiable decree of the rendering state, nonetheless, some courts have done so.

   e.g. Husband and wife were divorced in New Jersey. The New Jersey decree was modifiable both prospectively and retroactively. Husband moved to California, subsequently, and wife commenced an action there to enforce the New Jersey decree. Over the husband's objections, the California court entertained the wife's action for enforcement of the New Jersey decree. In so doing it held that "foreign-created alimony and support obligations are enforceable in this State. In an action to enforce a modifiable support obligation, either party may tender and litigate any plea for modification that could be presented to the courts of the state where the alimony or support decree was originally rendered." See Worthley v. Worthley, 44 Cal.2d 465, 283 P.2d 19 (1955).

   CAVEAT—The California court in *Worthley* elected to enforce the judgment, even though it was not bound to do so under the Full

Faith and Credit Clause.   In the future, the Supreme Court of the United States may well hold that there is an obligation under the Full Faith and Credit Clause to enforce such judgments, rather than merely the freedom to do so.

Case 56   *Obligations assumed after a divorce decree do not constitute alimony*

W and H are husband and wife.   W brings a divorce action against H in state X, their domicile, which has a statute stating that alimony provisions must be made part of the divorce decree and, if no provisions for alimony are made a part of the decree, the spouse is precluded from receiving any such payments after such decree.   H and W execute a separation agreement containing provisions for the division of their property and the payment of $15,000 by H to W in monthly installments.   Six days later W is granted a decree of divorce.   The court approves the property settlement, but does not make it part of the decree.   H now seeks to have the separation agreement declared void as an agreement to pay alimony after a decree of divorce.   Should his action be upheld?

Answer. No.   Alimony is the provision for the payment of money to a spouse as set forth by judicial judgment or decree of court.   Alimony in contravention of state law in state X would be payments imposed by a court *after* a final decree of divorce.   Such an action did not occur in this case.   Instead H entered into a contractual agreement with W.   Such contract is valid and, therefore, binding upon H.   Thus, H's action should be dismissed.

See *Francis v. Francis*, 412 S.W.2d 29 (Tex.1967).

Case 57   *Circumstances of the parties are determinative of alimony— standard of review*

H and W were married for over twenty-five years when W obtained a divorce from H.   W had never worked during her marriage and at the time of the divorce was ill, requiring much medical attention. W was awarded alimony by the trial court in the amount of $225 per month.   H earns between $833 to $916 a month.   W now appeals such alimony award, claiming it to be inadequate.   Where an alimony award is not clearly inadequate, will the appellate court overturn such award?

Answer. No.   In fixing alimony a court must look to all the circumstances of the case and fix an amount equitable to both parties. Courts should not force a husband to pay such an amount of alimony as to destroy his incentive to work and earn enough to pay any alimony.   Here, on the basis of the facts it cannot be said as a matter of law that the lower court erred in its alimony award.   Furthermore, *the appellate court will not substitute its decision for that of the trial court. W's appeal should be dismissed.*

See Bramblette v. Bramblette, 448 S.W.2d 44 (Ky.1969); Canady v. Canady, 30 Ill.2d 440, 197 N.E.2d 42 (1964).

Alimony award subject to modification   Case 58

H and W-1 were married until W-1 obtained a divorce from H. H was earning $10,000 a year at the time of the divorce, and W-1 was awarded alimony in the amount of $100 per week. H remarried and had three children with W-2, his second wife. He currently earns $13,000 a year, but his second wife is ill and requires medical attention. W-1 is unmarried, childless and earns $6,000 a year. H now petitions the court to lower the alimony award to W-1. Should his petition be granted?

Answer. Yes. There is no hard and fast rule concerning the determinative factors to be considered in weighing a motion to reduce alimony. The circumstances of each situation must be considered by the court in order to achieve an equitable balance. Alimony must not make a wife a drone and unjustly burden the husband. In considering an application for modification of the amount of a prior alimony award the court should consider any significant changes in circumstances which materially increase or decrease the financial burden on either spouse, and should attempt to achieve a balance between the parties in the exercise of the court's sound discretion. Here, in view of W-1's income and H's responsibilities, W-1's alimony was reduced to $40 a week.

See Covert v. Covert, 48 Misc.2d 386, 264 N.Y.S.2d 820 (1965).

Divisible divorce—an ex parte divorce does not affect   Case 59
alimony rights

H and W marry and four years later separate in state C. W moves to state D and establishes her domicile there. H files for and obtains a divorce from W in state N. W was not served with process and did not enter an appearance in the case. W now sues H in state D for alimony. H responds by entering a special appearance and stating that the court in state D under the Full Faith and Credit Clause of the Constitution should treat the divorce decree of state N as terminating the marriage and with it his duty of support. Does an ex parte divorce in a foreign state destroy the alimony rights of the wife in the state in which she resides?

Answer. No. Where a wife is not subject to the jurisdiction of a foreign state court rendering a divorce decree, such court has no power to extinguish any rights she may have for support from her *husband. It is a constitutional rule that a court cannot adjudicate a personal claim or obligation unless it has jurisdiction over the person of the defendant. Here, although the court of state N had the power to grant the divorce, the court did not have power to cut off W's right to alimony because it did not have personal jurisdiction over the wife. To the extent that the court of state N purported to do so, the court of state D was not obligated to recognize it. State N had "in rem" jurisdiction over the marital status, not the parties.*

See Vanderbilt v. Vanderbilt, 354 U.S. 416, 77 S.Ct. 1360, 1 L.Ed. 1456 (1955). Compare CASES 38 and 39.

NOTE—The result in this Case leads to what is called the "divisible divorce doctrine". This means that the subject matter of the divorce is divided into: (a) granting the divorce itself, and (b) dealing with the financial obligations of the parties. Because there was jurisdiction "in rem" over the status of the divorce, the court had jurisdiction or "power" to deal with it by granting a divorce. In this way the rights of the absent wife as to the marital relationship could be affected. However, since there was no personal jurisdiction over the absent wife there was no jurisdiction or "power" to affect her *personal* rights in financial matters.

Case 60   *Effects of an ex parte divorce decree on a prior alimony award*

H and W marry and live together in state Y for five years until H leaves W. A year later W files for a legal separation rather than for a divorce, H enters an appearance, and the court grants W such separation and awards her $180 per month as alimony. H then goes to state N and files for divorce. W receives constructive service, but does not enter an appearance. The court in state N grants H a divorce, but makes no provisions for alimony. After the decree H ceases to make any alimony payments to W. W sues in state Y for a judgment with respect to the alimony arrearage. H moves to eliminate the alimony provisions of the decree from state Y. Should his motion be upheld?

Answer. No. The court in state N could not adjudicate the property rights of a party under a judgment rendered in state Y, if there was no personal service on such party or an appearance by such party in state N. A judgment of a court having no personal jurisdiction to render it is not entitled to full faith and credit which the Constitution requires. Here, the court in state Y, having jurisdiction over both H and W, granted W a decree of alimony. This is an intangible property interest over which jurisdiction can only arise from control over the persons whose relationships are the source of the rights and obligations. State N cannot exercise in personam jurisdiction over a person not before its court. Therefore, the decree *of state N should only be given effect with respect to the dissolution of the marriage, but not with respect to alimony.*

See Estin v. Estin, 334 U.S. 541, 68 S.Ct. 1213, 92 L.Ed. 1561 (1948).

TERMINATION OF DUTY TO PAY ALIMONY

1. Alimony is generally required until the remarriage of the spouse. The basis for terminating alimony is:

   (a) a state statute,

   (b) the agreement of the parties, or

   (c) a modification of the alimony decree by a court because of the changed circumstances of the parties. See Appendix, Question 5.

2. Today, with the not uncommon practice of couples living together without benefit of clergy, some courts have held that absence of financial need can be shown by evidence of cohabitation by the spouse receiving alimony. See Meyer v. Meyer, 41 Md.App. 13, 394 A.2d 1220 (1978); Garlinger v. Garlinger, 137 N.J.Super. 56, 347 A.2d 799 (1975).

   e.g. A divorce decree required that H pay $35,000 annually, as support and maintenance to W. The obligation was binding until the remarriage or death of W. Subsequently, W met X who moved into W's home during various periods for three years. X used W's address as his own, and they traveled together registering in hotels as husband and wife. W admitted having sexual relations with X on a number of occasions. X did not make any contribution to W's support. In fact, W bought X clothes, paid both of their travel expenses and made money loans to him. When H learned of this he moved the court to relieve him of making further alimony payments to W because of the change in her marital status. The court said that if the alimony award was not solely for support, but was in settlement of some or all of the property rights of the parties, it may not be changed. In this case there is a separate provision for a property settlement so that the alimony award is severable and may be changed. An alimony agreement which is fair when made may be rendered manifestly oppressive, for example, where the custodian of children does not care for them, the receiver of alimony makes no attempt at self-support, or where the economic situation of either or both parties drastically changes. Post divorce unchastity or similar misconduct does not *per se* require a termination of alimony. However, it is a circumstance which should be considered. If a former wife is being supported by a paramour the former husband may have his obligation reduced or terminated. If the paramour resides with the wife without contributing anything to her support, then it may be inferred that the wife's alimony is being used, at least in part, for the benefit of her paramour, and the amount of alimony may be modified accordingly. The inquiry is whether the illicit relationship has produced a change of circumstances sufficient to modify the alimony award. In this case the trial court terminated all alimony, and in view of all the circumstances, that was not an abuse of discretion. Thus, the alimony award was modified to terminate H's obligations to W. See Wolfe v. Wolfe, 46 Ohio St.2d 399, 350 N.E.2d 413, 75 O.O.2d 474 (1976).

NOTE—A New York statute provides for the termination of alimony where the recipient habitually lives with another *and* holds herself out to be his spouse. This is a two part test. Cohabitation alone does not justify an inference that the parties are holding themselves out as man and wife. A holding out requires some assertive conduct such as "I am his wife," or a checking account listing his surname. See Northrup v. Northrup, 43 N.Y.2d 566, 373 N.E.2d 1221 (1978).

3. Homosexual cohabitation has also been used as a basis for terminating alimony. One court reasoned that the homosexual cohabitation made remarriage substantially less likely, thus creating a change of circumstance not considered when the initial provision for alimony was made. See Anonymous v. Anonymous, 5 F.L.R. 2127 (Minn.Dist.Ct., Ramsey Cty., 1978).

NOTE—The purpose of the court decisions in numbers 2 and 3, above, is not to impose a moral standard on persons or penalize a person for immoral conduct per se. The decisions are based on the economic reality that cohabitation without marriage can be used to obtain support unfairly when the ex-spouse is being supported by a resident paramour.

4. Although the duty to pay alimony terminates upon the remarriage of the spouse receiving payments, a problem may arise if the subsequent marriage is annuled.

(a) Where the second marriage is void, some courts will reinstate alimony from the date of the annulment. Other courts will not revive the obligation to pay alimony.

e.g. H and W were divorced and H was required to pay alimony to W. W married, but later discovered that her second husband was validly married at that time. W had her second marriage annulled because it was bigamous and void at all times. She asked to have alimony reinstated. The court refused to reinstate H's alimony obligations to W. However, a state statute allowed W to obtain alimony from her second husband even though that marriage was annulled. See Gaines v. Jacobsen, 308 N.Y. 218, 124 N.E.2d 290 (1954).

(b) Where the second marriage is voidable, most courts will not reinstate alimony.

e.g.   H and W were divorced, and H was ordered to pay alimony to W.   W remarried, but later had the marriage annulled on the ground of fraud.   The court said that W's right to alimony should not be revived.   Since W's new marriage was only voidable, redress by way of annulment might never be sought, and the marital status might continue indefinitely.   When W remarried, H was entitled to recommit his assets previously chargeable to alimony to other purposes.   It was W who brought herself and H into their present situation, and therefore, W should assume the responsibility for it.   See Sefton v. Sefton, 45 Cal.2d 872, 291 P.2d 439 (1955).

DETERMINATION OF CHILD CUSTODY

1. The children of a couple being divorced are innocent parties who are vitally affected by the divorce.   It is the interests of the innocent children which underlie the traditional rules as to child custody in a divorce.   Although modern courts have adopted new criteria in the granting of divorces they have been reluctant to deviate from traditional principles in determining child custody.

2. Child custody is generally determined by the court according to the best interests of the child.   Factors considered include:

   (a) the age of the child or children,

   (b) their health and emotional stability,

   (c) fitness to care for the child, including:

      (i)   the emotional stability of each parent, and

      (ii)   the misconduct of one spouse,

   (d) the financial situation of the parents, and

   (e) in some jurisdictions, the preference of the child or children.

3. In determining custody of children, the fact that the mother is living with a person to whom she is not married does not, by itself, disqualify her from being custodian of her children.   Courts have stated that it is not for them to approve or disapprove of such conduct, but only to determine its effect on the children. See Jarrett v. Jarrett, 64 Ill.App.3d 933, 21 Ill.Dec. 718, 382 N.E.2d 12 (1978).   See also CASE 61, below.

4. Child custody for fathers is becoming more common.   A few courts have provided for joint custody of children rather than the traditional award of sole custody to one parent.   Legislation is pending in other states which would create a presumption in favor of joint custody.

NOTE—An important factor in joint custody arrangements is the necessity for cooperation between the parents to make joint decisions in the child's best interests. The court must determine whether this is feasible before ordering joint custody.

5. The award of custody of illegitimate children is also changing, and fathers who have shown responsibility through care and support of the child are being considered equally with mothers. See CASE 74, below.

6. Court jurisdiction to determine custody of children is a problem in interstate child custody disputes.

   e.g. H and W are husband and wife domiciled in Oklahoma. They have a minor child, C who is living with them. W sues H in Oklahoma for divorce and custody of C. H is served with process in Oklahoma. The court grants the divorce, and decrees that each parent shall have custody of C for six months of each year, the first six months custody to go to W. The child is taken by W to Texas where W establishes her domicile. When the first six months has expired, H comes to Texas where W hands to H the child and immediately serves process on H in habeas corpus to regain possession of the child. H's defense is the Oklahoma decree. Must the Texas court give full faith and credit to the Oklahoma decree? Ans. No. A child custody decree deals with a changing situation; it may be materially different even in a period of six months. In this case the Texas court has jurisdiction of W, of H and of C. The court also has jurisdiction of the status of the child because its domicile is that of the mother who had custody in Texas. The ultimate issue before the court is the welfare of C in which the state of Texas has a paramount interest. The Texas court may invoke the change-of-circumstances rule under which it would examine the facts de novo to determine the custody of the child. If the Texas court determined that the child's best welfare was served by remaining with the mother, W, such decree may be made thus depriving H of the custody decreed by the Oklahoma court.

7. To avoid child custody conflicts the Uniform Child Custody Jurisdiction Act has been adopted by some states. Section 1(a) of the Act states that its purposes are to:

   "(1) avoid jurisdictional competition and conflict with courts of other states in matters of child custody which have in the past resulted in the shifting of children from state to state with harmful effects on their well-being;

   *   *   *

   "(2) assure that litigation concerning the custody of a child take place ordinarily in the state with which the child and his family have the closest connection and where significant evidence concerning his care, protection, training, and personal relationships is most readily available, and that courts of this state decline the exercise of jurisdiction when the child and his family have a closer connection with another state."

8. Principal provisions of the Act include:

(a) jurisdictional standards for courts,

(b) the requirements that courts recognize the custody decrees of foreign states which had the requisite jurisdiction,

(c) a forum non conveniens (inconvient forum) section designed to protect the interests of the child and avoid simultaneous proceedings in different states,

(d) procedures for modification of a custody decree of another state,

(e) procedures for enforcement of custody decrees of other states,

(f) taking testimony or conducting proceedings in another state, and

(g) methods of cooperation with courts in other states.

See Wadlington, pp. 858–861.

9. Most jurisdictions provide that at a certain age the child may elect which parent he desires to live with.

Best interests and desires of children determine custody award, not social mores   Case 61

Gay Christian obtained a divorce from her husband, H, and was awarded custody of their children, together with support payments. After the divorce H continued to live in Nevada but Gay moved to Colorado. During the following years Gay developed the characteristics of a male and became a transsexual. Gay changed her name to Mark and married a woman. A Colorado court set aside the initial Nevada custody decree and awarded custody of the children to H. H took the children to Nevada where they were forcibly confined in his home. The children ran away from H and returned to Colorado. They were apprehended by authorities and placed in a foster home pending a court determination of custody. At the trial Mark, formerly Gay, appeared to be a strong, healthy male with long sideburns and mustache. There was testimony at trial about homosexuality, lesbianism and other sex acts which were denied by Mark. Mark claimed to have established himself as a father image to the children, and stated that the children were devoted to himself and his wife. Was there a change of circumstances after the original decree sufficient to warrant an award of custody to H?

Answer. No. *The trial judge interviewed the children individually in chambers. They had been taught about their former mother's change of sex. They understood and appreciated it for the fact that it is. The children all expressed the desire to live with Mark and his wife. Based upon the desires of the children, and the evidence indicating that Mark and his wife would provide a better home for them, the court concluded "that despite social mores and old-fashioned attitudes, the welfare of the children will be best served by placing them with their former mother, and now the father-image, Mark Randall."*

See *Randall v. Christian,* No. 32964, 1st Dist., Carson City, Nev. (1973), reprinted in Krause, pp. 1081–1082.

CHILD SUPPORT

1. The usual standards for child support are need and ability to pay.

   e.g. Two children were beneficiaries of a testamentary trust established by their grandfather. When their parents were divorced, child support payments took into consideration income from the trust. May a court consider a child's own independent income when determining a parent's obligation for support? Ans. Yes. Parents bear the primary obligation to support their children and resort to the children's own resources for their basic needs may only be done if the parents are financially unable to fulfill that obligation themselves. However, a child's property and income may be used to supplement the primary obligation of the parents to supply the child's basic minimum support needs for more expensive matters, such as education and travel. See *Armstrong v. Armstrong,* 15 Cal.3d 942, 126 Cal.Rptr. 805, 544 P.2d 941 (1976).

2. Ordinarily the obligation to support children continues until they reach the age of majority. However, a state may not establish the age of majority at 21 for males and 18 for females in the context of a parent's obligation for support payments for children. Such a statute violates the Equal Protection Clause of the Fourteenth Amendment. See *Stanton v. Stanton,* 421 U.S. 7, 95 S.Ct. 1373, 43 L.Ed.2d 688 (1975).

   CAVEAT—The obligation of support may continue after the child reaches the legal age of majority if circumstances require. Thus, where a child suffered from dyslexia, a brain defect, requiring psychiatric care and prescription drugs for life, the duty of support and maintenance continued after the child reached majority. See *Elkins v. Elkins,* 262 Ark. 63, 553 S.W.2d 34 (1977).

3. Traditionally, the father was held primarily responsible for child support. In fact, the statutes in many states specifically placed that responsibility on the father.

4. The trend of more recent statutes and court decisions is to divide child support equitably between the mother and father. That trend is consistent with the policies of no fault divorce.

e.g. H and W were divorced. W was awarded custody of their child, and H was required to make support payments to W. Subsequently, W obtained employment in which she was paid more than H. H petitioned for a modification of his child support payments. W opposed the modification relying on cases which placed the primary duty of supporting a child with the father. The court held that established law which placed the duty of child support on the father was "a vestige of the past and incompatible with the present recognition of equality of the sexes." Thus, the old rule was rejected and child support responsibilities were divided equitably between the parents. See Conway v. Dana, 456 Pa. 536, 318 A.2d 324 (1974).

NOTE—The student should remember that an equitable division of child support does not necessarily mean an equal division. It means only that the court will consider all relevant circumstances of each spouse and then make a determination without consideration of the sex of each spouse.

5. The jurisdiction of a state over a nonresident spouse in a child support matter depends on the contacts of the nonresident spouse with that state. The test is whether there is sufficient contact with the state to make it fair and reasonable for the court to adjudicate the claim against the nonresident. See CASE 62, below.

Jurisdiction over nonresident parent for child support—   Case 62
contacts required

H and W, husband and wife, resided in New York for a number of years. They had two children, A and B. H and W executed a separation agreement in New York, after which W moved to California. By the terms of the agreement, A and B were to live with H in New York for nine months each year while attending school, and live with W for the other three months each year. The agreement also provided that H would pay W $3,000 for the children's support while they were living with her. Subsequently, W obtained a divorce in Haiti which incorporated the terms of the separation agreement. Thereafter, A asked to live in California with W during the school year and with H during vacations. H agreed. Two years later W arranged with B to move to California without H's knowledge. W then brought an action against H in California to increase H's child support obligations. H appeared through counsel in California to contest the jurisdiction of the California court over him. H contended that his contacts with California were not sufficient under the Due Process Clause to give the California court in personam jurisdiction over him.

H's defense was rejected. The court reasoned that since H had intentionally availed himself of the benefits and protection of California laws by sending A there, and later consenting to B's residence there, California courts could assert in personam jurisdiction over H to resolve the issue of child support. H appealed. Should the decision be upheld?

*   **Answer.** No. The Due Process Clause of the Fourteenth Amendment limits the power of state courts to assert personal jurisdiction over nonresidents. There must be certain minimum contacts with the forum state so that maintenance of the suit does not offend "traditional notions of fair play and substantial justice." Stated another way, a defendant must have sufficient purposeful contact with the state to make it fair and reasonable for the court to adjudicate the claim. In the present case California's jurisdiction was based on H's consent to have A live with W. H's decision was based on his personal, domestic relations and he derived no financial benefit from A's presence in California. Furthermore, H could not reasonably anticipate that his consent to A's living with W would be the basis of having to litigate the child support claim 3,000 miles away. Thus, H had insufficient purposeful contacts with California to provide a constitutional basis for its courts to exercise personal jurisdiction over him. W's suit was dismissed.*

*   See Kulko v. Superior Court of California, 436 U.S. 84, 98 S.Ct. 1690, 56 L.Ed.2d 132 (1978).*

NOTE—The Court pointed out that California had substantial interests in protecting the rights of resident children and in facilitating child support actions on their behalf. That interest can be met through application of the Uniform Reciprocal Enforcement of Support Act, which has been adopted in California and New York. Applying that Act to the present case, W could file a petition for support in California and have its merits adjudicated in New York without either W or H having to leave her or his own state. Thus, W has a means to vindicate her claimed right to additional child support from H and to collect any support payments found to be due her. See 9 Uniform Laws Ann. 476 (Supp.Pamph. 1977); Cal.Code Civ.Proc. § 1650 et seq.; N.Y. Domestic Relations Law § 30, et seq.

FEDERAL LEGISLATION AND CHILD SUPPORT

1. Practical experience has shown that the legal remedies available for non-support are more theoretical than real. In many situations they are either not effective, or cannot be used because the parent having the support obligation cannot be located.

2. When the parent with custody of the child cannot obtain support from the other parent, public welfare is often necessary to assist the parent and child.

3. Congress has recognized that many parents who do not live with their children fail to fulfill their support obligations. In 1974 and 1975 Congress amended the Social Security Act in order to provide a means to:

   (a) enforce the support obligations owed by absent parents to their children,

   (b) locate absent parents,

   (c) establish paternity, and

   (d) obtain child support.

   See Child Support and Establishment of Paternity amendments to the Social Security Act, 42 U.S.C.A. §§ 651–662.

4. The amendments established a program within the Department of Health, Education and Welfare (HEW) under which states could participate and receive funds under the Aid to Families with Dependent Children (AFDC) program.

5. Under the law, HEW has overall responsibility for the program. Specifically, its principal functions include:

   (a) establishment of standards for state programs for locating absent parents, establishing paternity, and obtaining child support,

   (b) review and approval of state plans for such programs,

   (c) audit state plans to assure conformity with federal standards,

   (d) provide technical assistance to states to establish paternity and collect child support payments, and

   (e) create a Parent Locator Service.

6. States are given latitude in developing their AFDC program. However, state plans must not conflict with the Social Security Act or valid HEW regulations issued in administering programs under the Act. See CASES 63 and 64 below.

   CAVEAT—Although states may not discriminate between legitimate and illegitimate children in granting benefits (see CASE 64, below), the circumstances of married and divorced women may be sufficiently different to warrant the granting of benefits to one class and not to the other class of persons.

   e.g. The Social Security Act grants benefits to a married woman under age 62 if she has a minor or dependent child in her care and her husband retires or becomes disabled. A divorced woman is not entitled to such benefits in the same circumstances. The Act was challenged on the ground that it arbitrarily discriminated against divorced wives in violation of the Due Process Clause of the Fifth Amendment. The Court noted that the challenged provision was not a general public assistance law designed to pay money to those who need it most. The primary objective of the Act was to provide workers and their families with some protection against hardships created by the loss of earnings due to illness or old age. To grant benefits to a married woman to meet the *additional need* created when her husband reaches old age or becomes disabled is consistent with the Act's objective. Furthermore, Congress could rationally decide that: (a) divorced spouses typically lead separate lives and are less dependent on each other than couples who remain married, and (b) the need of divorced women was less pressing than that faced by women who continue to live with their husbands. Congress had the discretion to spend money to improve the general public welfare in one way and not in another, so long as it had some reasonable basis for its action. The challenged provision is not unconstitutional merely because its classifications are imperfect. In view of the purpose of the statute, and the generally different circumstances between married and divorced women, the statutory classification was constitutional. The divorced plaintiff in the present case may be denied the benefits of the challenged section of the Act. See Mathews v. DeCastro, 429 U.S. 181, 97 S.Ct. 431, 50 L.Ed.2d 389 (1976).

7. In addition to the establishment of an acceptable program, the principal obligations of states are to:

    (a) establish paternity of the child,

    (b) locate absent parents with technical assistance from the federal government, and

    (c) obtain and enforce court orders for support.

8. The services of the program are not limited to families eligible for AFDC benefits. They may be used to locate and collect alimony or separate maintenance even though there are no children involved.

9. The wages of federal government employees, including military personnel, are subject to garnishment in support and alimony cases. This was accomplished by a waiver of sovereign immunity, and is an important and effective means of enforcing such obligations.

10. States are not required to participate in the program, but because of financial incentives, all states do, in fact, participate.

11. The Secretary of HEW is authorized to pay to each state 75 percent of the amounts expended by a state in the operation of its

approved plan, which must meet all HEW standards. See 42 U.S.C.A. § 655.

Eligibility for AFDC must conform to federal criteria   **Case 63**

The Social Security Act defines a dependent child as a "needy child . . . who has been deprived of parental support or care by reason of the death, continued absence from the home, or physical or mental incapacity of a parent, and who is living with" a specified relative. A regulation of the Department of Health, Education and Welfare (HEW) for the Aid to Families with Dependent Children (AFDC) program provided that "only income and resources that are, in fact, available to an applicant or recipient for current use on a regular basis will be taken into consideration in determining need and the amount of payment." A state law provided that payments to a "needy child" under the AFDC program will be computed after consideration of the income of the child's "stepfather or an adult male person assuming the role of spouse to the mother although not legally married to her." Thus, state law conclusively presumed that the need of a child for public welfare was reduced by the amount of income available from the man living with the child's mother. The amount of money actually given to the mother to meet the needs of the mother's dependent child was not considered. Mothers and children receiving AFDC benefits challenged the state law, contending that it was contrary to the applicable HEW regulation. May a state determine the "resources" of a child under the AFDC program by considering the income of persons not legally obligated to support the child?

Answer. No. The applicable HEW regulation negates the idea that the "resources" of a needy child should include income of: (a) a stepfather, that is, a man married to the child's mother but who has not legally adopted the child and is not legally required to support the child under state law, or (b) a man living with the mother assuming the role of spouse although not married to her. The Social Security Act requires that a parent of the needy child be continually absent from the home. Thus, if a stepfather or man assuming the role of spouse is considered a "parent" under state law, AFDC aid would not be available. However, the legislative history shows that Congress intended the term "parent" to include only those persons with a legal duty to support the child. If there is proof that a nonparent contributed to the child's support, then such contribution may be considered in determining the child's need. Since the state statute conclusively presumed that certain persons contributed to the child's support without actually determining whether any support was given, it was invalid.

See *Lewis v. Martin*, 397 U.S. 552, 90 S.Ct. 1282, 25 L.Ed.2d 561 (1970).

NOTE—The student should consider the following principles to be derived from CASE 63, above: (a) a state may not make children ineligible for AFDC benefits where a federal statute or valid regulation provides otherwise, (b) a state may not assume that a person living in the house of an AFDC recipient will provide financial support to the child, and (c) the need of the child must be based upon income actually available to the child, and not on assumed support by a person who is not legally obligated to support the child.

Case 64   *Eligibility for welfare benefits may not discriminate against illegitimate children*

A state program for "Assistance to Families of the Working Poor" provided financial assistance to certain families. Benefits were limited to families "which consist of a household composed of two adults of the opposite sex ceremonially married to each other who have at least one minor child . . . of both, the natural child of one and adopted by the other, or a child adopted by both. . . ." The statute was challenged as violative of the Equal Protection Clause of the Fourteenth Amendment because it operated to deny benefits to illegitimate children while granting benefits to legitimate children. Does the eligibility requirement of the statute unlawfully discriminate against persons otherwise entitled to welfare?

Answer. *Yes. "Although the challenged classification turns upon the marital status of the parents, as well as upon the child-parent relationship, in practical effect it operates almost invariably to deny benefits to illegitimate children while granting benefits to those children who are legitimate." It is illogical and unjust to impose legal disabilities upon illegitimate children because they are not responsible for and have no control over their status. The challenged welfare program provides important health benefits to children. The denial of such benefits to illegitimate children may not be justified on the ground that it preserves and strengthens family life. Thus, the eligibility requirement of the statute violated the Equal Protection Clause because it discriminated against illegitimate children.*

See New Jersey Welfare Rights Organization v. Cahill, 411 U.S. 619, 93 S.Ct. 1700, 36 L.Ed.2d 543 (1974).

SEPARATION AGREEMENTS   1. Parties to a marriage may agree to live separately. This may be done *without* obtaining a divorce. It may also be done without any judicial action. Customarily the rights and obligations of the parties, following separation, are provided for in a separation agreement between them.

2. The basis of all separation agreements is the discontinuation of cohabitation by the parties.

   See Harper, p. 390.

3. A separation agreement is an agreement voluntarily entered into by the parties to a marriage which does, in most instances, include provisions for the following:

   (a) the support of one of the parties to the marriage, generally the wife,

   (b) the adjustment of the property rights of the parties, and

   (c) the custody and support of the children born of the marriage.

4. Separation agreements, like other contracts, vary as to form and content, particularly under the emphasis of differing state laws. The following are typical provisions contained in such an agreement:

   (a) separation of the parties,

   (b) division of property, real and personal,

   (c) amount of alimony,

   (d) amount of child support,

   (e) delineation of custody and visitation rights,

   (f) medical and dental expenses of any children,

   (g) educational expenses of any children,

   (h) dependency claims with respect to children for tax purposes,

   (i) insurance to guarantee payment contained in agreement, and

   (j) legal fees and expenses.

5. In England, the courts enforce the support provisions and separate habitation provisions of separation agreements. By contrast, in the United States the courts enforce *only* the support provisions of separation agreements, not the separate habitation provisions.

6. Enforcement of the separate habitation provisions contained in a separation agreement would be against public policy in the United States which favors the preservation of the marital relationship. See Day v. Chamberlain, 223 Mich. 278, 193 N.W. 824 (1923).

7. Separation agreements are valid in all jurisdictions if they do not tend to induce divorce or separation. See Clark, p. 521.

   CAVEAT—Generally, any separation agreement entered into by parties who are living together as husband and wife and continue to do so after the agreement will be held to be void. See Garlock v. Garlock, 279 N.Y. 337, 18 N.E.2d 521 (1939).

8. The law of the jurisdiction in which the separation agreement is executed governs the validity of the agreement.

   NOTE—If the parties indicate that the law of a different jurisdiction is to govern the validity of the agreement, there are differing opinions as to whether or not such provision should be honored. See Reighley v. Continental Illinois Nat. Bank, 390 Ill. 242, 61 N.E.2d 29 (1945); Gessler v. Gessler, 273 F.2d 302 (5th Cir.1959). See also Goodrich pp. 202–207.

9. Generally a separation agreement under which the wife relinquishes all claims for support or receives a payment in lieu of support will be held to be valid. However, there are several jurisdictions which have exceptions to such rule:

   (a) In some jurisdictions lump sum payments under the terms of separation agreement in lieu of support have been held invalid.

   (b) In other jurisdictions any setting of support payments in separation agreements has been held invalid.

   See Clark, p. 529.

10. Separation agreements may be attacked on the following grounds:

    (a) fraud, and

    (b) duress.

    NOTE—Lack of full disclosure of financial circumstances will constitute fraud and subject a separation agreement to attack. See Clark, pp. 523–532.

11. The consequences of the execution of an invalid separation agreement are as follows:

    (a) If an agreement is found to induce divorce, it will be unenforceable by either party. See CASE 65, below.

    (b) If an agreement is not found to induce divorce, enforceability is dependent upon who is asserting the invalidity and whether partial or total performance of the agreement has occurred by the other party.

    e.g. H and W, husband and wife, entered into a separation agreement under which W relinquished her right of support and H relinquished all claims to W's property. W died and H sues for a portion of W's estate as the surviving spouse. Should his claim be upheld and the agreement invalidated due to W's release of her right to support? Ans. No. W's release of her right to support was invalid. However, no purpose would be served by invalidating the agreement since H had the benefit of her release of support and W had fully performed her part of the agreement. See Laleman v. Crombez, 6 Ill.2d 194, 127 N.E.2d 489 (1955). See also Clark, pp. 533–535.

12. If a separation agreement is presented for approval to the court in a divorce action, the court, after reviewing its provisions, may:

(a) accept it for incorporation into the divorce decree,

(b) reject it, or

(c) accept it for incorporation into the divorce decree, but subject to modifications.

Separation agreement in contemplation of divorce   **Case 65**

W and H were married but living apart. W had valid grounds for a divorce and did not intend to live with H again. Thereupon, after consultation with counsel for each of the parties, W and H entered into a separation agreement which provided for the settlement of the rights of the parties effective upon the obtaining of a divorce by one of the parties. W obtained a divorce and now sues for arrearages under such agreement. H claims the agreement is against public policy and void since it was entered into in contemplation of, and for the purpose of promoting divorce. Is a separation agreement enforceable which is entered into without collusion on the part of the parties and while the parties are separated, but which becomes effective only upon a divorce?

    Answer. *Yes. A separation agreement which is entered into without collusion after the parties are living apart is not invalid solely because it is to become effective upon a divorce. Such agreements made in contemplation of divorce are based on the assumption that divorce will follow and do not promote divorce. Public policy does not discourage divorce where the relations between a husband and wife are such that the legitimate objects of marriage have been completely destroyed. In this case, H should not be permitted to avoid the agreement where there was no collusion in the divorce proceedings, the parties were living apart, and W did not contract to obtain a divorce in the future.*

    See Hill v. Hill, 23 Cal.2d 82, 142 P.2d 417 (1943).

Payments in lieu of support while cohabiting   **Case 66**

H and W are husband and wife who voluntarily enter into an agreement where H agrees to pay W a specific amount annually in lieu of support for "her personal use and maintenance" unless and until W should begin divorce or separation proceedings. W lives with H after signing such agreement. Now W seeks to change the amount payable to her under such agreement. Should such a reformation be granted?

Answer. No. An agreement by a husband to pay a wife an annual amount in lieu of support while the parties live together is void as against public policy and by state statute which supports the premise that a husband may not be relieved from supporting his wife. Furthermore, reformation of void provisions in a contract will not be entertained. Therefore, W's petition should be dismissed.

See Lacks v. Lacks, 12 N.Y.2d 268, 238 N.Y.S.2d 949, 189 N.E.2d 487 (1963).

Case 67   *Enforcement of separation agreement by contempt proceedings*

H and W, domiciled in state Y, entered into a separation agreement in which provision was made for the transfer of certain property to W, and for the settlement of other property rights, including the payment by H to W of 40% of his net income, exclusive of capital gains, losses or distributions. W then obtained a default divorce decree in state N which incorporated the separation agreement and ordered performance thereof. H later married W-2. After such marriage, he was advised that "net income" meant net income for tax purposes, and that he only had to pay 40% of the community interest of himself and W-2. H, therefore, reduced payments, and upon W-1's remarriage, terminated such payments altogether. H claimed that the payments were alimony and terminable by remarriage. The lower court found that H had a continuing obligation and entered a judgment for arrearages as well as future performance. W-1 now seeks to enforce such judgment through contempt proceedings. Can the provisions of a divorce decree with respect to monetary payments which are not alimony be enforced by contempt proceedings?

Answer. No. A decree of alimony is subject to modification and enforceable by contempt proceedings. By contrast, payments which are viewed as a continuing obligation, and as an integral part of an adjustment of property rights, are not enforceable by contempt proceedings. To do so would be a violation of the state law forbidding imprisonment for debt. In this case H's payments were an inseverable part of an integrated adjustment of all property rights between the parties. Therefore, H cannot be held in contempt.

See Bradley v. Superior Court, 48 Cal.2d 509, 310 P.2d 634 (1957).

Case 68   *Cohabitation does not abrogate a separation agreement*

H and W were a married couple who during the pendency of a separation suit entered into a property settlement agreement in state C. Under the agreement W received property valued at $30,000, which was more than half interest in their community property. The agreement also provided that the parties would not contest each other's will and any reconciliation would not affect the terms of the agreement. H and W lived together as husband and wife, during which time H paid board to W. After seven years H moved to a former home in State A, where he lived for four years until his death. H's will left W the sum of $5.00 since she had already received a property settlement under an agreement. W now sues for a widow's portion of H's estate, claiming that the reconciliation of the parties abrogated the agreement. Does a subsequent reconciliation and resumption of marital relations abrogate a property settlement agreement?

Answer. No. It is well settled in State C that separation agreements, including property settlements, between estranged spouses are valid and enforceable. A subsequent reconciliation of the parties with a resumption of marital relations operates to avoid the agreement for separation with all provisions remaining executory. Here, the agreement contained no provisions concerning the separation of the parties but merely the property rights of the parties. With the transfer of the agreed property, the contract was completely executed and no executory features existed. The evidence does not tend to establish any intention by the parties to abrogate the agreement. Therefore, W's suit should be dismissed.

See Simpson v. Weatherman, 216 Ark. 684, 227 S.W.2d 148 (1950).

Enforceability of restrictions in a separation agreement

Case 69

H and W were married for over 20 years when they separated and entered into an agreement in state Y under which H was to pay W $100.00 a week for support and maintenance. The agreement further provided that such payments were to cease, if W engaged in a retail business within city N similar to one operated by H. W's sister and brother-in-law opened a business in city N which was similar to that operated by H. W was employed as manager of said business. H thereupon ceased payments to W. W now sues for arrearages and enforcement of the support provisions of the agreement. Is a provision in a separation agreement suspending support payments to a spouse, if such spouse engages in a business similar to one operated by the other spouse legal?

Answer. No. The obligation of a husband to support a wife is based on the marital relationship itself. He must support her in conformity with his circumstances. Under the law of state Y neither spouse may relieve the husband of this obligation. However, they may, if separated, enter into an agreement for regular, periodic payments to the wife as a measure of support. In this case, the provision restricting W relieves H of his duty of support and is in violation of the state law. Such provision is therefore void, and W's suit should be upheld.

See Haas v. Haas, 298 N.Y. 69, 80 N.E.2d 337 (1948).

BACKGROUND OF COMMUNITY PROPERTY LAW

1. Community property law defines the interests of spouses in *property acquired during* marriage. Generally, both the husband and wife are deemed to have an undivided, equal, present, vested interest in each item of community property. See generally, Mucklestone, pp. A-1–A-3.

2. Eight states have community property laws. These are: Arizona, California, Idaho, Louisiana, Nevada, New Mexico, Texas and Washington.

   CAVEAT—All of the community property laws in the eight states above, are not identical in operation.

   (a) In Texas, Idaho and Louisiana income from separate property is considered community property.

   (b) By contrast, in Arizona, California, Nevada, New Mexico and Washington income from separate property is considered separate property.

3. Community property law was transmitted to the United States during the colonization of the New World by the Spanish, who had derived such law from Germanic tribes during the Middle Ages. See generally, Burby, pp. 236–37.

4. The American territories in the Southwest, originally Spanish colonies, enacted legislation continuing community property laws upon their admission to statehood. Other states, such as Washington and Idaho, likewise enacted community property laws, possibly as an attempt to attract women to the area at the time. See Mucklestone, p. A-1.

5. Other states adopted community property laws due to the favorable tax advantages afforded married persons. However, with the enactment of the Revenue Act of 1948 with its equalization of taxes for persons in non-community property states, such states repealed their community property laws. These states were: Hawaii, Michigan, Nebraska, Oklahoma and Oregon.

   NOTE—Pennsylvania also enacted a community property law, but it was found to be unconstitutional. See Willcox v. Penn. Mut. Life Ins. Co., 357 Pa. 581, 55 A.2d 521 (1947).

   See generally, Foote, pp. 757–762.

BASIC PRINCIPLES OF COMMUNITY PROPERTY LAW

1. The time of acquisition of property is a determining factor in the classification of an asset as community property or separate property.

   (a) Property acquired *before marriage* is separate property.

   (b) Property acquired *after* the dissolution of a *marriage* is separate property.

(c) Property acquired *during marriage* is community property, except as noted in number 2, below.

See Burby, p. 242.

2. In general, the following types of property, if acquired during marriage constitute community property:

   (a) earnings,

   (b) damages awarded in a personal injury suit,

   (c) damages awarded in an industrial accident suit, and

   (d) rents and profits of separate property.

   See Burby, pp. 243–44.

3. The source of property during marriage is also a determining factor in the classification of an asset as community property or separate property.

   (a) Property acquired through *gift* to one spouse is separate property.

   (b) Property acquired through descent and distribution is separate property.

   (c) Property acquired through devise or bequest is separate property.

4. The classification of community property may be changed to separate property and vice versa by agreement between a husband and wife. See Tomaier v. Tomaier, 23 Cal.2d 754, 146 P.2d 905 (1944).

5. Property may be classified as partially separate property and partially community property.

   e.g. Life insurance purchased by a party before marriage and the premiums for which after marriage are paid out of earnings constitutes partially separate property and partially community property. See Modern Woodsman of America v. Gray, 113 Cal.App. 729, 299 P. 754 (1931).

COMMUNITY PROPERTY- MANAGEMENT AND CONTROL

1. In general, the husband possesses the power of control and management over community property. The wife, however, may be designated as the husband's agent with respect to community property and upon such designation, the wife's acts with respect to community property will be binding upon the husband. See Mucklestone, p. A-3.

2. In all of the community property law states, there are limitations imposed upon a husband's power of control over community property. Such restrictions include the following:

(a) The property must be managed for the spouses' joint benefit.

(b) A husband's right of control over community property may be forfeited, if he abandons his wife.

(c) In the majority of community property law states, a husband cannot convey community real property without the consent of his wife.

(d) In some of the community property law states, a husband may not give away community personal property without the consent of his wife.

3. In recent years, traditional community property laws have been criticized as discriminatory against women. Because of this some states have modified their laws.

e.g. In Washington each spouse has power to manage or sell certain community property. However, joint action is required for purchase or sale of real property, furniture and household goods.

See generally, Burby pp. 250–254; Foote, pp. 757–759; Mucklestone, pp. A-3–A-4.

COMMUNITY PROPERTY AND DIVORCE

1. In all of the community property law states, the parties to a marriage may enter into an agreement *before marriage* to the effect that there shall be no community property.

2. In all eight community property law states divorce terminates the community relationship. See Mucklestone, pp. A-8–A-9.

3. There is a lack of unanimity, however, among the statutes of the eight community property law states regarding the manner in which community property is to be divided between husband and wife upon divorce.

(a) In some states the community property is to be divided equally.

(b) In other states the community property is to be divided in a manner the court finds just.

(c) In some states the guilt of a spouse in a divorce action may result in the reduction of his or her share of the community property.

See Burby, pp. 260–261.

4. Separation agreements between husband and wife are recognized and held to be valid in community property law states.

CAVEAT—Where the power of control over community property lies with the husband, the husband must make full disclosure of the nature and extent of the community property. If the husband does not do so, a separation agreement may be set aside on the basis of fraudulent concealment. See Burby, p. 262.

5. Upon the divorce of the parties, if the community property has not been divided through a separation agreement or court judgment, the parties become tenants in common with respect to all property formerly held in a community relationship. See Mucklestone, pp. A-8—A-9.

INTRODUCTORY NOTE—The subject matter of federal income, estate and gift taxation is outside the scope of this Review. However, in the resolution of the financial aspects of most divorces and separation agreements the federal tax considerations frequently play a more important role than do the laws traditionally regarded as being the law of "domestic relations". For this reason the following sections are designed to give a brief outline of key tax issues in a divorce.

TAX ASPECTS OF DIVORCE

1. There are four aspects of divorce negotiations which can have far-reaching tax implications for the parties involved:

   (a) alimony,

   (b) child support,

   (c) transfer of property, and

   (d) legal fees.

2. Alimony and separate maintenance payments are deductible by the payor and included in taxable income by the recipient if made under a written agreement and paid at periodic intervals. See §§ 71, 215. See also Mahana v. U. S., 88 F.Supp. 285 (Ct.Cl.1950), cert. denied 339 U.S. 978, 70 S.Ct. 1023, 94 L.Ed. 1383, rehearing denied 340 U.S. 847, 71 S.Ct. 14, 95 L.Ed. 620 (1950).

3. To qualify as alimony, payments must be made pursuant to written agreement. This may be either a written decree of divorce or separate maintenance or a formal agreement incident to divorce or separation. However, if the agreement is not part of a *court* action for divorce or separation, payments will not qualify as alimony unless the parties are living apart and have not filed a joint return for the taxable year. In addition, only payments made *after* execution of an agreement or a court decree will be includible as income and deductible as alimony.

4. Deductible alimony must qualify as a "periodic payment" as opposed to lump-sum property settlements. A periodic payment is one which may be:

   (a) remitted at irregular unspecified intervals,

   (b) for uncertain or indefinite amounts,

   (c) extend over an indefinite period, or

   (d) must be paid for more than 10 years.

   NOTE—Under the "ten year rule" of Section 71(C)(2) if the amount is payable over a period in excess of ten years it may nevertheless qualify as "alimony" and be deductible by the husband. These payments, however, are subject to the "10% rule." Under that rule only 10% of the principal amount may be deducted by the payor in any one year. This treatment precludes any prepayment by the payor.

   e.g. Under a court decree of divorce, taxpayer husband is ordered to pay taxpayer wife $100,000 payable in lieu of alimony as installments over 15 years. During the first four taxable years, taxpayer husband pays $10,000 each year to taxpayer wife and claims the deduction. Taxpayer wife includes the payments as income each year. In the fifth and sixth years taxpayer husband makes payments of $15,000 each year. Since these payments exceed 10 percent of the principal sum, only $10,000 of each $15,000 payment is deductible to the husband and includible by the wife as income.

5. Contingent payments will also qualify as periodic. Alimony or support payments which are subject to termination in the event of remarriage, death, or a change in the economic status of the parties are not considered the discharge of a fixed debt and therefore qualify. Such payments are not subject to the 10 percent limitation. See Reg. § 1.71-1(d)(3).

   e.g. H and W agreed to the following settlement in connection with their divorce: H was to pay $3,000 to W as a lump sum settlement, and permanent alimony of $100 a month for 121 months. The alimony payments were to cease upon remarriage of W. The agreement also said that the alimony payments were to be deductible by H for tax purposes. Two years later W remarried. She brought an action to compel continuance of the monthly payments, alleging that they were a property settlement. Although the court recognized that the words used were not controlling, it rejected W's contention. The court reasoned that the agreement providing for permanent alimony installments to W, and a tax deduction for H, contemplated permanent alimony to W and not a property settlement. Only the initial $3,000 payment was a property settlement. Thus, H was not obligated to continue monthly payments to W after her remarriage. See Bisno v. Bisno, 239 Ga. 388, 236 S.E.2d 755 (1977).

6. Contingent payments will be considered "periodic" even though

   (a) they are payable for less than 10 years,

   (b) the total amount is specifically stated or may be calculated, or

   (c) the contingencies are set forth in the decree or imposed by local law.

   NOTE—Payment of a fixed sum in one or more installments within 10 years or less *does not* qualify as deductible alimony. There is, however, one exception. If in lieu of alimony a fixed amount is paid by installments extended more than 10 years from the date the obligation arose, these installments will be treated as alimony to the extent that the payments received in one year do not exceed 10 percent of the principal sum. If the amount received does exceed 10 percent of the principal sum, only that part of the payment equal to 10 percent of the fixed sum will qualify. The excess is neither includable as income or deductible as alimony.

7. Payments which meet the qualification of alimony need not be specifically designated as such. Dental or medical payments, insurance or other expenses if based upon the marital obligation of support and drafted to meet the standards of "periodic" may all be deductible expenses for the husband and includable as income to the recipient wife.

   NOTE 1—A lump sum payment is more in the nature of a property settlement, and therefore, it is neither deductible by the payor nor income to the recipient.

   NOTE 2—A property settlement is considered separable from alimony provisions and merely covering both in one agreement or decree is not sufficient to lump them together for tax purposes. Also, initial payments of legal expense or other specified expenses may be ruled non-recurring lump sum payments and as such, non-deductible.

8. The Tax Reform Act of 1976 changed alimony payments from an itemized deduction to a deduction taken from gross income. Because of this change a taxpayer may use the standard deduction, instead of itemizing deductions, and still deduct alimony.

9. The following are situations in which amounts paid by one spouse to the other will be deductible if they are "periodic" or subject to the "ten year rule":

    (a)   payments made pursuant to the terms of a decree of divorce,

    (b)   payments made pursuant to the terms of a separation agreement, and

    (c)   payments made pursuant to the terms of a decree for support.

10. Payments for child support are neither deductible by the husband nor includable by the wife in her gross income by virtue of the operation of Section 215(a).

e.g.   A divorce decree provided that H would pay $12,000 annually to W for the support, care, and maintenance of W and their two children. The agreement provided that when each child became 21 or married, the amount would be reduced by $3,500, and that the agreement was binding on the estate of H to the extent of $7,000 for the benefit of the two children. H deducted the full $12,000 from his income tax return as alimony. The Internal Revenue Service contended that $7,000 was for child support and not deductible. The court held that where the agreement either specifies or fixes a sum certain to be paid for the care, support, and maintenance of the children, the sum cannot be considered alimony. The reasonable interpretation of the agreement was that $5,000 was intended for W and $7,000 as support for the children. Therefore, H may not deduct the $7,000 which was support for his children. H may deduct only the excess paid to W as alimony. See Commissioner of Internal Revenue v. Gotthelf, 407 F.2d 491, cert. denied 396 U.S. 828, 90 S.Ct. 78, 24 L.Ed.2d 79 (1969).

11. Although child support payments are not themselves deductible, the individual providing more than 50% of the support of a child is entitled to claim that child as a dependent for purposes of an exemption on his federal income tax return.

12. Upon the division of jointly owned property between the spouses, which division accomplishes merely a partition of such property, any transfer of such property from one spouse to the other spouse, generally does not incur any income tax or gift tax consequences to either spouse. See Clark, p. 486.

CAVEAT—The mutual release of marital rights is not sufficient consideration for the transfer of property for gift tax purposes. The gift tax may be avoided by taking the gift tax marital deduction and the annual exclusion. It may also be avoided if the property settlement is: (a) part of the divorce decree issued by a court which has power to modify the settlement, or (b) part of a written agreement relating to marital and property rights and the parties are divorced within two years.

13. By contrast to the rule in number 12, when one spouse transfers property which has appreciated in value in full settlement of the

other's inchoate marital rights therein, under a decree of divorce, a taxable event occurs and the transferring spouse realizes a gain on the transfer.   The gain is equal to the difference between the transferring spouse's basis and the fair market value of the appreciated property at the time of the transfer.

14. Payments of legal fees by either party in a divorce action are *not deductible except:*

    (a) to the extent that they are for services that constitute the rendering of tax advice, or

    (b) to the extent that they are for services rendered to the wife in connection with the collection of alimony, which is taxable income to her.

    CAVEAT—Although the wife may not deduct the legal fees expended by her in obtaining the divorce, as a practical matter, in many cases, the husband pays the wife an amount as "additional alimony" which is deductible by him, and taxable to the wife, and the wife, in turn, pays for her own attorney's fees, which are *not* deductible to her.   This approach usually results from the disparity in the tax brackets between the parties, the husband typically being in a significantly higher tax bracket than the wife on the separate tax returns which are filed by each following the divorce.

    See *e.g.,*   Levine, "Successful Divorce Negotiations Require Careful Attention to the Tax Implications", *Taxation for Lawyers,* Jan.–Feb. 1974, pp. 232–238.

ADOPTION

Summary Outline

INTRODUCTION

1. Adoption is the legal procedure by which the status of parent and child is conferred upon persons who are not naturally so related.

2. The development of the law of adoption may be traced to antiquity:

    (a) Adoption was known in Ancient Greece and Rome where it was employed to ensure succession of property and title. It was this particular aspect of adoption that was stressed in modern civil law.

    (b) In furtherance of this concept, the French 1804 Civil Code provided for adoption, but only with respect to the adoption of persons who had reached their majority by persons who had attained fifty years of age and who had no legitimate lineal heirs.

    (c) It was not until this century that French adoption statutes provided for the inclusion of a minor through adoption into a normal family situation.

3. Although adoption legislation in the United States was late in development and enactment, all fifty states at present have passed statutes authorizing and governing adoption.

    (a) By contrast to European adoption law, the focus of such statutes has been directed toward the welfare of the adopted rather than toward the adoptive parent and his line of succession.

    (b) Such legislation has developed a procedure by which children whose natural parents cannot or will not properly care and provide for them are placed with persons who can suitably attend to them and their needs.

4. Adoption was not recognized at common law. Thus, there is no common law background for adoption. As a result, the adoption procedures in the United States are governed by statutes specifying the conditions, manner, means and consequences of adoption, as well as the rights and responsibilities of all parties involved.

5. Despite the judicial procedures and legal implications involved in adoption, social considerations are assuming an increasingly important role in the adoption process:

    (a) social welfare agencies charged with administration have developed agency policy considerations, and

    (b) social welfare agencies have developed agency procedures to be followed by all parties.

    See In the Matter of the Adoption of Reinius, 55 Wash.2d 117, 346 P.2d 672 (1959).

1. There are two basic types of adoption placement procedures, both of which are governed by statute:

    (a) the agency placement, and

    (b) the independent placement.

    See generally, Clark, pp. 638–652.

2. The *agency* placement is characterized by the following procedures:

    (a) Arrangements for the adoption of a child are made by a licensed public or private agency charged with the responsibility of placing children.

    (b) Generally, a thorough, detailed investigation is made with respect to the suitability of the adoptive parents and the background of the child involved.

    (c) In most cases the adoptive parents pay a fee to such agency. Such fee may depend upon the financial resources of such parents.

3. The *independent* placement, also known as the private placement, is characterized by the following procedures:

    (a) Arrangements for the adoption of a child are made by an individual, either the natural parent or an interested intermediary party who may represent the prospective adoptive parents or the natural parent.

    (b) Generally, a thorough investigation, *unless required by statute*, is not made of either the natural parents or the adoptive parents.

    (c) Usually the adoptive parents pay the medical expenses and fees of the natural mother as well as any legal expenses and fees.

4. In addition to the agency placement and the legal private placement, there is a "black market" in babies which affords childless couples a chance to obtain a child. See generally, Katz, pp. 1134–1153.

5. The term "black market" encompasses a wide variety of methods by which a child is procured from its natural mother and subsequently adopted by the adopting parents. These methods, which are illegal, generally arise from the extensive delays, complicated procedures of the agencies and courts, and the relatively small number of adoptable children vis-a-vis the number of individuals desiring to adopt a child.

6. The black market provides:

TYPES OF ADOPTION PLACEMENT PROCEDURES

(a) speed in the adoption procedure since there is no investigation, and

(b) secrecy to the natural mother.

7. Not infrequently the illegality of the "black market" adoption arises from the amount of payment which is made by the adopting parent to the natural mother. Although the natural mother may be reimbursed for the expenses of delivery and confinement, both prior to and subsequent to the delivery of the child, the mother may not receive a payment for the infant itself, since it is illegal to sell children.

8. The chief criterion with respect to the "black market" in babies is the ability of the adoptive parents to pay the price demanded by the black market operator.

9. There are distinct, definite advantages and disadvantages of both the private and the agency placement, which are illustrated in the CHART III below:

10. Statutes and agency rules concerning the suitability of adoption are relaxing in some jurisdictions while in others they are not.

    e.g. If a person is willing to adopt a hard-to-place child, rules are often waived whereas strict requirements must be met if a person desires to adopt an easily placed child.

11. The chief consideration in adoption is the welfare of the child. Therefore, some elements in determining who are suitable adoptive parents include:

    (a) religion,

    (b) race,

    (c) economic status,

    (d) home environment,

    (e) age,

    (f) health,

    (g) physical and character defects of adoptive parents, and

    (h) emotional factors.

    See generally, Foote, pp. 294–302.

    NOTE—These criteria, or some of them, are implemented in agency placements or in private placements where under state law the adoptive parents must be investigated.

SUBSIDIZED ADOPTION

1. States and the federal government have recognized the benefits of adoption as opposed to institutional care, but have often found it

---

CHART III. COMPARISON OF PRIVATE AND AGENCY PLACEMENTS

ADVANTAGES

Private Placement	Agency Placement
(a) permits adoption of a child by persons who might otherwise be subjected to a lengthy waiting period or who would not find a child available through the normal agency channels due to stringent requirements or nonavailability of children.	(a) provides a minimization of the risk of a non-healthy child; of discovery of the identity of the adoptive parents by the natural mother; of a change of mind by the natural mother regarding the adoption.
(b) provides a certain degree of privacy and anonymity for the natural mother.	(b) provides a rigorous investigation of the background of the natural parents as well as that of the adoptive parents to ensure suitability.
(c) permits the payment of medical expenses by the adoptive parents in the situation where the natural mother does not have adequate financial resources of her own to pay such expenses.	(c) provides, in most cases, a minimization of fees and costs with respect to the adoption.

DISADVANTAGES

Private Placement	Agency Placement
(a) risks the natural mother not actually completing the adoption procedure.	(a) involves lengthy and rigorous requirements established by the agencies with respect to the suitability of the adoptive parents.
(b) risks the discovery by the natural mother of identity of the adoptive parents and an attempt by her to claim the child.	(b) results in a limited number of children available for adoption.
(c) risks the adoption of a non-healthy child.	
(d) risks the non-suitability of the adoptive parents.	
(e) risks that such a procedure, if not strictly controlled, might lead to a "black market".	
See generally, Katz, 1146–1153.	

difficult to place children for adoption who have special needs. That includes children with physical, mental or emotional handicaps and children of various minority groups.

2. In recognition of those unfortunate circumstances a program of *subsidized adoption* has been developed in some states.

3. Under a subsidized adoption program the adoptive parents receive monthly reimbursement from a social agency according to a prior agreement.

4. The subsidy is designed to meet the special needs of the child. It may allow for specific medical or other costs.

5. The subsidy may continue for an indefinite period or be for a limited time only.

See generally, Krause, pp. 668–669.

PRIVACY OF ADOPTION RECORDS

1. The accepted rule is that adoption records are sealed to the child and the natural and adopting parents.

NOTE—There has been some litigation in this area, and there will undoubtedly be more litigation in the future. Suits will be brought by the adopted child who desires to know his "roots", and by natural parents who want to see their child.

2. Factors which courts must consider in such litigation include the interests of:

(a) the child,

(b) the natural parents,

(c) the adopting parents, and

(d) the adoption system of the state.

3. Courts have shown more willingness to order the release of adoption records in recent decisions than in the past. However, it is still difficult to establish the required "good cause" necessary to obtain such records.

e.g. One court stated that the right of an adopted child to inherit from natural parents and other blood relatives may constitute a compelling reason to unseal adoption records. However, most states do not provide for inheritance in such situations. See Massey v. Parker, 369 So.2d 1310 (La.1979).

CONSENT IN ADOPTION

1. Practically all adoption statutes require the consent of parents or guardian of the child to be adopted. Many of such statutes con-

tain detailed requirements regarding the form and procedure of such consent. If such formalities are so outlined, they must be strictly observed or the adoptive parents may find the adoption susceptible to attack later by the natural mother. See CASES 70 and 71, below. See also Foote, pp. 254–255.

2. Consents signed before or soon after the birth of the child have been particularly susceptible to attack by the natural mother. Despite sketchy evidence, findings of involuntary consent have been handed down in such cases due to the natural mother's physical and mental condition during such time. See Adoption of McKinzie, 275 S.W.2d 365 (Mo.App.1955).

3. If a child is legitimate, the consent of both parents is required for an adoption unless one parent has forfeited such right of consent. See Termination of Natural Parent-Child Rights and Duties, number 4, below.

4. Where a child is illegitimate, the natural father has certain rights. Recent United States Supreme Court decisions indicate that a state may impose only reasonable requirements for him to obtain rights comparable to those of the mother under the Equal Protection Clause of the Fourteenth Amendment. See CASES 73 and 74, below.

5. If a child has been legally placed with an agency, or has had a guardian legally appointed, the consent of the natural parents is not required. However, in many jurisdictions if a child has been placed with an agency, the consent of the agency is required. See CASE 75, below.

6. Revocation of consent by a natural parent to an adoption has been permitted in various jurisdictions under different circumstances:

   (a) the parent's surrender of the child and written consent constitute an irrevocable act and in the absence of fraud or duress cannot be altered,

   (b) after relinquishing the child the parent can revoke consent at any time *prior* to a final decree of adoption,

   (c) the parent can revoke consent within the discretion of the court whose chief consideration is the welfare of the child.

   See Annual Survey of American Law 1971–72, pp. 600f. See also In re: Adoption of Krueger, 104 Ariz. 26, 448 P.2d 82 (1969).

7. The majority of jurisdictions follow the approach stated in number 6(c), above. In some instances, the resulting decision provokes much criticism. See People ex rel. Scarpetta v. Spence—Chapin Adoption Service, 36 A.D.2d 524, 317 N.Y.S.2d 928, aff'd 28 N.Y.2d 185, 321 N.Y.S.2d 65, 269 N.E.2d 787, cert. denied, 404 U.S. 805, 92 S.Ct. 54, 30 L.Ed.2d 38 (1971).

   See generally, Foote, pp. 236–247; 252–255.

Case 70 *Adoption—formalities of consent must be strictly observed*

W gave birth to an illegitimate daughter, X. While W was in the hospital, an employee, A, approached her and said that A and her husband would like to adopt the child. A persuaded W to relinquish custody of X. W consented in writing and it was witnessed by one person. When A's lawyer saw that the consent was only witnessed by one person, he had another consent signed and witnessed. Neither consent contained the signatures of two witnesses as required by state law, but each document was witnessed by a different person. W delivered X to A. Thereafter, A and her husband petitioned for adoption of X, and W sought to regain custody of X. At a hearing the trial court concluded: (a) W's consent was valid, (b) A and her husband were fit adoptive parents, (c) W had no prospects of making a complete home for X, and (d) the best interests of X will be served by permitting her to remain with A and her husband. W appealed, contending that her consent was invalid, and in the absence of evidence that she was unfit, should be granted custody of her daughter. Should the appeal succeed?

Answer. Yes. The state statute provided strict safeguards for preventing children from being taken from their parents. The purpose of the statute is to prevent an ill-advised and impulsive decision by a parent at a time of physical and emotional distress, such as the present case where a child is born to an unwed mother. Pressure was brought on W by her physician, the welfare department, a hospital official, A, and her lawyer to agree to adoption. The statute requires a written consent, executed and acknowledged before two competent witnesses. W executed two consents, but separately they are ineffective because only one person witnessed each consent. Thus, there was a failure to comply with the statute. Further, a mother is presumed to be a suitable person to raise her child with a right superior to other persons. It is in the best interests of the child to be raised by the mother unless she is wholly unequal to such responsibility. The evidence showed that W is intelligent, has a good job, and apart from this single dereliction, is of good moral character. In a matter as intimate as the relationship between parent and child there must be strict adherence to the letter of the law. Since that was not done, the decision of the lower court was reversed, and W was awarded permanent custody of X.

See In re Alsdurf, 270 Minn. 236, 133 N.W.2d 479 (1965).

NOTE—CASE 70, above, involved independent or private placement adoption. That should be distinguished from agency placement in which a social agency assists the mother, obtains the consent, and attempts to locate suitable adoptive parents. See CHART III, above.

Revocation of consent by natural mother permitted   Case 71

Before the birth of C, M, the unmarried mother of C, had consulted a doctor for medical care. The doctor knowing of a couple that wanted to adopt a child, persuaded M that the best interests of her unborn child would be best served by placing such child, C, for adoption with the couple he knew. The doctor also told M that she would not be admitted to a hospital unless she signed a consent form to the adoption in blank. M signed such consent. Upon the birth of C, C was taken from M and placed in the home of the adoptive parents and adoption proceedings were begun. When served with notice of the hearing with respect to the adoption of C, M objected on the ground that her consent was invalid due to the manner in which it was obtained and that she had not abandoned C for six months as required for adoption without consent under the laws of that jurisdiction. Should M's objection be upheld?

Answer. Yes. Where the mother of an illegitimate child due to persuasion exerted upon her executes a consent to the adoption of such child in blank and her child is placed with persons for a period of over six months, an adoption decree will be reversed when the evidence indicates that the mother never had any intention of abandonment of the child. Here, M did not abandon C since she never had possession of C and since M attempted to revoke her consent when served with notice of the adoption. Thus, C should be surrendered to M by the adoptive parents.

See *Ashton Adoption Case,* 374 Pa. 185, 97 A.2d 368 (1953).

Consent cannot be revoked merely due to change of mind   Case 72

M and F are the parents of C, who was conceived before M and F's marriage. After the birth of C, M and F instituted and arranged with the Department of Welfare proceedings to place C for adoption due to their finances, social position and family considerations. At a hearing held before a referee M and F reaffirmed their wish to place C for adoption and were informed by the referee of the consequences of such an action. A final order of relinquishment was entered and C was placed for adoption. M and F then later upon the urging of M's mother instituted proceedings to revoke their consent. The trial court denied their petition. M and F now appeal urging revocation of their consent on the ground that they did not receive proper counseling. Are the surrender and consent proceedings void?

Answer. No. Where parents are aware of the consequence of a consent to adoption and give their consent freely, such consent cannot be revoked merely because they changed their minds. Once fully cognizant of the consequences of their actions, no attempt need be made to argue with the natural parents concerning their reasons for relinquishment. Thus, in this case the surrender and consent proceedings are valid.

See Smith v. Welfare Dept. of City & County of Denver, 144 Colo. 103, 355 P.2d 317 (1960).

Case 73 *Adoption—rights of unwed father may be limited*

The mother of an illegitimate child married a man who was not the child's father. The stepfather petitioned to adopt the child, and the natural father objected. State law required the consent of the mother for the adoption of an illegitimate child, thus giving her veto power by withholding her consent. To acquire the same veto power over an adoption as the mother, the father must legitimate his offspring, either by marrying the mother and acknowledging the child as his own, or by obtaining a court order declaring the child to be legitimate and capable of inheriting from the father. By contrast, where the child was born in wedlock both parents had the right to veto an adoption. The natural father did not attempt to legitimate the child until the adoption petition was filed. In opposing the adoption the natural father contended that the state statute prohibiting him from vetoing the adoption violated the Due Process and Equal Protection Clauses of the Fourteenth Amendment. Is that contention valid?

Answer. No. The Court held that the "best interests of the child" standard used by the lower court in granting the adoption petition did not violate any substantive rights of the natural father under the Due Process Clause. The natural father never sought custody of the child, and the adoption would recognize an existing family unit. In this case the court was not required to find anything more than that the adoption, and the denial of the legitimation petition, was in the "best interests of the child." The Equal Protection Clause is not violated merely because unwed fathers are not given the same veto power that married, divorced or separated fathers are granted. The two classes of fathers may be distinguished because married fathers have had significant responsibility at some time for the daily supervision, education, protection or care of their children. A different standard may be used for unwed fathers, since they have not borne such responsibility for rearing the child during the marriage. Thus, the state statute is constitutional and adoption may be granted.

See Quilloin v. Walcott, 434 U.S. 246, 98 S.Ct. 549, 54 L.Ed.2d 511 (1978).

Case 74 *Adoption—constitutional rights of unwed parents*

A and B lived together for several years without being married, and they had two children. A, the mother, left B and took the children with her. Subsequently, A married her present husband and they petitioned for adoption of the children. *B, who had lived with and supported his children for several years, filed a cross petition for adoption. State law permitted an unwed mother, but not an unwed father, to prevent the adoption of her children by refusing to consent. The unwed father could prevent adoption by the mother only by showing that such adoption would not be in the best interests of the children. The state court permitted A to adopt the children based upon state law. B, the father, appealed, contending that the state law violated the Equal Protection Clause of the Fourteenth Amendment because the statute bore no substantial relation to any state interest. Was the law constitutional?*

Answer. No. The law treated unwed parents differently according to their sex. Maternal and paternal roles are not always different in importance so that the mother should always be preferred over the father. Further, the gender-based distinction was not related to the achievement of any governmental objectives. Thus, the state statute violated the Equal Protection Clause of the Fourteenth Amendment. The state court decision which permitted A to adopt the children was based on the unconstitutional statute. Therefore, that decision was reversed.

See *Caban v. Mohammed*, 441 U.S. 380, 99 S.Ct. 1760, 60 L.Ed.2d 297 (1979).

NOTE—CASE 73 and CASE 74 may be distinguished. In the former case the father could acquire the same rights as the mother by merely acknowledging the child as his own. Since this procedure furthered a legitimate state interest and did not unreasonably interfere with any constitutional rights of the father, the statute was constitutional. In the latter case the father could not acquire the same rights as the mother under any circumstances. The statute violated the Equal Protection Clause because it discriminated on the basis of sex.

Consent may not be revoked after surrender of a child to a charitable agency

Case 75

M, mother of C, placed C with D, a charitable agency, for adoption. D placed C for adoption with adoptive parents. M then notified D that she wished to withdraw her consent to the adoption of C and demanded custody of C. May a mother after placing a child with a proper agency for adoption revoke consent?

Answer. No. Where a parent has surrendered a child to a charitable agency and given her written consent to the adoption of said child, such agency may place the child for adoption. The parent's consent can only be revoked if obtained through fraud, duress or misrepresentation. Furthermore, the burden of proof rests on the parent to show that the best interests of the child would be served by such revocation. Here, no fraud, duress or misrepresentation occurred. Thus, M's consent cannot be revoked.

See *Catholic Charities of Diocese of Galveston v. Harper, 161 Tex. 21, 337 S.W.2d 111 (1960).*

TERMINATION OF NATURAL PARENT-CHILD RIGHTS AND DUTIES

1. Adoption involves a two-step process:

   (a) *termination* of the rights and responsibilities of a child and his natural parents to each other, and

   (b) *creation* of the rights and responsibilities of parent and child between a child and his adoptive parents.

2. The termination of the rights and responsibilities between parent and child can be voluntary or involuntary.

3. *Voluntary* termination of natural parent-child rights and duties occurs when the natural parents consent to the adoption of the child in accordance with the controlling statutory requirements. Such consent, once given with full knowledge of the implications and without duress, cannot be revoked and is valid at the time such consent is granted.

   e.g. M, the natural mother of C, signed a consent to the adoption of C in the presence of two witnesses and complied with all requirements of the adoption statute of the jurisdiction with respect to giving C up for adoption. The names of the adoptive parents, however, were omitted from the consent form at the time M signed such form, and M was unaware of their identity. M cannot claim that the adoptive parents obtained custody of C without her consent since all statutory requirements were met. A consent for adoption is valid even though the names of the adoptive parents are not set forth when the natural parent signs the form. See McKinney v. Weeks, 130 So.2d 310 (Fla.App.1961).

4. *Involuntary* termination of natural parent-child rights and duties occurs when the natural parents of a child are judged unable or unfit to care for their child. If such a ruling is rendered, consent of the natural parents to the adoption of the child is not necessary.

   (a) When M, mother of C, was declared mentally ill and committed to a state institution a guardian was appointed for C. M was given no reasonable expectation of recovery from her illness and C's natural father had died. Consequently, under the provisions of a law of that jurisdiction allowing a guardian of a child whose mother has been mentally ill for at least three years to consent to the adoption of the child, C can be placed for adoption by the court-appointed guardian without the consent of M. See People ex rel. Nabstedt v. Barger, 3 Ill.2d 511,

121 N.E.2d 781 (1954). See also State v. Blum, 1 Or.App. 409, 463 P.2d 367 (1969).

(b) W and H were married, but W had a child, X, who was not the child of H. Paternity was never established. W was diagnosed as having multiple sclerosis when X was born. Because W was unable to care for X, he was placed in a foster home. The foster parents petitioned for adoption, but W refused to consent even though she was a paraplegic at that time. The court noted that a parent has no property right in a child, and the right of custody is not absolute. Where it is shown by "clear and convincing" evidence that parental consent to adoption of a child is being withheld contrary to the "best interest of the child" parental rights may be terminated. Since W depended on others for most of her physical needs, could not care for X, and had never known X in a parent-child relationship, the petition for adoption was granted. See Matter of Adoption of J. S. R., 374 A.2d 860 (D.C.App.1977).

(c) M gave birth to an illegitimate child. M agreed to foster care for the child, but refused to consent to adoption or assume custody of the child herself. The child's father, a foreign national student had left the country and could not be located. The welfare agency petitioned the court to terminate M's rights so that the child, who was then 1½ years old, could be placed for adoption. During the next two years hearings were held regarding the future of the child, and to give M time to formulate plans with respect to the future of the child. At a final hearing M said that she wanted custody of the child, but since M had made no plans for the child's care, the court terminated M's rights. On appeal the court said that although a natural parent has the right to have custody of the child if such custody is desired, in the absence of a parental decision to take custody, a court may terminate that right if it will be in the best interests of the child. Since M had neglected the child for four years, and failed to show that she could give the child adequate care at the time of the final court hearing, the trial court did not abuse its discretion by terminating M's right to custody. See In re Lem, 164 A.2d 345 (D.C.Mun.Ct.App.1960).

5. A divorce granting *custody* of a child to one parent does not terminate the other natural parent's rights and responsibilities with respect to such child. Normally both parents must consent to any adoption of the child.

e.g. M married H-2 her second husband, who petitioned to adopt M's two children by H-1, her first husband. H-1, the children's father, objected, but the adoption nevertheless was granted. On appeal, the decree was overturned since in the case of divorce one parent is granted custody of the child or children of the marriage based on the welfare of the child or children involved. However, custody based on such standard does not terminate the necessity of consent by the parent not having custody of the children to the subsequent adoption of the children. Without consenting there must be some conduct on the part of the nonconsenting parent which demonstrates an intent to abandon the child or children or forfeit the natural rights of parenthood. In this case circumstances were not of such a nature and the constitutional rights of the father involved could not be ignored. See In the Matter of Adoption of Smith, 229 Or. 277, 366 P.2d 875 (1961).

6. Due process requires that notice and an opportunity to be heard be given to the natural father in custody cases before termination of his rights.

e.g. A state law permitted adoption of a child by a stepfather without the consent of the natural father if the natural father had failed to contribute to the child's support to the extent of his ability for two years. On facts similar to those above, number 5, the statute was held unconstitutional as violative of the Due Process Clause of the Fourteenth Amendment. See Armstrong v. Manzo, 380 U.S. 545, 85 S.Ct. 1187, 14 L.Ed.2d 62 (1965).

NOTE—The notice requirement stated in number 6, above, applies to unwed fathers. See State ex rel. Lewis v. Lutheran Social Services of Wisconsin, 59 Wis.2d 1, 207 N.W.2d 826 (1973).

7. In most jurisdictions, the fact that the natural parents have not reached the age of majority is not a cause for revocation of consent.

JURISDICTIONAL ASPECTS OF ADOPTION

1. A valid adoption may be created either:

   (a) in the state where the child to be adopted has his or her domicile,

   (b) in the state where the adoptive parents are domiciled when the child is before the court, or

   (c) in a state where the adoptive parents and either the adoptive child or the person having legal custody of such child are subject to its personal jurisdiction.

   See Goodrich, p. 287. See also Restatement, Conflict of Laws, Second, § 142.

   CAVEAT—Most cases, in which jurisdictional issues are raised, are concerned with the requirements of the local statute and the application thereof.

2. Jurisdictional issues, if any, of an adoption proceeding are generally raised:

(a) at the time of the inception of the adoption proceedings to determine whether the court has jurisdiction to grant the adoption, or

(b) at a time after the entry of the decree of adoption to determine whether the adoption decree should be given recognition.

e.g. M and F, Connecticut residents, gave custody of their child, C, to P and her husband, now deceased, since they were unable to provide adequately for C. M also gave P and her late husband C's birth certificate and a letter granting permission to P and her husband to take C out of Connecticut. P then moved to New Jersey and later petitioned the court there for the adoption of C. M and F opposed such adoption and raised the jurisdictional question of whether a New Jersey court was the proper forum for the adoption proceeding. It was held that a New Jersey court could entertain such adoption proceeding since P, who had legal custody of the child, C, was domiciled there. Thus, personal jurisdiction over P was sufficient, even though the domicile of C is that of her natural father who resides in Connecticut. See A v. M, 74 N.J.Super. 104, 180 A.2d 541 (1962). See also number 1(c), above.

Full faith and credit given to sister state adoption statute　　　　Case 76

H and W, husband and wife are domiciled in Michigan. Child, C, is abandoned on their doorstep. H and W, in compliance with the laws of Michigan, adopt C, through a proceeding in which all three appeared in court. H, W and C then moved to Connecticut where they established a new domicile and C grew to adulthood. H and W die intestate in Connecticut and C claims to be their heir under a Connecticut statute permitting an adopted child to inherit from his or her adoptive parents as though a natural born child. S, a sister of H, claims to be their heir, asserting that the adoption proceedings in Michigan were invalid, and thus C may not claim as an heir. Does S have a well-founded claim?

Answer. No. Since C was validly adopted under the laws of Michigan, the law of domicile at the time of the adoption will be given full faith and credit in Connecticut. C, an adopted child under Michigan law, is recognized as an adopted child under Connecticut law and can inherit from his or her adoptive parents under the laws of Connecticut as though a natural child. In so doing C will prevail over S, who would take by intestacy if H and W had no children at the time of their death.

See Woodward's Appeal, 81 Conn. 152, 70 Atl. 453 (1908). See also Goodrich, pp. 287, 289, 291.

ABROGATION OF ADOPTION DECREES

1. Courts do not look with favor on suits to abrogate adoption decrees since permanency and finality are viewed as a necessity to such decrees.

   e.g. H and W adopted a child, but concealed the fact that they were having marital difficulties from the adoption agency. At the time of the adoption W believed that a reconciliation had been effected. Subsequently, H and W were divorced, and the adoption agency sought to set aside the adoption because of fraud. The court said that the failure to disclose marital difficulties to the placing agency was not such fraud as to permit a revocation of the decree of adoption. The petition of the agency was denied. See In re Adoption of O, 88 N.J.Super. 30, 210 A.2d 440 (1965).

2. If circumstances warrant such action, however, an adoption decree may be set aside on the following grounds:

   (a) fraud,

   (b) lack of notice to an interested party, such as a natural parent, or

   (c) welfare of the child.

   See Clark, pp. 668–71.

3. In most cases to abrogate an adoption, the natural parent is the party attacking the adoption decree in order to regain custody of the child. See Clark, p. 668.

4. However, *adoptive parents* in some instances do attempt to abrogate the adoption decree. In jurisdictions which do not have statutes regulating such an action, courts are reluctant to set aside a judgment of adoption.

   e.g. A court will not set aside an adoption decree simply because the adopted child was mentally retarded. It must be shown that abrogation of the adoption would be in the best interest of the child. See In re Adoption of G, 89 N.J.Super. 276, 214 A.2d 549 (1965); Allen v. Allen, 214 Or. 664, 330 P.2d 151 (1958).

5. A small number of jurisdictions have statutes authorizing abrogation of adoption decrees, upon the petition of the adoptive parents, if certain conditions are found. Among such conditions are:

   (a) willful desertion by the child,

   (b) racial differences, and

   (c) epilepsy, feeble-mindedness or insanity developed by child.

   NOTE—Some jurisdictions impose a five years statute of limitations with respect to the abrogation of an adoption.

   See generally, Clark, pp. 666–69.

1. The adoption of adults is governed by statute and the judicial construction of such statute. The provisions of such statutes vary from jurisdiction to jurisdiction:

   (a) some statutes expressly limit adoption to minors,

   (b) some statutes expressly provide for adoption of adults,

   (c) some statutes merely provide for the adoption of "children:"

      (i) certain courts have found such terminology to mean "minors";

      (ii) other courts, by contrast, have found it to mean a relationship, thereby including adults.

   NOTE—Forty-four states have some type of law permitting adoption of adults.

2. In jurisdictions where adult adoption is permitted, a husband may adopt his wife in order to permit inheritance through him.

   e.g. In a state where adult adoptions were allowed by statute a court held that a fifty-six year old man could adopt his forty-five year old wife so that she could inherit under a testamentary trust established by his mother. The principal of such trust upon his death was to be distributed to his "heirs at law". Under the statutes of that jurisdiction an adopted child is regarded as an heir unless specifically disinherited. See Bedinger v. Graybill Ex'r., 302 S.W.2d 594 (Ky.1957).

   NOTE—Such adoption was held not to have constituted an incestuous relationship.

3. The purpose of adult adoption, in most instances, is to provide an inheritance device. See Clark, pp. 652–53.

   NOTE—Some states have passed "designation of heir" statutes rather than adult adoption statutes to achieve a similar result without the need for an adoption.

4. When an adult is adopted, there is no duty to support the adoptee as there is when a child is adopted.

5. The procedures for adopting an adult are not as complicated as those for adoption of a minor.

   (a) The adopting adult is not investigated.

   (b) There is usually no need for a court determination that the adoption is in the best interest of the adoptee.

   (c) Only the consent of the adult to be adopted is usually required.

   See generally, Areen, pp. 1179–1181.

ADOPTION OF ADULTS

Case 77 *An unmarried adult may adopt an unmarried adult*

W, an unmarried 56 year old W.A.C. sergeant, petitioned the court, in a jurisdiction which by statute permits the adoption of any person, whether a minor or an adult, to adopt C, an unmarried 35 year old W.A.C. captain, who consented to such adoption. The purpose of the adoption was allegedly for reasons of inheritance and maternal feeling. The trial court without a hearing dismissed the petition on the grounds that the consequences of an adoption by an unmarried adult would be to make the adopted person "illegitimate". W appeals. Was the dismissal by the trial court correct?

Answer. No. The law provides for the adoption of any person regardless of the age of the adoptee. The effect of the law, if the adoptee is an adult, is the same whether or not the "adoptor" is married and the adoptee is treated as an heir. Furthermore, in adult adoptions for purposes of inheritance, there is no change in the social or domestic relationship of the parties. Thus, the adoption of an adult by an unmarried adult would not cause the adoptee to be illegitimate. Here, the trial court erred by not hearing evidence with respect to the appropriateness of the adoption.

See Ex parte Libertini, 244 Md. 542, 224 A.2d 443 (1966).

INHERITANCE RIGHTS OF ADOPTED CHILDREN

1. The statutes governing adoption in the various jurisdictions do not follow a uniform scheme with respect to:

   (a) *whether an adopted child may inherit from his natural parents*, and

   (b) the *order in which persons inherit from the adopted child.*

2. The modern trend is to treat the adopted child solely as a member of the adoptive family and to terminate all rights of inheritance between such child and his natural family, except where the child is adopted by the spouse of one of the natural parents.

   e.g. C is the child of H-1 and W, who are divorced. W marries H-2 who adopts C. C's inheritance rights from W are not cut off, while such rights from H-1 are cut off. See Uniform Probate Code 2–109.

   CAVEAT—Adoption statutes can dictate the inheritance rights of a child and his parents, both natural and adoptive. However, they cannot dictate to whom a person may leave property. Under the example given in number 2, above, despite the fact that C does not have inheritance rights to H-1's property, H-1 may, nevertheless, make C an heir under a will.

3. The following principles relate to inheritance by an adopted child.

(a)   An adopted child may inherit *from* adoptive parents through intestate succession.

(b)   An adopted child may inherit *through* adoptive parents in most states.

e.g.   M was a beneficiary of a testamentary trust which provided that in the event of her death, income would be paid to M's "lawful issue or descendents." M adopted X, and that fact was known to the testator. After M died the question arose whether X was entitled to trust income. The court said that the words "issue" and "descendant" when used in a will include adopted children when the testator knows of such adoption, unless the testator clearly indicates an intention that the adopted children be excluded. Thus, X is entitled to the trust income. See Matter of Upjohn, 304 N.Y. 366, 107 N.E.2d 492 (1952).

4. The treatment of inheritance rights *from* the adopted child varies from jurisdiction to jurisdiction and include the following:

(a)   only natural relatives inherit,

(b)   only adoptive relatives inherit,

(c)   both natural and adoptive relatives share equally, or

(d)   adoptive relatives take property which came from the adoptive family with natural relatives taking the remainder.

NOTE—The majority of states provide for the adoptive parents and relatives to inherit from the adopted child, rather than the natural parents and family.

See generally, Clark, p. 661; *Smith's Review, Wills and Trusts*, Chapter I, "The Effect of Adoption and Designated Heirship on the Right to Inherit."

IX ILLEGITIMACY

Summary Outline

A. Common Law Background of Illegitimacy
1. child had no rights
2. parents had no duty to support

B. Modern Approach to Illegitimacy
1. harsh common law rights abandoned
2. child has right to support and to inherit
3. Equal Protection Clause protection
4. state statutes provide for legitimization

C. Artificial Insemination and Illegitimacy
1. common law did not provide for artificial insemination
2. child legitimate by statute if donor not married to woman

D. Inheritance Rights of Illegitimates
1. traditional rule
2. recent Supreme Court decisions

COMMON LAW BACKGROUND OF ILLEGITIMACY

1. Illegitimacy is the state of being born out of wedlock or unlawfully begotten.

2. *At common law* a child was considered illegitimate:

   (a) if his parents never married, or

   (b) if his parents married *after* his birth.

   NOTE—Conversely, a child was considered legitimate, even if conception took place before the marriage, as long as the marriage took place *before* its birth.   See Clark, p. 156.

3. *At common law* a child of a married woman was presumed to be legitimate.   However, this presumption could be rebutted if it was proved that the husband of such a married woman was impotent or "beyond the four seas".

4. *At common law* a child of an annulled marriage, whether void or voidable, was considered illegitimate since the annulment decree was retroactive to the date of the marriage.

5. *At common law* an illegitimate child was considered a child of no one and had no right to inherit from or through his parents.

6. *At common law* the parents of an illegitimate child had no duty to support him.

   (a) This particular characteristic of illegitimacy was altered in 1576 by the English Poor Law which provided for a quasi-criminal procedure against the natural father of an illegitimate child for the support of such a child.

   (b) The Poor Law was designed to relieve the general public of the support of such children and was quasi-criminal in nature because the failure to support is an offense against society as well as a wrong to the child.

   NOTE 1—The quasi-criminal aspect of the procedure under the English Poor Law can be found today in some jurisdictions of the United States even at the present time.   See generally Clark, p. 155.

   NOTE 2—Problems relating to custody, support and adoption of illegitimate children are considered elsewhere in this Review. See Chapter VII, *Determination of Child Custody* and *Federal Legislation and Child Support*, and Chapter VIII, *Adoption*, above.

MODERN APPROACH TO ILLEGITIMACY

1. Most of the harsher aspects of common law treatment of illegitimate children, such as limitations on rights to support and to inherit have been changed.   The Equal Protection Clause of the Fourteenth Amendment has been the vehicle utilized in most of such modifying decisions.

e.g. The law in Texas provided for a judicially enforceable right of support for a legitimate child from a natural father. No such right was afforded to an illegitimate child. C, an illegitimate child, through her guardian sued her natural father for support, claiming that the Texas statute was discriminatory and violated the Equal Protection Clause of the Fourteenth Amendment. Should C's claim be upheld? Ans. Yes. Once a state recognizes a judicially enforceable right of children to needed support from their natural fathers, there is no constitutionally sufficient justification for denying such right to a child merely because her natural father has not married her mother. For a state to do so is illogical and unjust. The law violated the equal protection guarantees of the Fourteenth Amendment. C is entitled to support from her natural father. See Gomez v. Perez, 409 U.S. 535, 93 S.Ct. 872, 35 L.Ed.2d 56 (1973). See also Chapter X, *Illegitimacy*, below.

2. An illegitimate child may not maintain an action against his parents for damages for being born illegitimate.

    e.g. P was born illegitimate and brought suit against D, his father. P alleged that D seduced P's mother by promising to marry her, but D could not keep his promise because he was already married. P sought damages for deprivation of the right to be born a legitimate child, to have a legal father, to inherit from P's paternal ancestors, and for being stigmatized as a bastard. The court acknowledged that D had committed a willful tort and that P had suffered an injury. The court reasoned that to recognize P's claim would create a new tort: a cause of action for wrongful life. The legal and social implications of such a tort would be enormous. It is more appropriate for the legislature to study and declare its policy on suits than for the courts. P's suit was dismissed. See Zepeda v. Zepeda, 41 Ill.App.2d 240, 190 N.E.2d 849 (1963).

3. Modern statutes provide for legitimization of children born out of wedlock. Legitimization then is the legal procedure by which such children may be declared to be legitimate.

4. All fifty states have passed some type of statute providing for the legitimization of children born out of wedlock. These statutes are quite divergent and can be classified roughly as follows:

    (a) statutes which recognize all children as the legitimate children of their natural parents,

    (b) statutes which recognize the subsequent marriage of an illegitimate child's natural parents as a method of legitimization,

    (c) statutes which recognize the subsequent marriage of an illegitimate child's natural parents along with some form of acknowledgment of paternity by the natural father as a method of legitimization,

(d) statutes which recognize a child born out of wedlock as being legitimate if such child is acknowledged by his natural father and taken into such father's family, and

(f) statutes which recognize a child born out of wedlock as being legitimate if such child is declared legitimate in a prescribed court proceeding.

See generally, Paulsen, p. 669.

5. Acknowledgment is the admission by a natural father that an illegitimate child is his child. Acknowledgment can take many forms and its validity is dependent upon statutory requirements.

e.g. Where acknowledgment must be in writing, any written document containing an admission of paternity will generally suffice. It is not necessary that such document was written for the purpose of providing acknowledgment of the child involved. Where acknowledgment is not required to be written, oral admission of paternity to friends and acquaintances is sufficient to meet statutory requirements. See Clark, p. 160.

6. The law of the domicile of the parent of an illegitimate child determines whether or not an act of such parent has legitimized such child.

e.g. F, domiciled in state R, is the father of an illegitimate child, C, whose domicile is with C's mother in state M. By the law of state R, the natural father's domicile, an acknowledgment in writing by a natural father that an illegitimate child is his offspring will make the child the legitimate child of the father. Such is not true under the law of state M, the child's domicile. F writes a letter in state R in which he addresses C as Dear Son C and sends such letter to C in state M. F dies intestate and C claims to be an heir of F under a statute which permits only legitimate children to inherit from their fathers. May C inherit as an heir of H? *Ans.* Yes. The act of F acknowledging C to be his child took place in state R, the domicile of F the parent. If such act complies with the requirements for the legitimization of a child in the state of the domicile of the parent, the status of the child is thereby changed from one of being illegitimate to that of being legitimate, regardless of where the child is domiciled.

See Goodrich, pp. 281–284.

See generally, Chapter X, *Illegitimacy*, below.

ARTIFICIAL INSEMINATION AND ILLEGITIMACY

1. Artificial insemination is the impregnating of a woman with semen of a donor through means other than sexual intercourse. The donor can be the woman's husband or a third party.

(a) If the donor is the *husband* such artificial insemination is referred to as "AIH" (artificial insemination by husband).

(b) If the donor is a *third party*, which usually is the case, such artificial insemination is referred to as "AID" (artificial insemination by donor).

(c) If the sperm of the husband is mixed with that of a third party, such artificial insemination is referred to as "CAI" (confused artificial insemination). This method is used principally for psychological reasons.

2. Artificial insemination was not contemplated under the common law. As a result it raises many questions concerning legitimacy of the resulting children.

3. Children conceived through AIH obviously have natural fathers who are married to their natural mothers and, therefore, are not illegitimate.

4. Case law concerning the status of children conceived through AID and the conduct of their mothers is scanty and conflicting as well. Compare CASES 78 and 79, below.

5. Many jurisdictions have enacted legislation providing for a conclusive presumption that a child conceived as a result of artificial insemination by a third party donor with the consent of husband and wife is legitimate. See Ga.Code § 74–101.1 (1973); Okla.Stat.Ann. tit. 10, § 551–3 (1973); Kan.Stat.Ann. ch. 23–128 (1973). See also Uniform Parentage Act § 5.

See generally, Foote, pp. 534–539; Krause, pp. 722–728; Wadlington, pp. 682–691.

Resulting child of artificial insemination is illegitimate   **Case 78**

H filed for an annulment of his marriage to W. W counterclaimed for an annulment. Testimony and medical evidence sustained W's allegation that the marriage had never been consummated. Evidence further showed that due to infirmities of H, the parties had decided and agreed in writing to have W artificially inseminated. As a result of such insemination, a child, C, was born to W. H now claims that C is not issue of the marriage and that H, therefore, has no duty of support with respect to C. Is C who was conceived by a married woman through the means of artificial insemination, with the consent of her husband, legitimate?

Answer. No. Unless it can be construed from a statute concerning children born out of wedlock that there is an intention to modify the well settled concept that a child who is begotten through a father who is not the mother's husband is illegitimate, it must be presumed that offspring conceived by AID are illegitimate. The statute involved in this case classifies children born out of lawful matrimony as illegitimate. Such language must be interpreted to refer to any child *whose natural father was not married to its mother regardless of the marital status of the mother.* However, although C is considered illegitimate, H must support C whether on the basis of implied contract or equitable estoppel, since his conduct and consent to the artificial insemination implied a promise to support any offspring born from such insemination.

See *Gursky v. Gursky,* 39 Misc.2d 1083, 242 N.Y.S.2d 406 (1963). Compare CASE 79, below.

NOTE 1—The Gursky case appears to be the only published decision which specifically concludes that AID children are illegitimate. The case has been criticized because of its reliance on principles developed before the use of artificial insemination. See Foote, p. 537.

NOTE 2—A later New York case characterized the Gursky case as unpersuasive when the issue arose in a slightly different context. H-1 and W were married. They consented to artificial insemination by a donor and a child, C, was born with H-1 listed as the father. Subsequently, H-1 and W were divorced. W remarried, and her second husband, H-2, petitioned to adopt C. H-1 refused to consent. H-2 contended that H-1's consent was not necessary because H-1 was not the father of C. The court noted state policy, reflected by laws providing that a child born of a void marriage, even if the marriage is knowingly bigamous, incestuous or adulterous, is legitimate and entitled to all the rights of a child born during a valid marriage. The court concluded that it would be absurd to hold illegitimate a child born during a valid marriage, of parents desiring but unable to conceive a child, and both consenting to the impregnation of the mother by a carefully and medically selected anonymous donor. Therefore, the petition for adoption was dismissed. See In re Adoption of Anonymous, 74 Misc.2d 99, 345 N.Y.S.2d 430 (1973).

Case 79   ***Resulting child of artificial insemination is legitimate***

H and W were married fifteen years. W was artificially inseminated because H was sterile. H consented to the procedure. A child, C, was born to W, and H was named as C's father on the birth certificate. W and H separated four years later with W having custody of C. H filed for divorce. W consented to the divorce which did not provide for child support, but did provide that the court retain jurisdiction over the support obligations of H. Upon W later becoming ill and no longer being able to work, she received public assistance. H refused to pay support for C demanded by the district attorney. The municipal court thereupon found H guilty of failure to support a minor under the Penal Code. H appeals claiming that he is not the lawful father of C and therefore should not have to support C. Is H responsible for C's support as C's lawful father?

Answer. *Yes. The intent of the provision of the Penal Code is to provide support to a minor child, no matter how conceived, and to require such support from the child's lawful parent. One who agrees to artificial insemination becomes the lawful parent of the resulting child and is obligated to support such child. The interpretation placed upon the word "father" is not a distortion of the statutory language and achieves the purpose of such statute. Thus, although C does not have a "natural" father, C has a "lawful" father, H, who is obligated to support C.*

See People v. Sorensen, 68 Cal.2d 280, 66 Cal.Rptr. 7, 437 P.2d 495 (1968).

1. At common law an illegitimate child was deemed a child of no one, and had no right to inherit. No one other than his or her own issue had the right to inherit from an illegitimate person.

INHERITANCE RIGHTS OF ILLEGITIMATES

2. The rule which developed in the United States was that an illegitimate child was the child of the mother and could inherit from her and from her relatives, and they from him.

3. The general rule prior to CASE 82, below, was that an illegitimate child was not treated as a child of the father unless legitimated or acknowledged by the father.

4. The trend is toward liberalizing the rights of illegitimate children to inherit from their natural fathers. A recent United States Supreme Court decision held that a statute which discriminated against illegitimate children in intestate inheritance violated the Equal Protection Clause of the Fourteenth Amendment. See CASE 82, but compare CASE 81, below.

5. Recent United States Supreme Court cases, by reason of the Equal Protection Clause of the Fourteenth Amendment, have raised serious questions as to the ability of the states to enact classifications which discriminate on the basis of illegitimacy. Such classifications were held *not* to be justified on the basis:

(a) that they promoted legitimate family relationships,

(b) that difficulties in proving paternity justify total disinheritance of illegitimates, or

(c) that the father could have provided for the child by will.

See CASES 80, 81, and 82, below.

6. The issue of parents whose marriage is void, nevertheless are legitimate.

e.g.   If H marries W-1, by whom he has children, A and B, and then contracts a bigamous marriage with W-2 by whom he has children, C and D, the children of both marriages are legitimate even though H's marriage to W-2 is void.   See Uniform Probate Code 2-109.

7. When a man has children by a woman and afterward marries her, such issue will be legitimated either:

(a) by the subsequent marriage alone, or

(b) by the subsequent marriage and acknowledgment of the father.

NOTE—A legitimated child is treated the same for inheritance purposes as any other child of the parent.

Case 80   *Discrimination against illegitimate children as denial of equal protection*

A state statute provides a right of recovery for wrongful death of a deceased parent in favor of the surviving children of the deceased. The deceased, D, left five surviving illegitimate children.   The supreme court of that state held that a surviving "child" under the statute did not include an illegitimate child.   On appeal to the United States Supreme Court the children contend the statute denies them equal protection under the Fourteenth Amendment of the United States Constitution.   Is their contention correct?

Answer.   *Yes.   Illegitimate children are "persons" within the meaning of the Equal Protection Clause of the Fourteenth Amendment and as such the state court's interpretation of the statute is an invidious classification denying without reason rights which other citizens enjoy.   "Legitimacy or illegitimacy of birth has no relation to the nature of the wrong allegedly inflicted on the mother."   The children of D, though illegitimate, were dependent on her since D cared for them and nurtured them.   By her death they suffered a wrong in the sense that any dependent would.   Since the state statute was interpreted to deny illegitimates the opportunity to recover for the wrongful death of a parent the same as legitimate children, it violated the Equal Protection Clause.   The children may recover.*

See Levy v. Louisiana, 391 U.S. 68, 88 S.Ct. 1509, 20 L.Ed.2d 436 (1968).

Case 81   *Discrimination against illegitimate children in state's intestate scheme—sustained*

Intestate was survived only by collateral relatives and X, an illegitimate daughter, who had been acknowledged but not legitimated by the intestate. The jurisdiction has a statute which provides, "Illegitimate children though duly acknowledged cannot claim the rights of legitimate children"; and one which reads: "Natural children are called to the inheritance of their natural father, who has duly acknowledged them . . . to the exclusion only of the state." The father could have left the child property by will. The child claims that the intestate succession laws which bar an illegitimate child from sharing equally with legitimate children constitute a violation of the Equal Protection and Due Process Clauses of the United States Constitution. Is the illegitimate child entitled to inherit equally with legitimate children under the applicable state law?

*   **Answer.** *No. The statutory scheme is valid. It is within the state's power to establish rules for the protection and strengthening of family life and for the disposition of property. The rule in question is reasonable in achieving such result within the requirement of equal protection. The case is to be distinguished from the situation in CASE 80, above, where the state creates a statutory tort and provides for the survival of a decedent's cause of action so that a large class of persons injured by the tort could recover damages in compensation for their injury and excludes from the class potential plaintiffs. In this case the father could have left property by will to the illegitimate child. The state, therefore, has not prevented the child from inheriting. Rules of intestate succession attempt to reflect the intent of a decedent, and such schemes as the state allows which do not constitute an insurmountable barrier are constitutional.*

    See Labine v. Vincent, 401 U.S. 532, 91 S.Ct. 1017, 28 L.Ed.2d 288 (1971).

---

*Statute discriminating against acknowledged child in intestate   **Case 82**
inheritance held unconstitutional*

D died intestate survived by his parents and an illegitimate daughter, X. D had been under a court order to support X. The state statute relative to inheritance provides that an illegitimate child is the heir of his mother. Only if the parents marry, and the father acknowledges the child, is an illegitimate child treated as legitimate and able to inherit under the statute of descent and distribution. X claims the state statute is unconstitutional in that it discriminates between legitimate and illegitimate children. Does the statute violate the Equal Protection Clause?

*   **Answer.** *Yes. X should receive the property. The statute violates the Equal Protection Clause of the Fourteenth Amendment. Imposing sanctions on children does not bear a rational relationship to promoting a legitimate family relationship. Since D was ordered to support X, paternity had already been established, and for this*

class of child there was little danger of spurious claims to upset the orderly settlement of estates.

See Trimble v. Gordon, 430 U.S. 762, 97 S.Ct. 1459, 52 L.Ed.2d 31 (1977).

NOTE—The court attempted to distinguish the Trimble case from Labine v. Vincent, CASE 81, above, by distinguishing the legislative plans in the two states. However, the Court aknowledged that it subjected the statute involved in the Trimble case to more careful scrutiny than the statute in the Labine case. There is serious doubt about the continued vitality of the Labine case, as Trimble may be read as impliedly overruling it or at least limiting Labine to its facts.

TRENDS IN FAMILY LAW

Summary Outline

A. Introduction

B. Divorce
   1. changes in attitudes towards divorce
   2. enactment of no fault divorce laws

C. Property Settlement and Alimony

D. Child Custody and Support

E. Adoption

F. Illegitimacy

G. Marriage, Divorce, and Cohabitation

H. Trends in Rights of Women

I. Proposed Equal Rights Amendment

J. Rights of Juveniles in Criminal Law

INTRODUCTION **1.** Beginning in the late 1960s and continuing through the 1970s there have been revolutionary changes in Family Law, both statutory and judicial. This was the period when the gap between social mores and the law narrowed.

  2. The changes in the legislative and judicial philosophy toward all aspects of Family Law resulted, in substantial part, from recognition of equality of the sexes.

  3. Those changes have affected the following aspects of Family Law:

   (a) divorce,

   (b) property settlements,

   (c) alimony,

   (d) child custody,

   (e) child support,

   (f) adoption,

   (g) rights of illegitimate children and their unwed parents,

   (h) rights of unmarried persons who cohabit, and

   (i) the right to marry.

  NOTE—Most of the trends in these areas have been analyzed in previous chapters. They are collected in this Chapter so that the student may quickly identify trends and specific aspects of Family Law which have changed recently.

  4. This Chapter also considers:

   (a) the rights of women,

   (b) the proposed Equal Rights Amendment, and

   (c) criminal responsibility and constitutional rights of juveniles.

DIVORCE **1.** The recent years have witnessed a change in society's attitudes toward the permanency of marriage. Divorce has become more acceptable and in some areas and groups, even a way of life.

  2. A reflection of the growing acceptance of divorce and the rejection of any stigma attached thereto can be seen in the revision of the divorce statutes in most states. All states but two have enacted some form of no fault divorce statute.

   (a) In some states, incompatibility has been added as an additional ground for divorce.

   (b) In some states, living apart for a certain length of time, such as two years, will be sufficient to allow a divorce without "fault" being placed on either party.

(c) In other states, the "irretrievable breakdown" of the marriage has become the sole ground for dissolution of a marriage and no fault is placed on either party.

3. In many respects a divorce granted on the ground of the "irretrievable breakdown" of the marriage can be classified as a "no fault" divorce.

(a) Neither spouse can be accused of any wrongdoing in the petition for divorce.

(b) The relative culpability of either spouse is not considered in the awarding of alimony.

(c) In many of the states granting a divorce on this ground, the defenses of condonation, connivance, collusion, recrimination and insanity have been eliminated.

CAVEAT—Although a proceeding for divorce on the ground of the "irretrievable breakdown" of the marriage is "nonadversary" in nature, a divorce will not be granted merely on demand or submission of affidavits. A hearing must be held to determine if such a breakdown has, in fact, occurred. The same principle applies where the ground for divorce is the irreconcilable differences of the parties. See McKim v. McKim, 6 Cal.3d 673, 100 Cal.Rptr. 140, 493 P.2d 868 (1972).

1. Where property acquired during the marriage is divided at the time of divorce, the contribution of each spouse is considered. The services of a full time housewife were recognized as a substantial contribution and often the property is divided equally regardless of which spouse earned the money to buy it.

2. Marital property which some courts have found to be divisible is increasing.

e.g. One court held that the "good will" of a physician's practice was an asset upon divorce which was subject to division. See In re Marriage of Lukens, 16 Wash.App. 481, 558 P.2d 279 (1976).

3. The philosophy of no fault divorce has been applied to alimony. The present trend is to base alimony on the need and abilities of each spouse, not on the degree of fault of one spouse.

4. Rehabilitative alimony has been awarded in some recent cases. This assists one spouse in finding meaningful employment suited to her or his abilities.

PROPERTY SETTLEMENT AND ALIMONY

5. Husbands may now be awarded alimony in appropriate circumstances.   State laws permitting an award of alimony only to women violate the Equal Protection Clause of the Fourteenth Amendment.   See CASE 54, above.

6. Traditionally, the duty to pay alimony continued until remarriage of the wife.   Today many courts will consider cohabitation without marriage as evidence of the lack of need for alimony.   Courts reason that the person paying alimony should not be forced to support an exspouse who is being supported by a lover.

CHILD CUSTODY AND SUPPORT

1. The new legislative attitudes toward divorce and judicial interpretations of the Equal Protection and Due Process Clauses of the Fourteenth Amendment have brought about changes in traditional policies with respect to child custody and support.

2. Child custody is becoming more common for fathers.   In addition, joint custody or split custody is being ordered more frequently by courts than historically.   The reason is a recognition that the father should be treated equally with the mother in considering custody.

3. Fathers of illegitimate children are being accorded rights more equal to those of the mother, at least where the father has shown responsibility through care and support of the child.   See CASE 74, above and CASE 83, below.

4. The Uniform Child Custody Jurisdiction Act has been adopted by some states.   The purpose is to avoid conflicting decisions in different states regarding the custody of children.

5. The usual standards for child support are need and ability to pay.

6. Traditionally, the father was held primarily responsible for child support.   The trend of recent decisions and statutes is to divide child support equitably between the two parents.

7. Absent unusual circumstances the support obligation continues until the child reaches the age of majority.   However, a state may not establish different ages of majority for males and females under the Equal Protection Clause of the Fourteenth Amendment.

8. The federal government has attempted to correct some child support problems by amending the Social Security Act to provide a means to:

    (a) enforce child support obligations owed by parents,

    (b) locate absent parents,

    (c) establish paternity, and

    (d) obtain child support.

1. The number of children available for adoption in recent years has **ADOPTION** decreased drastically for some of the following reasons:

   (a) Many couples today who live together and have children out of wedlock do not give up such children for adoption.

   (b) The stigma of bearing and raising a child born out of wedlock has lessened considerably.

   (c) Abortion is more widely accepted and utilized.

   (d) Birth control information and devices are readily available.

2. Due to the scarcity of available white infants for adoption two trends can be discerned regarding adoption:

   (a) religion is an important factor in the choice of adoptive parents; and

   (b) race is no longer an important factor in the choice of adoptive parents.

3. Recent cases have upheld the constitutionality of religious considerations in adoption, thereby requiring religion matching of parents and child as well as preventing adoption by atheists. See Matter of Adoption of "E", 59 N.J. 36, 279 A.2d 785 (1971); Dickens v. Ernesto, 30 N.Y.2d 61, 330 N.Y.S.2d 346, 281 N.E.2d 153 (1972); Wilder v. Sugarman, 385 F.Supp. 1013 (S.D.N.Y.1974).

4. Adoption of hard to place children, such as those with handicaps, has been encouraged by giving financial assistance to the adoptive parents based on the special needs of the child. This is called subsidized adoption.

5. Traditionally, adoption records have been sealed to the child, the natural parents, and to the adopting parents. Litigation in this area is beginning, and courts appear more willing now than in the past to divulge such information if a special need for it can be shown.

6. Unwed fathers are entitled to certain rights concerning adoption of their children. State statutes which limit their rights may violate the Equal Protection Clause of the Fourteenth Amendment. See CASES 73 and 74, above.

7. The Due Process Clause of the Fourteenth Amendment requires that unwed fathers be given adequate notice and an opportunity to be heard before their children are placed for adoption. See CASE 83, below.

Custody rights of an unwed father **Case 83**

M and F never married, but lived together for 18 years during which time three children were born to them. M died while the three children were still minors. The children became wards of the state and were placed in the homes of court-approved guardians. No hearing was held regarding the suitability of F as a guardian. The law of the jurisdiction requires such a hearing in the case of married or divorced parents or unwed mothers. F, the unwed father, filed suit claiming that a hearing should have been held concerning his suit- ablity, and asserting that failure to require such a hearing was a denial of F's rights under the Equal Protection Clause of the Fourteenth Amendment. The state court upheld the statute and found that F's rights had not been denied. F appeals. Was the failure to hold a suitability hearing for F a denial of F's rights?

Answer. Yes. *The statute presumed that an unwed father was an unfit parent without notice and a hearing. Administrative inconvenience cannot justify the denial of a hearing when important interests of a parent and child are involved. The failure to hold a hearing with respect to F's suitability as a guardian for his own children regardless of his marriage status, when such a hearing would have been available to M, was a violation of the Equal Protection Clause and the Due Process Clause of the Fourteenth Amendment. The state statute was held invalid.*

See *Stanley v. Illinois, 405 U.S. 645, 92 S.Ct. 1208, 31 L.Ed.2d 551 (1973).*

ILLEGITIMACY
1. Historically the law governing illegitimate children has been based on the premise that fathers of illegitimate children are irresponsible and are unconcerned about the welfare of such children. Under such laws unwed fathers had no rights with respect to their children in the areas of custody, adoption or visitation. See Chapter IX, *Illegitimacy*, above.

2. With the discernible shift in attitudes towards marriage among some groups and the conscious decision of some couples to live together outside the marriage relationship, such a premise is not well-founded.

3. Courts are now recognizing the fallacy of traditional notions and are beginning to uphold the rights of the concerned, unwed father with respect to his children.

4. A statutory classification of children based upon whether they are legitimate or illegitimate may be unconstitutional, depending on the circumstances.

   (a) State classifications may violate the Equal Protection Clause of the Fourteenth Amendment.

   (b) Classifications by the federal government may violate the Due Process Clause of the Fifth Amendment which encompasses the principles of the Equal Protection Clause.

CAVEAT—The classification of individuals according to whether or not they are legitimate is not a suspect classification subjecting it to strict scrutiny by a court. In determining whether the classification is valid under the Equal Protection Clause or the Due Process Clause the statutory classification must bear a rational relationship to a legitimate state or federal government purpose. See *Smith's Review, Constitutional Law,* Chapter XVII, "Equal Protection Clause—Application to Persons."

5. In a series of cases the United States Supreme Court has found that various statutes which discriminate against illegitimate children violate the Equal Protection Clause.

   (a) A state may not exclude illegitimate children from sharing equally with other children in the recovery of workmen's compensation benefits for the death of their parent. See CASE 84, below.

   (b) A state may not create a right of action in favor of children for the wrongful death of a parent and exclude illegitimate children from the benefit of such a right. See CASE 80, above.

   (c) Once a state grants a judicially enforceable right on behalf of children to needed support from their natural father, there is no constitutionally sufficient jurisdiction for denying such an essential right to illegitimate children. See Gomez v. Perez, Chapter IX, *Modern Approach to Illegitimacy,* above.

   (d) State welfare legislation may discriminate against illegitimate children by limiting benefits to households of married adults and their children. See CASE 64, above.

   (e) A state intestate inheritance scheme which deprives acknowledged illegitimate children of inheritance rights granted to legitimate children may constitute unconstitutional discrimination against them. See CASE 82, above.

6. Federal laws which discriminate against illegitimate children have been held violative of the Due Process Clause of the Fifth Amendment.

   (a) Illegitimate children born after the onset of their parent's disability were divided into two classes for purposes of determining eligibility for disability insurance benefits under the Social Security Act. Those which had been acknowledged or legitimized could receive benefits without showing that they were dependent upon their disabled parent. Other illegitimate children were conclusively denied benefits even though they were dependents. The plaintiffs were illegitimate children born after the disability and were dependent on their disabled father for support. The Court held that to deny them benefits which were available to illegitimatized children without a showing of need denied the former class equal protection of the law guaranteed by the Due Process Clause of the Fifth Amendment. See Jimenez v. Weinberger, 417 U.S. 628, 94 S.Ct. 2496, 41 L.Ed.2d 363 (1974).

(b) Survivors' benefits, as opposed to disability benefits in the Jimenez case, under the Social Security Act were challenged as unlawfully discriminating against illegitimate children. Acknowledged or legitimized children qualified, but other illegitimate children had to prove actual dependence on the deceased to receive benefits. The Court found that the purpose of the statute was to replace support which was lost by the dependents at the time of death. Thus, the requirement of showing actual dependency was reasonable, and the statute was upheld. The Jimenez case was distinguished because all illegitimate children born after the disability were excluded without the opportunity to establish dependence. In this case, since all illegitimate children could receive benefits if they could prove dependence, there was no unconstitutional discrimination. See Mathews v. Lucas, 427 U.S. 495, 96 S.Ct. 2755, 49 L.Ed.2d 651 (1976).

See generally, A. R. Fine and J. J. Dickson, "Constitutional Protection of Illegitimates," 1977 Annual Survey of American Law, pp. 239–261.

Case 84 *Rights of an illegitimate child protected by the Equal Protection Clause of the Fourteenth Amendment*

Decedent, F, a resident of state M, died as a result of injuries incurred during the course of his employment. F left four legitimate children, A, B, C and D, and one unacknowledged illegitimate child, X, as well as Y, a posthumously born illegitimate child. Under the provisions of the appropriate state workmen's compensation statute legitimate children and acknowledged illegitimate children recovered on an equal basis. Unacknowledged illegitimate children could only recover if there were not enough surviving dependents in the preceding classifications to exhaust the maximum allowable benefits. The four legitimate children were awarded the maximum allowable compensation under the statute, while the two illegitimate children, X and Y, received nothing. X and Y now challenge the award and statutory benefit scheme. They claim that the statute violates the Equal Protection Clause of the Fourteenth Amendment. Should their claim be upheld?

__Answer.__ Yes. When statutory classifications deal with sensitive and fundamental personal rights, the Court examines them more closely than classifications which involve economic and social reg-

ulations. The essential inquiry concerns the state interest which the classification seeks to promote and the fundamental personal rights which the classification might endanger. In this case the state interest in legitimate family relationships is not served by the classification. It bears no significant relationship to those recognized purposes of recovery which workmen's compensation laws serve. Thus, the denial of equal recovery rights to unacknowledged illegitimate children violated the Equal Protection Clause of the Fourteenth Amendment.

See Weber v. Aetna Casualty and Surety Co., 406 U.S. 164, 92 S.Ct. 1400, 31 L.Ed.2d 768 (1972).

1. The right to marry has been recognized as protected by the United States Constitution.

    (a) The essence of the right to marry is freedom to join in marriage with the person of one's choice. This right to marry is a right, not of racial groups, but of individuals. Thus, a segregation (miscegenation) statute relating to marriage impairs this fundamental right. See Perez v. Lippold, 32 Cal.2d 711, 198 P.2d 17 (1948). This California case is the forerunner of Loving v. Virginia, 338 U.S. 1, 87 S.Ct. 1817, 18 L.Ed.2d 1010 (1967) where the Supreme Court struck down a Virginia miscegenation statute and held that " . . . restricting the freedom to marry solely because of racial classifications violates the central meaning of the Equal Protection Clause". The Court also found that such statutes deprived the Lovings of "liberty" without due process of law.

    (b) Unreasonable restrictions may not be placed on the right to marry. See CASE 85, below.

2. The statutory scheme for obtaining a divorce must allow access to the courts by all persons without unreasonable restrictions.

    e.g. A state statute required payment of court fees and costs when a petition for divorce was filed. Plaintiffs could not pay such fees because of their indigency, and the court clerk returned their divorce papers to them. They challenged the statute as violative of the Due Process Clause because access to the courts was denied solely because of their inability to pay. The Court noted the basic importance of marriage to society and the necessity of judicial approval to dissolve a marriage. A state must afford to all individuals a meaningful opportunity to be heard under the Due Process Clause. To withhold that right because of inability to pay is the equivalent of denying them an opportunity to be heard and to dissolve their marriages. The law violated the Due Process Clause of the Fourteenth Amendment. Indigents should have access to

MARRIAGE, DIVORCE AND COHABITATION

divorce courts without prepayment of fees. See Boddie v. Connecticut, 401 U.S. 371, 91 S.Ct. 780, 28 L.Ed.2d 113 (1971).

3. Along with the erosion of the concept of the permanency of marriage, the entire institution of marriage presently is being questioned and, in some segments of society, even rejected.

4. As a result of such rejection, a growing number of people live together outside any marriage relationship, formal or informal. Such living arrangements obviously have had, and will in the future have, an effect on the mores and attitudes of society towards marriage.

5. Traditionally, courts have refused to enforce contracts between nonmarital partners if it involved an illicit relationship. Such contracts were viewed as contracts for prostitution, and therefore, illegal or contrary to public policy.

6. A number of courts have recognized the prevalence of nonmarital relationships in modern society, and the social acceptance of them. Accordingly, one court held that certain theories may be applied to couples living together so that one person may recover from the other.

  (a) An express contract between nonmarital partners should be enforced except to the extent that the contract is explicitly founded on the consideration of meretricious sexual services.

  (b) Courts may imply a contract, agreement of partnership, or joint venture between the parties based upon their conduct.

  (c) Courts may employ the doctrine of quantum meruit, or equitable remedies such as constructive or resulting trusts, when warranted by the facts of the case to permit recovery.

  See CASE 86, below.

Case 85   *Unreasonable restriction on right to marry held unconstitutional*

A state statute provided that residents, who were required by any court order or judgment to support children not in their custody, could not marry without court approval. The statute specified that court permission could not be granted unless the marriage applicant could prove that the children covered by the support order were not then and were not likely thereafter to become public charges. P was over $3,700 in arrears in support payments to his illegitimate child who had been a public charge since birth. For that reason P could not comply with the statute and he was denied a marriage license. P brought a class action challenging the statute as violative of the Due Process and Equal Protection Clauses of the Fourteenth Amendment. Was the statute constitutional?

Answer. No. The right to marry is of fundamental importance for all persons. It is part of the fundamental right of privacy implicit in the Due Process Clause of the Fourteenth Amendment. When a statutory classification interferes significantly with the exercise of a fundamental right, it cannot be upheld unless it is supported by sufficiently important state interests and is closely tailored to effectuate only those interests. The state contended that the statute furnished the opportunity to counsel the applicant and to protect the welfare of out-of-custody children. However, the statute did not require counseling, and the state could enforce support obligations by wage attachments, civil contempt proceedings and criminal penalties. Furthermore, preventing an applicant to marry does not achieve the objectives of the state. Thus, the means selected by the state unnecessarily impinged on the fundamental right to marry. In addition, the statute interfered with the right to marry by creating a classification of persons who must prove financial means to support their children in order to marry and violated the Equal Protection Clause. P and others similarly situated may marry without regard to the unconstitutional statute.

See *Zablocki v. Redhail*, 434 U.S. 374, 98 S.Ct. 673, 54 L.Ed.2d 618 (1978).

NOTE—Not every statute which regulates the prerequisites for marriage must be subjected to rigorous scrutiny as the Court did in the Zablocki case, above. The Court said that reasonable regulations that do not significantly interfere with decisions to enter into the marital relationship may legitimately be imposed.

Enforceability of agreements involving nonmarital relationships   Case 86

F and M lived together for seven years without being married. After they separated F brought suit against M for one-half of the property acquired by M while they were living together and for support payments. F contended that she had made an oral contract with M to share equally all property either should acquire while they were living together. It was also alleged that they agreed to hold themselves out as husband and wife, and that F would render "services as a companion, homemaker, housekeeper and cook" to M. Finally, F alleged that she agreed to give up her career as a singer, and that M agreed to provide for all F's financial support and needs for the rest of her life. M moved to dismiss principally on the ground that the alleged contract was so closely related to the supposed "immoral" character of the relationship between F and M that enforcement of the contract would violate public policy. M's motion was granted and F appealed. Are all contracts between nonmarital partners, which are made in contemplation of a common living arrangement, invalid?

Answer.   *No.*   *The fact that a man and woman live together without marriage, and engage in a sexual relationship, does not in itself invalidate agreements between them relating to earnings, property or expenses.   A "contract between nonmarital partners is unenforceable only to the extent that it explicitly rests upon the immoral and illicit consideration of meretricious sexual services."   Thus, a court will not enforce a contract if it is explicitly and inseparably based upon sexual services.   However, where other services are part of the contract, and they are supported by independent consideration, that part of the contract will be enforced if it is severable from that part of the contract involving sexual services.   The court reasoned that "judicial barriers that may stand in the way of a policy based upon the fulfillment of the reasonable expectations of the parties to a nonmarital relationship should be removed."   Therefore, an express contract will be enforced unless it rests on an unlawful meretricious consideration.   Furthermore, in the absence of an express agreement there are other remedies courts may consider to protect the lawful expectations of the parties: (a) the conduct of the parties may evidence an implied contract, joint venture or other tacit understanding, (b) courts may apply the principles of constructive trust or resulting trust where appropriate, and (c) quantum meruit recovery for the reasonable value of household services rendered, less the reasonable value of support received, if one person can show that such services were rendered with the expectation of monetary reward.   M's motion to dismiss was denied and the case was remanded for trial.*

See Marvin v. Marvin, 18 Cal.3d 660, 134 Cal.Rptr. 815, 557 P.2d 106 (1977).

NOTE 1—M raised other grounds in support of his motion to dismiss. (a) M contended that the contract violated public policy because it impaired the community property rights of his wife. (M began living with F before divorcing his wife.) That argument was rejected because a contract involving the improper transfer of community property is not void ab initio, but merely voidable at the option of the aggrieved spouse. M's wife had the opportunity to protect her rights in her divorce action and that decree fixed her interest in M's property. (b) M also contended that the oral contract could not be enforced because state law required that "All contracts for marriage settlements must be in writing." However, the statute refers to an agreement in contemplation of marriage in which each party agrees to release or modify property rights which would otherwise arise from the marriage. Since the contract involved in the present case was not made in contemplation of marriage the statute did not apply.

NOTE 2—The Marvin case attracted national publicity when it was tried, not only because of the issues involved, but also because the defendant was the famous movie star Lee Marvin. His female companion, who had legally changed her name to Marvin, sought one-half of the $3.6 million that Lee Marvin earned while they were living together. At the trial no contract, express or implied, was found to have been made by the parties. However, the judge awarded Miss Marvin $104,000 for her rehabilitation as a career woman. The news media reported at the time that her attorney, who took the case on a contingent fee basis, was entitled to 1/3 of that amount, and presumably, reimbursement of $60,000 in expenses.

NOTE 3—It has been reported that 17 states have followed the Marvin decision and only four states, Arizona, Arkansas, Florida and Georgia, have rejected it. See L. Bodine, The National Law Journal, Vol. I, No. 31 (April 16, 1979), p. 14.

NOTE 4—In a *Marvin* type situation a common law marriage may exist if such marriages are recognized by the state and there is a holding out by the couple that they are married. The element of consent by the parties to the marriage is not required by all states which recognize common law marriages. If a common law marriage exists, the parties must obtain a divorce before either may remarry. See *Common Law Marriages*, Chapter III, above.

INTRODUCTORY NOTE—The legal position of women, married and unmarried, has changed greatly due to statutory and case law from that under the common law. Although the change has not evolved quickly enough or completely enough in the opinion of many persons, significant progress has been made and should be recognized. Nevertheless, pockets of discrimination against women exist and will require the further attention and action of courts and legislatures.

TRENDS IN RIGHTS OF WOMEN

1. At common law when a woman married, she exchanged a number of rights for the protection of her husband. They included:

   (a) the right to make contracts,

   (b) the right to hold property, and

   (c) the right to sue or be sued.

   See generally, Clark, pp. 220–222.

2. At common law a married woman's personal property became a possession of her husband and upon his death was transferred to his personal representative, except for her clothing and jewelry which returned to her. See Clark, p. 220.

3. At common law a married woman's real property interests were affected as follows:

   (a) Her *estates of inheritance* belonged to her husband during the marriage and he received the rents and profits therefrom during the marriage. If a child was born of the marriage, the husband received the rents and profits for life.

(b) Her *life estates* became those of her husband and he was entitled to the use of rents and profits from them.

(c) Her *leaseholds* became the property of her husband.

See Clark, pp. 220–221.

4. At common law a married woman's loss of property rights was balanced by the following:

(a) She became entitled to dower or a one-third interest in her husband's land.

(b) She was entitled to support from her husband.

(c) Her husband was responsible for her antenuptial debts.

(d) Her husband was responsible for her torts, whether committed before or after her marriage.

See Clark, p. 221.

5. In England by the 17th and 18th Centuries, the courts started to modify the common law rules concerning women's rights and liabilities.

6. In the United States the courts demonstrated a reluctance to follow their counterparts in England, so by 1850 the legislatures of various jurisdictions passed statutes modifying the common law position. These statutes were called "Married Women's Property Acts". See Clark, p. 222.

7. Today, such legal disabilities affecting women have been removed. The American woman has achieved more freedom than in any other period of western history. See CHART IV, below.

8. Controversial areas which have been altered, and which afford greater freedom to women are the right to obtain birth control information and abortions.

(a) D operated a Center where information, instruction and medical advice was given to married couples as to the means of preventing conception. This was contrary to state law and D was convicted of a misdemeanor and fined. D appealed contending that the law was unconstitutional. The Court held that the law violated a right of privacy which was implied from the penumbras of the Bill of Rights and made applicable to the States through the Fourteenth Amendment. See Griswold v. Connecticut, 381 U.S. 479, 85 S.Ct. 1678, 14 L.Ed.2d 510 (1965).

(b) A state statute permitted married persons to obtain contraceptives to prevent pregnancy, but prohibited distribution of contraceptives to unmarried persons for that purpose. D was convicted under the statute, and filed a writ of habeas corpus contending that the law violated the Equal Protection Clause of the Fourteenth Amendment. The Court held that the statute was unconstitutional. (i) If the purpose of the law is to prevent fornication, a misdemeanor, there is no reason to make violation of the statute a felony. In addition, the punishment for fornication is not pregnancy and birth of an unwanted child. (ii) If the purpose of the law is the protection of health, there is no basis to distinguish between married and unmarried persons. (iii) The law cannot be viewed as a prohibition on contraception per se for then the rights of married and single persons would have to be the same. (iv) If distribution of contraceptives to married couples cannot be prohibited under Griswold v. Connecticut, a ban on the distribution to unmarried persons is also impermissible because the constitutionally protected right of privacy extends to individuals, not just married couples. If Griswold does not prohibit distribution, then the state could not treat married and unmarried persons differently. Thus, there is no constitutional basis for the statute. See Eisenstadt v. Baird, 405 U.S. 438, 92 S.Ct. 1029, 31 L.Ed.2d 349 (1972).

(c) Based upon a constitutional right of personal privacy and personal liberty the Supreme Court has also recognized the right to an abortion. Although this right may be limited to the period when the fetus is not viable, other limitations to that right have been held unconstitutional. See CASES 87 and 88, below.

9. Discrimination and de facto segregation against women in employment is prohibited by the United States Constitution, federal and many state laws. Discrimination based upon sex is prohibited:

(a) to the federal government by the Due Process Clause of the Fifth Amendment,

(b) to the states by the Equal Protection Clause of the Fourteenth Amendment, and

(c) to private employers, employment agencies and labor unions by Title VII of the Civil Rights Act of 1964, as amended by the Equal Employment Opportunity Act of 1972.

See *Smith's Review, Labor Law and Employment Discrimination*, Chapter XIII, "Other Laws Governing Labor Relations"; *Smith's Review, Constitutional Law*, Chapter X, "Fifth Amendment—Due Process Clause," and Chapter XVII, "Equal Protection Clause—Racial and Other Discrimination."

10. Laws and practices which discriminate against women have been struck down as women assume a more equal role in society.

(a) A school board established a mandatory rule which required pregnant teachers to take maternity leave four months prior to the expected birth. Another school board required leave five months before the expected birth. Pregnant public school teachers challenged the rule as violating rights under the Due Process Clause of the Fourteenth Amendment. Both rules were held unconstitutional. They were arbitrary and violative of due process since they had no valid relationship to a state interest. The Court stated that the school boards' administrative convenience alone could not justify the rule. Another rule, which prohibited teachers from returning to work until after the child was at least three months old, was also held invalid for the same reason. See Cleveland Bd. of Education v. LaFleur, 414 U.S. 632, 94 S.Ct. 791, 39 L.Ed.2d 52 (1974).

(b) A state statute denied a wife power to alienate or mortgage her lands without the consent of her husband. However, a husband could convey his land without the consent of his wife though the grantee would take subject to the wife's dower interest. W contracted to sell land to P. When W refused to perform, P sued for specific performance. W defended on the ground that she could not sell because her husband refused to consent. P contended that the state law relied upon by W violated the Equal Protection Clause of the federal and state constitutions because it discriminated against a wife in favor of the husband. The court noted that single, divorced, and widowed women, and all men, were free to convey or alienate their property; only married women were restricted, theoretically to protect them against their own actions. However, the law cannot be justified on the myth that married women need their interests protected more than other adults. The statute denied married women rights exercised by other adults, and therefore, denied them equal protection of the laws. The court held that the law violated the state constitution, but noted that equal protection rights were the same under both the federal and state constitutions. Thus, W may not rely on the statute as a defense to P's suit. See Peddy v. Montgomery, 345 So.2d 631 (Ala.1977).

11. Sex discrimination is prohibited under Title VII of the Civil Rights Act, as amended by the Equal Employment Opportunity Act.

(a) An employer had a policy of not hiring women with preschool age children, but it hired men with pre-school age children. A woman who was refused employment on that basis brought suit under Title VII. The lower courts found no unlawful sex discrimination because 75% to 80% of those hired to fill the job applied for were women. The United States Supreme Court reversed. It said that Section 703(a) required that persons of like qualifications be given equal employment opportunities irrespective of sex unless sex is a bona fide occupational qualification reasonably necessary to the normal operation of a business. Since there was no evidence that women with pre-school age children were less able to perform the job than men with pre-school age children, the employment policy violated the Act. See Phillips v. Martin Marietta Corp., 400 U.S. 542, 91 S.Ct. 496, 27 L.Ed.2d 613 (1971).

(b) Female employees filed suit against their employer under Title VII alleging that the employer's disability insurance plan discriminated on the basis of sex because disabilities arising from pregnancy were excluded. The employer contended that the same sickness and accident plan was provided for all employees, and, therefore, there was no discrimination. The Court held that there was no unlawful discrimination in the absence of evidence that the exclusion of pregnancy disability was a pretext for discriminating against women. The plan did not exclude anyone from eligibility because of sex, but merely removed one physical condition, pregnancy, from the list of compensable disabilities. The employer's insurance package covered some risks and excluded others. The same insurance "package" was offered to all employees. There was no risk from which men were protected and women were not; there was no risk from which women were protected and men were not. That the "package" did not include all risks did not render it unlawful. Although pregnancy-related disabilities constitute an additional risk unique to women, the failure to compensate them for this risk did not destroy parity of benefits to men and women under the plan. "To hold otherwise would endanger the commonsense notion that an employer who had no disability benefits program at all does not violate Title VII even though the 'underinclusion' of risks impacts, as a result of pregnancy-related disabilities, more heavily on one gender than upon the other. Just as there is no racial gender based discrimination in that case, [where the employer has no benefits plan] so, too, there is none here." The suit was dismissed. See General Electric Co. v. Gilbert, 429 U.S. 125, 97 S.Ct. 401, 50 L.Ed.2d 343, petition for rehearing denied 429 U.S. 1079, 97 S.Ct. 825, 50 L.Ed.2d 800 (1977).

NOTE 1—In a subsequent case the Court held that an employer's policy of denying employees returning from pregnancy leave their accumulated seniority while on leave deprived them of employment opportunities because of their sex in violation of Title VII. The Court explained that the employer's policy was more than the mere refusal to extend a benefit to women as in General Electric v. Gilbert, but it imposed on women a substantial burden which men need not suffer. Therefore, it violated Title VII. See Nashville Gas Co. v. Satty, 434 U.S. 136, 98 S.Ct. 347, 54 L.Ed.2d 356 (1977).

NOTE 2—In 1978 Congress amended the Act to specifically prohibit discrimination because of pregnancy. The effect of the amendment was to nullify the holding in General Electric v. Gilbert, above.

12. To comply with present law companies follow these procedures with respect to maternity leave:

   (a) a leave of absence for maternity is granted,

   (b) the length of such leave is determined by the employee, and

   (c) at the end of the leave, the employee is permitted to return to her job without loss of seniority.

CHART IV. RIGHTS OF MARRIED WOMEN
COMMON LAW AND MODERN COMPARED

At Common Law	Under Modern Statutory and Case Law
1. Could not contract with husband or others.	1. Can contract with husband (except where contracts go to the essence of the marital relationship) as well as with others.
2. Could not sue or be sued without joining husband.	2. Can sue and be sued without joining husband.
3. Could not make a will.	3. Can make a will.
4. Could not vote.	4. Can vote.
5. Could not serve on juries.	5. Can serve on juries.
6. Could not hold public office.	6. Can hold public office.
7. Could contract as husband's agent.	7. Can contract as husband's agent.
8. Could pledge husband's credit for necessaries.	8. Can pledge husband's credit for necessaries.
9. Personal property became a possession of the husband.	9. Personal property remains the property of the owner.
10. Rights with respect to her real property were severely limited.	10. Rights with respect to her real property are not limited.

Constitutional right of privacy permits abortion before fetus is viable   Case 87

Texas statutes made it a crime to procure an abortion except for the purpose of saving the life of the mother. P, who was pregnant but unmarried desired to terminate her pregnancy by an abortion "performed by a competent, licensed physician, under safe, clinical conditions." P alleged that she was unable to get a "legal" abortion in Texas because her life did not appear to be threatened by the continuation of her pregnancy, and that she could not afford to travel to another jurisdiction in order to secure a legal abortion under safe conditions. P contended that the Texas statutes were unconstitutionally vague and that they abridged her right of personal privacy, protected by the First, Fourth, Fifth, Ninth and Fourteenth Amendments. Was P deprived of her constitutional rights by the statutes?

Answer. Yes. Although the Constitution does not explicity mention any right of privacy, the Court has recognized a right of personal privacy in certain areas "in the penumbras of the Bill of Rights." The Court explained: "This right of privacy, whether it be founded in the Fourteenth Amendment's concept of personal liberty and restrictions upon state action, as we feel it is, or, as the District Court determined, in the Ninth Amendment's reservation of rights to the people, is broad enough to encompass a woman's decision whether or not to terminate her pregnancy. The detriment that the State would impose upon the pregnant woman by denying this choice altogether is apparent. Specific and direct harm medically diagnosible even in early pregnancy may be involved. . . . The Court's decisions recognizing a right of privacy also acknowledge that some state regulation in areas protected by that right is appropriate. As noted above, a State may properly assert important interests in safeguarding health, in maintaining medical standards, and in protecting potential life. At some point in pregnancy, these respective interests become sufficiently compelling to sustain regulation of the factors that govern the abortion decision. The privacy right involved, therefore, cannot be said to be absolute." The Court emphasized that where certain "fundamental rights" are involved, such as P possessed in the present case, laws limiting those rights can be justified only by a "compelling state interest." The Court attempted to balance the interests of the pregnant female and those of the state by dividing the term of pregnancy into three stages. During the first trimester of pregnancy a woman is free to determine with her physician whether the pregnancy should be terminated. An abortion may then be performed without interference by the state. During the second trimester until the fetus is viable, a state may regulate the abortion procedure only to protect the health of the mother. Such regulation may relate to the qualifications of the person performing the abortion and the facility where it is performed. This state action is permissible because the danger to the mother's health is greater during this period.

When the fetus becomes viable, which is approximately the third trimester, the state has a "compelling" interest in protecting the life of the fetus. Therefore, a state may prohibit abortions during that period except where it is necessary to preserve the health of the mother. The Texas abortion statute failed to meet these standards which balanced the interests of the parties based upon a tripartite division of pregnancy. Therefore, the statute was held unconstitutional.

See Roe v. Wade, 410 U.S. 113, 93 S.Ct. 705, 35 L.Ed.2d 147 (1973). See also Doe v. Bolton, 410 U.S. 179, 93 S.Ct. 739, 35 L.Ed.2d 201 (1973).

Case 88 *Limitations on right of state to regulate abortions*

After the Supreme Court decision in Roe v. Wade, CASE 87, above, Missouri enacted a statute to control and regulate abortions. The statute: (a) defined the term "viability" as "that stage of fetal development when the life of the unborn child may be continued indefinitely outside the womb by natural or artificial life-supportive systems," (b) required the woman to certify in writing that she freely consented to the abortion if it occurred during the first 12 weeks of pregnancy, (c) required the consent of the spouse during the first 12 weeks unless the abortion was necessary to preserve the life of the mother, (d) required the consent of one parent if the woman was not married and under the age of 18, unless the abortion was necessary to preserve the life of the mother, (e) prohibited the method of abortion known as saline amniocentesis after the first 12 weeks of pregnancy, (f) imposed various record keeping requirements and (g) required the physician to exercise professional care "to preserve the life and health of the fetus." Two physicians and a facility where abortions were performed brought suit alleging that the statute deprived them and their patients of various constitutional rights, including the right to privacy in the physician-patient relationship, the physician's right to give and the patient's right to receive medical advice and treatment, including the method of termination of the pregnancy, the female's right to determine whether to bear children, and the physician's right to practice medicine according to the highest standards of medical practice. What sections of the statute, if any, violate the Due Process Clause of the Fourteenth Amendment or other constitutional guarantees?

Answer. *(a) The definition of "viability" reflects the fact that viability varies with each pregnancy, and that determination is a matter for the judgment of the attending physician. The definition was constitutional since it did not circumvent the limitations on state regulation of abortions. (b) The decision to abort is important, and it is desirable that it be made with full knowledge of its nature and* consequences. *Since the woman is the person primarily concerned, her awareness of the decision and its significance may be assured, constitutionally, by requiring her prior written consent. (c) The consent of the spouse cannot be required during the first 12 weeks of pregnancy. The state cannot prohibit abortions during that period and, therefore, it cannot delegate veto power to a spouse. (d) For substantially the same reason the consent of a parent where the female is under 18 and unmarried cannot be required. Minors, as well as adults, are protected by the Constitution. Those rights do not come into being upon reaching the state-defined age of majority. Although a state has broader authority to regulate the activities of minors than of adults, the Court found no significant state interest which would warrant imposition of the parental consent requirement. (e) The saline amniocentesis method of abortion was prohibited after the twelfth week of pregnancy. That is the most commonly used abortion procedure and is considered the safest. Since safer methods have not been developed, and the statute contains an outright prohibition of saline amniocentesis, the regulation is unreasonable and arbitrary, having the effect of inhibiting the vast majority of abortions after the first 12 weeks. Thus, it is unconstitutional. (f) Reporting and recordkeeping provisions can be useful to the state in protecting the health of its female citizens and may be of medical value. The records are confidential and do not interfere with the abortion decision or the physician-patient relationship. The requirement is reasonable and it is valid. (g) The standard of care provision requires the physician to preserve the life of the fetus whatever the stage of pregnancy. It does not limit the duty to pregnancies where the fetus is viable and is unconstitutional. Thus, a state may require written consent of the pregnant woman before an abortion and prescribe reasonable recordkeeping requirements. However, a state may not require the consent of a spouse or parents before an abortion, prohibit abortions by medically recognized methods, or prescribe an unreasonable standard of care.*

See *Planned Parenthood of Central Missouri v. Danforth*, 428 U.S. 52, 96 S.Ct. 2831, 49 L.Ed.2d 788 (1976).

1. The proposed constitutional amendment popularly known as the Equal Rights Amendment will, if ratified, become the Twenty-Seventh Amendment to the United States Constitution. The Amendment states:

> "Section 1. Equality of rights under the law shall not be denied or abridged by the United States or any state on account of sex.

> "Section 2. The Congress shall have the power to enforce, by appropriate legislation the provisions of this Article.

PROPOSED EQUAL RIGHTS AMENDMENT

"Section 3.   This Amendment shall take effect two years after the date of ratification."

2. The Amendment forbids federal, state and local governments to use sex as a factor in determining the rights of men and women.

3. The Amendment does not impose any new obligations on private organizations or individuals.   However, if a private group is performing a governmental function it would have the same obligations as a state under the state action doctrine.

4. Under the state action doctrine, where a private group performs a governmental function they must accord individuals the same constitutional rights as the state would be required to do.   This is also known as the governmental function theory.

   NOTE—In applying this principle, courts reason that a state has the duty to see that its constitutional responsibilities are fulfilled, whether it delegates authority or merely permits private parties to take some action.   This is true even if the action taken by the private group has no binding legal effect, so long as it is a proper governmental function.   See *Smith's Review, Constitutional Law,* Chapter XVIII, Fourteenth Amendment, and Chapter XIX, Right of Citizens to Vote."

5. The principle of equality embodied in the Amendment does not mean that the sexes must be regarded as identical.   Presumably courts will permit a reasonable separation of the sexes in certain circumstances.

   (a)   A state may continue to exercise its traditional power to regulate cohabitation and sexual activity by unmarried persons. This would include sleeping quarters at coeducational colleges, prison dormitories, and military barracks.

   (b)   People will continue to enjoy their right of privacy in places such as public toilets and sleeping quarters of public institutions.

6. The original date for ratification of the proposed Amendment was March 22, 1979.   However, in 1978 Congress voted to extend the deadline to June 30, 1982.   Whether this extension is constitutionally permissible may eventually have to be determined by the Supreme Court.

7. As this Review goes to press 36 states have ratified the Amendment.   Ratification by three-fourths of the states, or 38, is required for passage of the Amendment.

   CAVEAT—Ratification of the Amendment has been complicated by the fact that three states, Idaho, Nebraska and Tennessee, have rejected the Amendment after having ratified it.   The ratification of two other states is also questionable: (a) the Kentucky legislature rescinded its approval, but the rescission was vetoed by the acting governor, and (b) South Dakota declared its ratification null and void because of the expiration of the original ratification deadline. Whether or not these ratifications are valid is a "political question" for Congress to determine. See Coleman v. Miller, 307 U.S. 433, 59 S.Ct. 972, 83 L.Ed. 1385 (1939).

See generally, *Equal Rights for Men and Women*, S.Rep.No. 92–689, Senate Committee on the Judiciary, 92d Cong., 2d Sess. (1972).

RIGHTS OF JUVENILES IN CRIMINAL LAW

1. A child is not criminally responsible for his acts or omissions unless he is old enough and has sufficient intelligence to be capable of having a criminal intent as to such acts or omissions. The test is whether the child understands the nature of the act and whether it is right or wrong.

2. At common law:

    (a) A child under seven years of age is conclusively presumed to be incapable of committing a crime.

    (b) One between the ages of seven and fourteen is presumed incompetent. The state has the burden of overcoming such presumption.

    (c) One over the age of fourteen is presumed capable of committing a crime, but the defendant may overcome such presumption by showing either mental or physical incapacity.

    CAVEAT—The student should be careful to distinguish the rules relating to criminal capacity with those relating to civil liability for tortious conduct.

3. The common law presumptions extend only insofar as chronological age is concerned. Mental age or evidence of mental incompetency is generally admissible to prove that the accused did not have the required intent to commit the crime with which he is charged.

4. Practically all states today have statutes creating juvenile courts which have all but dispossessed the criminal courts of jurisdiction over infants up to 16 or 18 years of age. See Model Penal Code § 4.10.

    (a) Some juvenile statutes extend the old English Chancery jurisdiction to the juvenile courts thus enabling the state to assume the protection of neglected children. Such statutes have for their purpose the rehabilitation of children, and not their punishment. They are constitutional under the police power of the state.

(b) Some states give jurisdiction to criminal courts instead of juvenile courts in the case of all felonies or certain named felonies.

(c) The jurisdiction of juvenile and criminal courts is concurrent in some states. In those states the juvenile court must waive jurisdiction before the juvenile can be tried as an adult in a criminal court.

NOTE—As to any given defendant, where concurrent jurisdiction exists, the juvenile court judge determines in his discretion, usually based upon statutory guidelines, whether to waive the jurisdicton of the juvenile court and have the juvenile tried as an adult.

5. Traditionally, it has been said of juvenile court proceedings that they are neither adversary in nature, nor are they criminal trials.

6. The concept which underlies traditional juvenile court and delinquency law is that there is a need to protect and rehabilitate a wayward youth. Such a youth is not a defendant who is on trial for a crime for which he will be punished if he is found guilty. The Court is seen as acting in the role of benevolent, understanding parents.

7. Consistent with these ideas, an objective of juvenile procedures has been to "hide youthful errors from the full gaze of the public and bury them in the graveyard of the forgotten past." For this reason statutes have provided that findings against a child are not a "crime", to help protect the child's future.

8. In practice, with respect to the same conduct, an individual may be subject either to the jurisdiction of a juvenile court, or to that of the normal adult criminal courts. As a result, from the inception of the juvenile court system, wide differences have been tolerated, if not insisted upon, between the procedural rights which are accorded to adults and those which are accorded to juveniles.

9. The juvenile court may waive its "exclusive jurisdiction and send the juvenile to an adult criminal court for trial. However, before a juvenile is tried as an adult he is entitled to a hearing, including access by his counsel to the social records and probation reports which, presumably, are considered by the court, and to a statement of the reasons for the juvenile court's decision. See Kent v. United States, 383 U.S. 541, 86 S.Ct. 1045, 16 L.Ed.2d 84 (1966).

10. Where a person is tried for an offense as a juvenile and found guilty of violating a criminal statute, the Double Jeopardy Clause of the Fifth Amendment as made applicable to the states through incorporation into the Due Process Clause of the Fourteenth

Amendment, bars a subsequent trial of the juvenile as an adult for the same offense. Even though the defendant never risked more than one punishment, he was twice put in jeopardy which is unconstitutional. See Breed v. Jones, 421 U.S. 519, 95 S.Ct. 1779, 44 L.Ed.2d 346 (1975).

11. The leading case in the field of juvenile justice is the decision in In re Gault, CASE 89, below. In Gault the Supreme Court considered the claim by the juvenile that he had been deprived of six basic constitutional rights in the proceedings by which a determination was made as to whether he, a juvenile, was a "delinquent", as a result of his alleged misconduct, with the consequence that he could be committed to a state institution. The Supreme Court held that at least four Bill of Rights safeguards apply to protect a juvenile accused in a juvenile court on a charge under which he can be imprisoned for a term of years:

(a) Timely notice must be given sufficiently in advance of the hearings, of the specific issues to be heard, as required by the Sixth Amendment.

(b) The child and his parent must be notified of the child's right to be represented by counsel retained by them, or if they are unable to afford counsel, that counsel will be appointed to represent the child, as required by the Sixth Amendment.

(c) The constitutional privilege against self-incrimination is applicable in the case of juveniles, as it is with respect to adults, as required by the Fifth Amendment.

(d) The right to confrontation and cross-examination of witnesses against the juvenile must be afforded, as is required by the Sixth Amendment.

12. The Supreme Court has given at least some retrospective effect to the Gault decision. The Court reversed an appeal from a finding of delinquency which was dismissed by a state supreme court two months *before* Gault, as to which certiorari was granted *after* Gault. In the Whittington case the Court remanded "for further consideration in light of In re Gault" because the state court had not had an opportunity to assess the impact of the Gault decision. See In re Whittington, 391 U.S. 341, 88 S.Ct. 1507, 20 L.Ed.2d 625 (1968).

13. The Due Process Clause of the Fourteenth Amendment requires the standard of proof beyond a reasonable doubt in state criminal cases. This standard applies to the adjudicatory stage of a juvenile court delinquency proceeding in which a youth is charged with an act that would be a crime if committed by an adult. See Matter of Winship, 397 U.S. 358, 90 S.Ct. 1068, 25 L.Ed.2d 368 (1970).

14. The Supreme Court has not ruled that all rights constitutionally assured to an adult accused are to be imposed in a juvenile proceeding. Thus, a trial by jury is not constitutionally required in the adjudicative phase of a state juvenile court delinquency proceeding. See McKeiver v. Pennsylvania, 403 U.S. 528, 91 S.Ct. 1976, 29 L.Ed.2d 647 (1971).

CAVEAT—Since the Gault decision the Supreme Court, some lower federal courts, and lower state courts, have begun to explore and resolve such questions as: Whether Gault should be retroactive; the right of juveniles to jury trial; requirements of bail; burden of proof; and those issues which the Supreme Court considered, but did not resolve initially, such as the requirement of appellate review and transcript of proceedings. See e.g., Hall et al., pp. 1347–1353. On any given set of facts the student must carefully consider the implications of Gault with respect to those issues not specifically resolved by it.

Case 89   *Constitutional rights of juveniles—proceedings determining delinquency*

D, a fifteen year old boy, was taken into custody as a result of a verbal complaint of a neighbor about a phone call in which lewd or indecent remarks were made. No notice was given to D's parents. A petition was filed with the state juvenile court alleging that D was a delinquent minor. This petition was not served on D's parents. A hearing was held the next day. D's father was not present. The complaining witness was not there. No one was sworn at the hearing. No transcript or other record was made of the hearing. No memorandum or record of the substance of the proceedings was prepared. No decision was reached at this hearing, and another hearing was held a few days later. Once again, the complaining witness was not present. At the end of the hearing the judge adjudged D a juvenile delinquent and committed him to the state industrial school until he reached age 21, unless sooner discharged by due process of law. Thus, in the juvenile proceeding he was committed to custody for a maximum period of six years. By contrast, the penalty in the state criminal code, applicable to an adult for the same offense, is $5 to $50, or imprisonment for not more than two months. Since no appeal is permitted under state law, a petition for a writ of habeas corpus was filed, asking that D be released from custody because at the proceedings at which he was adjudged a "delinquent" the following basic rights were denied: (a) notice of the charges; (b) right to counsel; (c) right to confrontation and cross examination; (d) privilege against self-incrimination; (e) right to a transcript of the proceedings; and (f) right to appellate review. Will habeas corpus issue?

Answer. Yes. The Supreme Court sustained D's contention that he had been deprived of the first four of the basic rights, listed above, and determined that through the due process clause of the Fourteenth Amendment these rights are applicable to juveniles in state court proceedings. The Court established that although the hearing did not have to conform with all of the requirements of a criminal trial, the following rights, afforded by the Fifth and Sixth Amendments, must be present: (a) Notice must be given sufficiently in advance of scheduled court proceedings so that reasonable opportunity to be prepared will be afforded, and such notice must set forth the alleged misconduct with particularity. (b) The child and his parent must be notified of the child's right to be represented by counsel retained by them, or if they are unable to afford counsel, that counsel will be appointed to represent the child. (c) Confrontation and sworn testimony by witnesses available for cross-examination are essential for a finding of "delinquency" and an order committing D to a state institution for a maximum of six years. (d) The constitutional privilege against self-incrimination is applicable in the case of juveniles as it is with respect to adults. The Court did not reach a decision on points (e) and (f). Based upon the denial to D of these four basic rights, D's adjudication of delinquency and commitment were reversed.

Even though the Court imposed certain criminal procedural safeguards on juvenile proceedings, it made it clear that such proceedings were not being equated with criminal proceedings. The Court refused to repudiate the basic rehabilitative theories of juvenile law. The Court stressed the concept of rehabilitation in the juvenile law process, and made it clear that the juvenile delinquent is not a convicted criminal.

See In re Gault, 387 U.S. 1, 87 S.Ct. 1428, 18 L.Ed.2d 527 (1967).

APPENDIX:

EXAMINATION QUESTIONS AND ANSWERS

SUGGESTED APPROACH TO ANSWERING ESSAY EXAMINATIONS IN LAW

1. Remember that you are taking an essay examination. The complete essay examination answer must contain not only the "answer" to the question, but of greater importance, must also contain your analysis, the applicable black letter law, and an explanation of how you have applied the black letter law to the facts and reasoned to the "answer."

2. Begin by reading the question, thoroughly.

3. Next, reread the question; read it as it is written, not as you think it is written.

4. As you read, spot key concepts, ideas, issues and applicable legal terms, principles and concepts.

5. Organize your thoughts into an orderly logical sequence.

6. Analyze the fact pattern and the key issues, terms, principles and concepts which you have spotted.

7. Work out a game plan for your answer, including the sequence of those things which you are going to write about, the priority for writing, the space to be allocated to each and an allocation of your time for writing.

8. Make a brief word-phrase outline of your proposed answer.

9. Use at least 25% of the time allotted for answering the question to all of the things outlined above before you begin to write the answer.

10. Begin writing with a short clear decisive answer to the question precisely as it is asked. For example, if the question reads: "Rule on plaintiff's motion," your answer should be: "Motion granted," or "motion overruled." The balance of your answer explains how you reasoned to that conclusion.

11. Write your answer in clear, professional, lawyer-like English prose using full and complete legal terminology. Remember: This

is an essay examination, in the English language, at the graduate level, in a learned profession.

12. Be certain to include full sentences of black letter law on each of the key issues.

13. Do not merely rehash the facts. A complete answer requires analysis, black letter law and application of that black letter law to the facts. Rehashing of the facts is not enough.

14. Use short, complete, simple sentences. Avoid long, wandering, convoluted sentences which deal with several issues and subjects.

15. Reason to a lawyer-like conclusion. If you have time and space, add a wrap-up concluding sentence to your answer.

16. Reread your answer to make certain that you have made no unintended errors or omissions, and to ensure clarity and completeness of your answer.

17. Use the full time allotted for the question—no more and no less.

EXAMINATION QUESTIONS AND ANSWERS

The following questions have been selected from various examinations of Professor Paul McLane Conway of Georgetown Law Center, Washington, D.C., and are reprinted here with his permission. Their inclusion in this Review is designed to acquaint the student with the kinds of questions which may be found on law school examinations. The original questions have been renumbered for convenience. Suggested answers, which have been prepared by the authors of this Review, are printed following the questions.

QUESTIONS

1. Tarzan and Jane have been dating for many years. When Jane becomes pregnant, she suggests they marry. Tarzan resists the idea of marriage, fearful that settling down with one woman would tarnish his image as a "swinger." Jane becomes furious with Tarzan's irresponsibility and issues an ultimatum: either Tarzan settles down or she takes off.

"But dear," protests Tarzan, "marriage is such a hassle. And you know how messy it can get if the marriage goes sour—the resentment, the pain, the endless litigation . . . And the husband always gets shafted in the end!"

Jane, a determined woman, comes up with a solution to calm Tarzan's fears. She suggests they sign a contract limiting the amount to which she would be entitled should their marriage falter. Jane hastens to assure Tarzan that she has no thoughts of ever leaving him, and that the separation agreement is merely a device "to take those silly worries out of your head." Tarzan is impressed by Jane's quick thinking and agrees to marry her.

The two marry and subsequently sign an agreement providing for a lump-sum of $20,000 payable to Jane, along with a weekly payment of $100 for the support of their daughter, Girl "in the improbable event that we, the undersigned, decide to split."

The years pass. By chance Tarzan is spotted by a visiting Mutual of Omaha film crew and receives a lucrative screen contract. His income quadruples and he, Jane and Girl live a life of un-accustomed luxury.

The pressures of stardom take their toll on the family. Tarzan is away from home much of the time. To fill up her lonely hours Jane acquires a job as a tour guide in a local escort service. One night Tarzan returns home unexpectedly to find Jane giving a "tour" of the bedroom to Marlin Perkins, Jr., alias Buster Crabbe. "I'll teach you to 'Cheeta' on me," grunts Tarzan. He promptly sues Jane for divorce on the ground of adultery.

(a) In the divorce proceeding Tarzan argues that the separation agreement governs his obligations to Jane.

Respond.

Assume that the separation agreement is approved by the court and merged in the divorce decree:

(b) If Tarzan fails to make the lump sum and child support payments, may he be held in contempt?

(c) For fifteen years Tarzan faithfully makes the child support payments. At the end of that period he petitions the court to reduce the amount he must pay for child support, claiming that he quit his acting job and can no longer afford to pay $100 per week. What result?

Would your answer be different if the agreement had been incorporated by reference, but not merged, in the divorce decree?

2. Husband seeks an injunction restraining his wife from interfering with the continuance of their seven year old child in a private school. The wife wishes to have the child attend a public school. This is part of a family dispute. There is no question concerning the custody of the child since the parents and child are living together as a family group. In the absence of a statute does a court of equity have "inherent jurisdiction" to resolve the dispute as to which school the child should attend?

3. June Green and Mulhamid Mulhamid met in Cairo, Egypt where June was on vacation. She was an American. He was a citizen of Egypt and wished to emigrate to the U.S. but was unable to obtain a visa. He offered to pay her $20,000.00 if she would marry him for the purpose of getting him into the U.S. on a

permanent basis. The immigration laws permitted the entry of spouses of American citizens outside the usual quotas. June agreed on the condition that they would never live together as husband and wife. Mulhamid paid her the money, the marriage was performed and they both came to the United States. Upon their arrival in New York they part. Two years later June hears that Mulhamid has become a very successful oriental rug dealer and is earning large sums of money. As a result she brings an action for maintenance and support. What result?

4. Discuss briefly the key elements of proof in an action for adultery based on circumstantial evidence.

5. Would the following events entitle either spouse to a modification of alimony?

(a) The wife married a second husband, who was much less wealthy than her first. Her first husband moved to terminate alimony payments, arguing that this should follow automatically from his wife's remarriage.

(b) The wife met and fell in love with another man, but her attorney advised her that if she married him, she would risk losing her alimony, so she and her new boy friend moved into an apartment together without bothering to marry, although they represented themselves as being married. The husband moved to terminate alimony.

(c) At the time of the divorce the husband's income was $18,000 per year, and the court awarded alimony in the amount of $500 per month. Two years later the husband invented a valuable electronic device and his income from patent royalties, together with his salary, became $60,000 per year. The wife moved for an increase in alimony, giving evidence also that inflation had produced an increase in her living expenses.

(d) The alimony order read that the wife was to receive $500 per month "until further order of this court". The husband died some years later leaving a substantial estate. His executor refused to make any further payments of alimony. Six months after the husband died, the executor moved to terminate the alimony. Does the divorce court have the authority to order periodic alimony which is to continue beyond the husband's death, particularly since, if they had remained married, the wife would have had no right to be supported beyond his death?

(e) The alimony order gave the wife $500 per month. Two years later the parties made an agreement by which she agreed to accept $300 per month in full satisfaction of her claims for the future. The husband then moved for a modification of the original award to $300 per month. Must the court grant his motion? Alternatively, assume that the husband made no such motion, but thenceforth paid at the rate of $300 per month. Three years later the wife brought a proceeding for enforcement of the original order of $500 per month. Could she prevail in this proceeding?

6. On what basis may a court distribute property following an annulment?

7. (a) In a Reciprocal Enforcement of Support action the initiating court must find two things. Name them.

   (b) In Reciprocal Support actions what role does the Full Faith and Credit Clause of the U.S. Constitution play?

8. Having opened your office pursuant to the general practice of law and in particular specializing in Family Law or Domestic Relations, Mrs. D consults you saying that she has information to the effect that Mr. D is about to flee the marital abode and the jurisiction. What action would you consider on her behalf to prevent Mr. D's fleeing?

9. Briefly define the following terms:

   (a) divorce *a mensa et thoro*

   (b) affinity

   Answer the following questions [10–13] true or false and give a short statement defending your position.

10. Jack and Jill agreed to an amicable divorce. The decree did not mention alimony which Jill neither needed nor wanted at that time. Eight months later Jill becomes seriously ill and she petitions the court to revise and modify the decree to provide for alimony. Jill invokes the continuing jurisdiction of the court and states that unless she is granted relief she will become a public charge. Jack will prevail.

11. H & W lived together as a married couple in State X, which has a no-fault divorce law and in which adultery is not a ground for divorce. Because of H's adultery W leaves and moves to State Y where adultery is a ground for divorce. W sues for divorce in Y on the ground of adultery and H defends. H will prevail because X was the center of gravity, because he had done no act or omission within State Y and because H & W were residents of State X during the time of the alleged breach of the marital duty.

12. An unconsummated ceremonial marriage is no more than an engagement to marry.

13. "Clear and convincing" proof of cohabitation and reputation will sustain a common law marriage.

14. What changes or additions would you make on the following text?

<u>PRE-DIVORCE TAX PLANNING</u>

Under certain circumstances alimony payments may be taxable to the recipient spouse and correspondingly deductible by the disbursing spouse. In order to receive such treatment under Section 71(a)(1) of the Internal Revenue Code, the parties must be divorced and the payments must be periodic.

Principal Sum—Generally, installment payments of a principal sum specified in a decree or agreement in terms of money or property are not considered periodic payments qualifying for the special treatment of Section 71(a)(1) (i.e. $10,000 in four annual installments of $2500.00 each). There are two exceptions to this general rule:

1. principal sums payable over a period of more than 10 years are treated as periodic payments, but the deduction is limited to an annual maximum of 10% of the principal sum. (i.e. $30,000 over a 12 year period payable in installments of $4,000 per year for the first three years and $2,000 per year thereafter; only $3,000 of the $4,000 payments qualifies as a periodic payment).

2. payments are considered periodic payments if they are subject to one or more of the contingencies of a) death of either spouse, b) remarriage of the wife or c) change in the economic status of either spouse, (i.e. $300 per month for 60 months, unless terminated by the wife's death or remarriage).

Noncash Payments—Premium payments of a life insurance policy on a husband's life may be deductible alimony to the wife, provided that the wife is made the beneficiary and the actual owner of the policy. To so qualify, the transfer must be under an obligation established by the decree or agreement incident to the divorce; it cannot merely be a gratuitous act.

Mortgage payments, if the property has been transferred to the wife under the decree, for more than ten years can be alimony taxable to the wife. This may be disadvantageous to the wife, however, since she will not be permitted to deduct the interest portion or the mortgage payment.

Alimony obligations may also be discharged by an alimony trust established by the husband. The trust income so distributed is deductible by the trust (not the husband) and taxable to the wife.

Child Support—Payments earmarked for child support are neither taxable to the recipient spouse nor deductible by the disbursing spouse. Where a decree comingles alimony and child support, the entire amount is treated as alimony; under such circumstances, the husband would be denied any dependency exemptions for such children.

Property Settlements—The husband has a taxable gain if he transfers appreciated property to his wife; on the other hand, the transfer of depreciated property does not give rise to a recognizable loss. With regard to depreciable assets, the husband is better off selling the assets on the open market (thus, recognizing the loss) and paying the cash realized on such sale to the wife.

Counsel Fees—Generally, legal expenses incurred by parties to a divorce action are personal expenses and, therefore, are non-deductible by either spouse. There are a few exceptions to this rule: 1) the wife may deduct that portion of her attorney's fees attributable to the production of taxable alimony; 2) either party to a divorce action may deduct that portion of the attorney's fees attributable to tax research and advice in connection with the divorce and the property settlement. Neither spouse may deduct legal fees paid on behalf of the other spouse; therefore, the husband would be better off paying the wife a higher alimony payment and allowing her to pay her own attorney's fees.

1(a). A separation agreement made when the parties are actually separated or are about to separate is usually valid. However, in the example the agreement was made shortly after marriage when there was no intention of separation. The agreement so states and it was many years before actual separation. In such circumstances the separation agreement is usually held to be unenforceable because of public policy: it may encourage separation or divorce. See Chapter VII, *Separation Agreements*; above; Clark, pp. 521–523; Caldwell v. Caldwell, 5 Wis.2d 146, 92 N.W.2d 356 (1958).

It should be noted that a separation agreement is a contract and it must be supported by consideration. If Tarzan and Jane made mutual promises of some kind in the agreement, that requirement would be satisfied. For example, Jane may have promised to care for Girl which would be sufficient consideration for her.

1(b). Where the separation agreement has been merged into the divorce decree, alimony and support orders are enforceable by contempt. Thus, in the example, the child support payments are enforceable by contempt. Property settlement orders such

SUGGESTED ANSWERS TO QUESTIONS

as the lump sum payment in the example are not enforceable by contempt.

An effect of the merger of the settlement agreement in the divorce decree is to extinguish the private contract rights of the agreement which become part of the court order (judgment). The duty of Tarzan to make support payments may be enforced by contempt proceedings because they violate a court judgment. Courts regard alimony and child support payments as a statement of the husband's obligation to support his family and not as the payment of a debt. Thus, the constitutional prohibition of imprisonment for a debt does not apply to alimony and child support. Tarzan may be held in contempt for failure to make the $100 per week child support payments. Lump sum payments are generally regarded as a property settlement rather than alimony. This would be especially true in this example because the amount of the payment has no relation to Tarzan's duty to support Jane or her needs. A property settlement is in the nature of a debt, and since it is unconstitutional to imprison a person for failure to pay a debt, that obligation cannot be enforced by contempt proceedings. See Clark, pp. 553–556.

1(c). A court would not permit Tarzan to evade his child support obligations by quitting his job and refusing to find employment elsewhere. It would deny Tarzan's petition, and he could be held in contempt if payments were not made. If the loss of income is only temporary, lasting until Tarzan finds other employment, the court would still deny Tarzan's petition. A temporary loss of income is not a valid basis upon which to reduce child support payments. See Clark, pp. 496, footnote 75, 498, 557–563.

Courts will modify child support provisions when it is in the best interests of the child regardless of whether the agreement has been merged into the divorce decree. Therefore, even if there were a valid reason to modify the amount of child support, the answer given in the preceding paragraph would not be changed. Tarzan's petition should be denied because the refusal to work, or the temporary loss of income, is not a sufficient reason to modify child support payments.

2. A court of equity would have jurisdiction to hear and decide the dispute, but it would not exercise its jurisdiction. The general rule is that courts will not resolve family disputes while the spouses are living together and have no grounds for separation or divorce. One reason for the rule is that there is no assurance that a judge would be able to resolve the dispute better than the spouses. Therefore, a court should not inject itself into a family problem while they continue to live together.

See CASE 28, above; Clark, p. 186.

3. June would lose her suit under the decisions of many courts which have held that a marriage contracted for the sole purpose of immigration is invalid. Where parties consent to marriage in a ceremony but do not have the intent to assume the status of a married couple a court should find the marriage invalid. The reasons for the rule include the failure to consummate the marriage and the lack of intent to establish a life together and assume the responsibilities which married status entails. Some courts, however, have upheld such limited purpose marriages. See Chapter II, *Elements of a Valid Marriage*, above; Clark, pp. 114–118.

4. Adultery may be established by circumstantial evidence. When this is done two elements must be shown: (a) the spouse charged had a disposition to commit adultery, and (b) there was an opportunity to commit it. One court concluded that there was sufficient evidence to establish adultery where the parties were seen together in a tavern and later on the same night in an automobile. That occurred on three different occasions late in the evening and in the early morning hours. They were seen embracing, petting and kissing on those occasions. When the couple was in the car no one else was around, and there was sufficient time and opportunity for them to have had sexual relations. The facts, summarized above, show the two elements: disposition and opportunity. See Ermis v. Ermis, 255 Wis. 339, 39 N.W.2d 485 (1949).

Other evidence may be available to show adultery. A wife may be shown to have committed adultery by blood tests establishing that her husband was not the father of her child or by establishing non-access of the husband when the child was conceived. A prima facie case of adultery may be made against a husband if he contracts a venereal disease during the marriage. See Clark, pp. 330–331.

5(a). Some states have statutes which automatically terminate the obligation to pay alimony upon remarriage. In other states the decree must be modified by the court to end the obligation. Remarriage is recognized as a change of circumstances which warrants termination of alimony. The reasons are that upon remarriage new support obligations arise between the parties, and public policy requires a termination of support from the earlier marriage. A reason given by some courts is that the claim for alimony is "abandoned" by the subsequent marriage. See Clark, p. 457.

5(b). Under traditional rules the fact that the spouse receiving alimony was cohabiting with a person of the opposite sex was not a sufficient reason to terminate alimony. That rule has been questioned in recent decisions. The termination of alimony is not automatic under the modern rule; it is a circumstance which should be considered by the court. Where the alimony is for support only and completely independent (severable) from any property settlement, issues arise as to whether there is a need to continue the alimony and whether part of the alimony is being used to support the lover of the ex-spouse. In the example the ex-wife held herself out to be married. If that occurred in a state which recognized common law marriages the alimony should be terminated as of the time of the common law marriage. A court might also be inclined to terminate alimony because the ex-wife is attempting to enjoy the benefits of marriage by cohabiting with a man and not enter into an actual marriage in order to avoid loss of alimony. Thus, the mere holding out as being married may be sufficient to terminate alimony in some states. See Chapter VII, Termination of Duty to Pay Alimony, above.

5(c). A general increase in the cost of living is a sufficient reason to increase the amount of alimony due the wife, so long as the husband is financially able to pay the increased amount. In this example it is clear that he can pay such increase, so alimony would be increased to compensate her for increased cost of living expenses. However, alimony may not be raised merely because the husband later earns substantially more money. The reason is that the purpose of alimony is to provide for the needs of one spouse, and assuming that the original alimony award provided adequate support, the mere ability to pay more does not justify modification of the initial award. If the original award was less than the spouse reasonably needed, but was set low because the husband could not afford to pay more, then a court may increase the amount if the husband subsequently earns more. See Arnold v. Arnold, 332 Ill.App. 586, 76 N.E.2d 335 (1947).

5(d). Most courts have found authority to order periodic alimony payments after the death of the husband from their interpretation of the applicable alimony statute; courts do not have inherent power to order alimony. However, when the spouse paying alimony dies courts are reluctant to order the continuation of alimony unless it conforms with the intent of the parties. This is so because requiring the estate to be held open for a long period to make alimony payments may cause hardship on others and frustrate the distribution of the estate in accordance with a will. The fact that the husband's obligation to support his wife would have ended with his death had they remained married does not control because in that event the wife would have been entitled to a share of her husband's estate. In the example there was no clear language to show that alimony should survive the husband's death, so the court should not order the alimony continued. See Clark, pp. 461–463.

5(e). When the parties mutually agree to modify alimony payments it should be submitted to the court for approval in order for it to be binding on them. Although the court is not obligated to accept the modification, it will normally do so unless there is evidence of fraud or overreaching by one party. If court approval of the alimony modification is not obtained, then the agreement to modify it is not binding. If the husband in the example did not move the court to change the amount of alimony payable, the wife could later enforce the original order. She would be entitled to the additional $200 per month. See Clark, pp. 464–465.

6. A court should distribute property equitably following an annulment. This may mean an equal distribution, but not necessarily. For example, if most of the marital property was given to the couple by the wife's father, then most of the property should be awarded to the wife. In states where no alimony may be awarded after an annulment, the property division may be very favorable to the spouse who would otherwise receive alimony. In this way a court may use the property division as a substitute for alimony. See Clark, p. 136.

7(a). In an action under the Uniform Reciprocal Enforcement of Support Act a complaint is filed by the person seeking to enforce the support obligation. The court in the initiating state must find that: (a) the complaint sets forth sufficient facts from which the duty of support may be imposed, and (b) a court in another state (the responding state) may obtain jurisdiction over the defendant. If the court in the initiating state finds those two essentials, it certifies its decision and transmits copies of the complaint, its certification and the Act to the court in the responding state which has jurisdiction over the defendant. It should be noted that such action by the court in the initiating state does not constitute a finding that support is due, but only that further proceedings are warranted. See CHART II, above; Clark, pp. 207–208.

7(b). The defendant may raise any defenses he may have before the court in the responding state, but no counter-claims may be raised. The court then determines the merits of the claims of the parties and may either dismiss the complaint or enter an order of support. Support orders may be registered as provided by the Act and enforced by contempt or other means. Insofar as such support order (decree) is final it must be given full faith and credit by other states. Usually accrued installments, even though not paid, are considered final and the support order may be modified only as to future support. If the plaintiff brought a second action under the act to increase the amount of support, the Full Faith and Credit Clause could be used as a defense to modification of the initial support order for accrued support payments in jurisdictions where they are considered a final judgment. See Clark, pp. 210–211.

8. A writ of ne exeat should be considered to prevent Mr. D from leaving the jurisdiction. The object of such a writ is to keep a defendant within the court's jurisdiction so that he may be compelled to perform court orders and decrees where that is necessary to the preservation and enforcement of the plaintiff's rights. The writ may also be used to prevent the defendant from taking property out of the jurisdiction. The granting of the writ is discretionary, and evidence must be presented to the court to show that the defendant intends to leave the jurisdiction or take property out of the jurisdiction, and that granting the writ is necessary to protect the plaintiff's rights. Should the writ issue the defendant may be required to post a bond. See Kirby v. Kirby, 185 Tenn. 408, 206 S.W.2d 404 (1947).

9(a). A divorce a mensa et thoro is a divorce from bed and board, or a legal separation. Ecclesiastical courts granted such a limited divorce without a right to remarry for adultery or cruelty. A divorce a mensa et thoro should be distinguished from a divorce a vinculo matrimonii, which is a divorce from the banns of matrimony or absolute divorce.

9(b). A marriage is permitted between unrelated persons. The prohibited relation may be by consanguinity (blood) or by affinity. A relationship by affinity occurs where one of the partners is related by marriage to a blood relative of the other. For example, under the common law a man could not marry the sister of his deceased wife because he was related to her by his earlier marriage. About one-half of the states prohibit such marriages, but the trend is to eliminate affinity as a ground to prohibit a marriage. See Ploscowe, pp. 198–199.

10. True, assuming that the court had personal jurisdiction over the parties to award alimony when the divorce was granted. The reason is that the matter is res judicata. If Jill could have asserted her claim for alimony in the divorce action she may not later put her former husband to the expense of a second suit on the same claim absent fraud or mistake. However, there are statutes in some states which permit a claim for alimony to be raised at any time. In those states Jill will prevail. See Clark, pp. 433–439.

11. False. So long as W has met the residency requirement of State Y she may sue for divorce in that state. H's defenses are not

valid. The fact that H and W had lived in State X and that H's adultery occurred in State X do not limit divorce actions to that state. See Clark, pp. 285–286.

12. False. Consummation of a marriage means to have sexual intercourse. So long as there is a ceremonial marriage the couple is validly married regardless of whether the marriage is consummated. If a common law marriage were involved the answer would be different. Since a common law marriage requires cohabitation as husband and wife, such a marriage must be consummated to be valid. See Clark, p. 40.

13. True. This is the test used by many courts. A lesser standard of proof is sufficient in some jurisdictions. At common law evidence of consent or agreement of the parties was also necessary, but courts which continue to adhere to that requirement infer the consent or agreement from the fact of cohabitation. See Chapter III, *Recognition of Common Law Marriages*, above; Clark, pp. 47–50.

14. The following changes or additions could be made: The parties must be divorced or legally separated for payments to receive alimony treatment.

Premium payments on a life insurance policy on a husband's life may be deductible alimony to the wife provided that the wife is made the irrevocable beneficiary and the absolute owner of the policy.

Mortgage payments, if the property has been transferred to the wife under the decree, and if the mortgage payments are not subject to ermination within ten (10) years can be alimony taxable to the wife.

With regard to assets which have depreciated in value, the husband is better off selling the assets on the open market (thus, recognizing the loss) and paying the cash realized on such sale to the wife.

Neither spouse may deduct legal fees paid on behalf of the other spouse; therefore, if the husband is in a significantly higher tax bracket on a separate tax return he would be better off paying the wife a higher alimony payment (which would be deductible to him and taxable to her) and allowing her to pay her own attorney's fees.

The title of the question is: "Pre-divorce tax planning." The thrust of the material is that the financial negotiations between the parties and the drafting of the separation and property settlement agreement should take these rules into account to make certain that the tax result is as anticipated, to both parties, and so that the optimal collective tax advantage to both parties may be obtained through the payment of the smallest possible total number of dollars.

See Chapter 7, Financial and Other Aspects of Divorce, pp. 129–133, above.

TABLE OF CASES

References are to Pages

When case name contains In re, Estate of, Ex parte, Adoption, Succession, or Matter of, see under name of party.

INDEX

References are to pages